Mavericks

Mavericks:
The Lives and Battles of Montana's Political Legends

John Morrison
and
Catherine Wright Morrison

With a Foreword by Pat Williams

University of Idaho Press
Moscow, Idaho
1997

Published by the University of Idaho Press
Moscow, Idaho 83844–1107
Printed in the United States of America

01 00 99 98 97   5   3   2   1

Library of Congress Cataloging-in-Publication Data

Morrison, John, 1961–
    Mavericks : the lives and battles of Montana's political
  legends / John Morrison and Catherine Wright Morrison ;
  with a foreword by Pat Williams.
        p.   cm.
    Includes index.
    ISBN 0-89301-199-1 (alk. paper)
    1. Politicians—Montana—Biography. 2. Montana—
  Politics and government. 3. Montana—Biography.
  I. Morrison, Catherine Wright, 1962– . II. Title.
  F731.M67   1997
  978.6'03'0922—dc21   [B] 96-52420
                                                      CIP

*For my dad, who taught me the
importance of courage in politics.
—J.M.M.*

Contents

Illustrations

Foreword

Montana, the place, molds its people. Its political leaders grew and learned in a state that is still what America started out to be: a place of magnificent sky, land, and water, fragile but full of riches, beautiful but sometimes severe; a place where civilization sprang up in a wild and rugged country and people of character are born; a place where folks take issues seriously and still call elected officials by their first names.

The splendor and the harshness of Montana's mountains and high plains prompt humility, empathy, loyalty. In such a place one is compelled to seek the truth, and in politics that seeking requires courage.

Montana's political leaders—the best of them—have sought to know the truth about the connection between activist government and resultant improvement in the lives of individual citizens; about the threat of government invasion into individual privacy; about the misuse and abuse of power; about the nature of fundamental rights, freedoms, and responsibilities.

It has been in that seeking that Montana's political leaders have often demonstrated the courage to move ahead of the ranks to lead as well as the courage to turn and stand against the mistaken but fleetingly popular public mood.

John Morrison and Catherine Wright Morrison have in these pages collected a century of Montana politics and have captured the golden thread of courage that runs through it. Here then is the drama of those hundred years and of nine distinguished Montanans whose tireless pursuit of truth in public affairs breathed life into democratic government and advanced the common good.

Congressman Pat Williams
Democrat (MT)

Acknowledgments

Our acknowledgments must begin with a special thanks to Professor Robert Swartout, history professor at Carroll College. His encouragement in the early stages and many hours devoted to reviewing chapters allowed this project to get off the ground. Of nearly equal importance were our research assistants, Anne Sturdevant and James Scott, senior students of the history department at Carroll College. Their compilation of source materials formed the foundation for the chapters that follow. Dave Walter of the Montana Historical Society, an accomplished historian himself, not only provided considerable source material for this book through his own writings but also generously shared his knowledge, insights, and advice on many occasions. Dave also read and edited the entire manuscript when the first draft was completed and provided invaluable guidance during the revisions. Other personnel at the Montana Historical Society Library spent many hours helping us locate and identify books, articles, and more obscure references. Dale Johnson and other members of the staff of the Mansfield Library in Missoula helped us wade through and cull materials on Mike Mansfield from his extensive papers and photo collection. Professor Harry Fritz of the University of Montana offered direction when this work was still only an idea and helped select the people profiled.

Although original sources were referenced and analyzed in connection with the preparation of each chapter of this book, the breadth of our subject matter required us to rely heavily on the work and knowledge of those historians who have studied our subjects in the greatest depth. Without the work of these principal biographers, this book would not have been possible. We are grateful to each of them and have acquired a new appreciation for the commitment of time and energy that their books represent. We wish to especially thank Jules Karlin, Donald Spritzer, Jim Ludwick, and Charles Hood, who took the time to read our chapters and offer helpful comments and suggestions. We are grateful to Ambassador Mike Mansfield as well, for reading the Mansfield chapter and confirming the accuracy of certain biographical details. We also wish to thank

Donna Metcalf, who provided firsthand historical information about her husband, Lee Metcalf, and who, as a skillful editor herself, read and critiqued the Metcalf chapter.

Finally, special thanks must go to those who helped in the preparation of the manuscript. Gayle Parrish, Suzanne Hunger, and Rick Newby provided editorial guidance in the first few chapters. Beverly McDonald read and edited the first full draft. Leslie Torgerson, Denice Cochran, and Jerri Woodring spent countless hours typing, revising, organizing, and printing the manuscript prior to its submission for publication. Sharon Morrison carefully edited the first galleys. Heidi Kruckenberg performed the tedious task of preparing an index and together with Peggy Pace and others at the University of Idaho Press, capably and cheerfully transformed our manuscript into this book.

As is the case with any formidable undertaking, the generous help of others, and especially the people named above, has been indispensable. We literally could not have done it without them. To each of them, we express our deepest gratitude. Any remaining errors are the authors' own.

Introduction

Montana's political landscape has been trekked by a parade of extraordinary public leaders. Their names are familiar to us because each of them, in some meaningful way, changed our world. Hundreds of other Montana politicians have successfully won election and contributed honorably to society, but the nine characters profiled in this volume are legendary. As Americans search for a reason to reinvolve themselves in government, the lives and careers of these paragons remind us of the qualities that underpin effective leadership.

President Grover Cleveland, who signed the legislation granting statehood to the people of Montana, once growled: "What's the use of being elected and re-elected unless you stand for something?" The lives and careers of Montana's political legends echo President Cleveland's rhetorical query. It is a remarkable heritage: nine nationally known men and women who exemplified the progressive and populist ideals that lifted social justice to a prominent place on the national agenda and helped to define the character of twentieth-century America.

Joseph Toole electrified Congress and captured the national spotlight with his impassioned plea for statehood and then laid the foundation for Progressive reform as Montana's first governor. Ella Knowles won for women the right to practice law in Montana, became the nation's first woman candidate nominated by a major party for statewide office, and earned recognition as the preeminent woman lawyer in America. Joseph Dixon challenged the establishment of the Republican Party, ran the Bull Moose effort nationally, and imposed the first meaningful tax on powerful mining interests.

Thomas Walsh cracked the Teapot Dome scandal, championed confirmation of the first Jewish Supreme Court justice, chaired two consecutive Democratic National Conventions, and was appointed attorney general of the United States by President Franklin Roosevelt. Jeannette Rankin became a leader in the national women's suffrage movement, the first American woman elected to Congress, and the only member of Congress to vote against America's entry into both world

wars. Burton K. Wheeler resisted war hysteria and defended
due process as the nation's youngest U.S. attorney, bolted the
Democratic Party as a U.S. senator to run for vice president on
the Progressive Party ticket, unveiled corruption in the Harding justice department, and led the opposition to Roosevelt's
legislative attempt to "pack" the Supreme Court.

James Murray helped engineer the New Deal and fathered
the first major legislative initiatives devoted to full employment, national health insurance, and federal aid to education.
Mike Mansfield, as the longest serving majority leader of the
United States Senate, delivered the nation's first comprehensive civil rights act and relentlessly fought against American
involvement in Vietnam, before completing his public career
as ambassador to Japan. Lee Metcalf founded and led the legislative crusade to preserve wilderness and protect forests,
while probing and exposing excesses of the massive private
power industry.

They came from Kentucky, New Hampshire, North Carolina, Wisconsin, Massachusetts, Canada, and New York; only
Rankin and Metcalf were native Montanans. Seven of the nine
were lawyers, most of them trial lawyers, and all of the nine
possessed a deep respect for the process of American law as a
means to the end of justice. All nine were college educated.
Two were Republicans, six were Democrats, and one represented the Populist Party. Eight of them served in the United
States Congress. Five of the eight who served in Congress held
elective positions in Montana state or county government before ascending; Walsh, Rankin, and Mansfield did not. Despite
differences in background and style, all of the nine shared a
commitment to the integrity of government and the interests
of common men and women. Each of the nine, in his or her
own way, grappled with enormous antagonists in the name of
social justice.

The stories of these people are inextricably interwoven with
Montana political history. Their careers were launched and
their values hewn in a state rich with populism, progressivism, and activism. By populism we mean the political philosophy that demands that the power in a democratic society
rest with the citizens. By progressivism we mean the political
drive to improve society by government policies that correct
social inequities. By activism we mean the grassroots commit-

ment of people with common interests to influence elections and public policy. These features have been prominent in Montana politics, more or less, since Abraham Lincoln signed the act creating the Montana Territory in 1864, and they characterize a common vein that runs through the careers and causes of the men and women whose profiles occupy these pages.

Because the subjects of our book all, save one, served in the Congress, many of the bold crusades recounted here occurred at the national level and bore no special relationship to the provincial interests of the Treasure State. Moreover, the focus of our survey of these remarkable political lives centers on the courage and fierce commitment they brought to their endeavors and the serious moral purpose with which they approached the pressing issues of their day. Yet neither these people nor their causes can be fully understood without some discussion of the tradition of populism, progressivism, and activism from which they emerged.

Montana's first populist movement grew up around dissatisfaction with territorial conditions and the consequent cry for statehood. The white male voters that peopled Montana before 1890 were recalcitrant spirits who had spurned the safe institutional existence of the country's more established communities to chase dreams of freedom and riches on the raw western frontier. They were also largely composed of Irish and other immigrants who were not tied to entrenched families and who moved from states within or near the confederacy on the heels of the Civil War. They teased and despised the eastern "dudes" that Washington's Republican presidential administrations imposed upon them and demanded to control their own destiny.

In 1866 the restive frontiersmen elected delegates to Virginia City to devise a constitution. The campaign failed and statehood eluded Montana for two decades, a function of national political conditions that foreclosed congressional approval. The populist embers were not extinguished though, and the rekindled movement in the 1880s set the stage for the first great Montana statesman, Joseph K. Toole. On Toole's tall shoulders, the state of Montana opened its doors in 1889.

Statehood alone did not answer the demands of agitators for democratic self-determination. The first legislative elections were smeared with claims of precinct-level corruption, and the assembly's Democrats and Republicans stubbornly met separately, squandering the opportunity to conduct meaningful public business and embarrassing the new state. At the same time, Montanans remained more akin to subjects of a colony than citizens of a state, as the big mining companies manipulated state affairs.

The feud between Marcus Daly and William A. Clark, the two "kings" of the state's new copper mining industry, increasingly dominated state politics. In 1894 the titans clashed in a bitter runoff campaign for location of the state capital. Daly, who wanted to seat the government in Anaconda, and Clark, who fought to make Helena the site, poured money into the race, sometimes paying voters directly for their support. Clark confessed, "I never bought a man who wasn't for sale." The two bought up newspapers to promote their respective agendas, sowing resentment and distrust among citizens who were denied the fundamental public right to a free press.

Clark's ambitions to win a place in the United States Senate also tainted the political process. The state legislature at that time determined who would represent Montana in the highest federal lawmaking body. Clark was accused, probably rightly, of bribing legislators to support his Senate bids in 1893 and 1899. In the latter year he succeeded, but was ushered out of office by the Senate leadership, which, after a committee investigation, rejected his unlawful election. Clark promptly captured control of the Democratic Party, influencing the next legislative elections, and was returned to the Senate by the legislature of 1901.

In 1892 the Populist Party, a movement sparked in the South and Midwest, called for radical policy changes to help struggling farmers. As the movement swept into Montana and other western states, the party also rejected the gold standard and demanded free unlimited coinage of silver dollars, which drew miners to the cause. This seminal version of the enduring liberal farm-labor alliance chose the young suffragette-lawyer Ella Knowles as its candidate for attorney general, marking the first nomination of a woman for a statewide political office in Montana.

The Panic of 1893 and depression that followed fueled the Populist fire. In 1896 the party fused with the Democrats, solidifying a coalition of activists that attacked banks, railroads, and other wealthy capitalists as the enemies of the working man, while pressing the free silver platform. The Populist seeds of antiestablishment, anticorporate sentiment were sprouting. The campaign for free silver won support in the Republican Party as well, splitting the GOP and creating a progressively inclined faction known as the Silver Republicans. From these ranks emerged Joseph Dixon, a Missoula lawyer who entered the state legislature in 1900 and helped ignite an era of progressive legislation in Montana. Dixon was elected to Congress in 1902 and joined the allies of the young progressive Republican president Theodore Roosevelt.

In 1899 Standard Oil Company executives, led by Henry Rogers and William Rockefeller, acquired the Anaconda Copper Mining Company from Daly and created Amalgamated Copper, which would become known simply as the Company. Daly, who died the next year, had actually been relatively benevolent to his workers, if only to preserve their loyalty throughout his battles with Clark. Amalgamated, in contrast, was immediately cast in a hostile light. When Clark sold his empire to the monstrous new holding company, only one obstacle remained to interfere with the Company's hegemony. The clever and wildly successful mining magnate F. Augustus Heinze maintained close friendships with the district judges in Butte and effectively tangled the Amalgamated in litigation, while pirating its copper veins. In 1903 the Company flexed its muscle by closing the gates of its various operations, leaving half the state's workforce jobless in a single day, while demanding a special session of the legislature to enact a law permitting litigants to demand a change of venue without reason. With this law, the Company could escape the Butte courts and the influence of Heinze. The government complied on bended knee, Heinze was squeezed out, and the Company's monopoly was complete.

Corrupt elections, legislative shenanigans, a captive press, and Company hardball tactics intensified class-war ideology in the electorate. Meanwhile, the Progressive movement emerged nationally as a response to the ugly underbelly of the industrial revolution: occupational disease and injuries, child labor, pollution, and fabulous disparities of wealth between rich capitalists and struggling wage earners. Montanans had witnessed these evils firsthand in a state dominated by big, hard industry. Among them was future United States senator James Murray, nephew of an early Butte mining mogul. Despite financial privilege, he worked in the mines as a young man side by side with men whose lungs wheezed from silicosis and men who lost limbs and lives laboring for the Company.

The Progressive movement embraced not only the progressive notion that government power must be mobilized to meet social needs but also the populist idea that corrupt special interests could best be curbed by vesting decision-making power directly in the citizens. By the turn of the century Montanans were ripe for Progressive change. The legislature enacted a flurry of reforms in a fifteen-year period. The State Board of Health was created in 1901. The State Bureau of Child and Animal Protection was conceived in 1903 and was followed in 1904 by legislation restricting child labor and creating a compulsory school law. The eight-hour workday was also codified in 1904. In 1906 the initiative and referendum process was established, empowering citizens directly to decide major political issues. The problem of youth delinquency was addressed with juvenile court legislation in 1907. The Leighton Act in 1911 allowed counties to be created upon petition of the people, nearly doubling the number of counties in the coming years and taking another step toward decentralization of authority. Primary nominating elections were enacted in 1912 along with campaign spending limitations, the direct election of United States senators, and the presidential preference primary. The Railroad and Public Service (utility) Commission was created in 1912 and the workmen's compensation system in 1915.

Helena trial lawyer Thomas Walsh launched his political career in the heart of the Progressive era. In 1906 he won the Democratic nomination for Congress, campaigning on the Progressive platform, but met defeat in the general election in the face of Company opposition. In 1910 he lost a bid for the United States Senate due to Company control of the legislature. A lone maverick legislator, Burton K. Wheeler of Butte, boldly proclaimed his support for Walsh and the Progressive agenda. Walsh tried again in 1912 and, helped by new rules that gave the electorate a direct say, was elected.

Progressive forces in Montana were fortified by the influx of tens of thousands of dryland homesteaders—"honyockers"—between 1906 and 1918. Many of these settlers, thought by legend

my grandparents (Mary & Frank)

to be simply rugged individualist loners, actually advocated active federal government relief programs and espoused anti-corporate and moralistic ideas. By the 1910s, the Non-Partisan League, rolling west from North Dakota, rallied distressed farmers by advocating public ownership of banks, grain elevators, insurance companies, and utilities and by urging strict government oversight of railroads and other large corporations. In the same time period Socialists were elected to city government offices in Anaconda, Butte, Red Lodge, and Livingston, and Butte elected a Socialist mayor.

The bedrock of Montana's Progressive movement was the implacable presence of organized labor unions. Butte stood out as a center of American unionism. The Butte Miners' Union and the Western Federation of Miners were born in Butte, and the radical Industrial Workers of the World (IWW) counted Butte as a critical center. Wobblies (members of the IWW) advocated overthrow of the entire capitalist system and ownership of the means of production by a single, unified international industrial workers' army. The prevalence of unions fostered the adversarial relationship between big-business owners and regular working people and put workers behind the Progressive agenda.

Another by-product of industrialization was the creation of a leisure class of women who had the time to meet and discuss their grievances and organize to seek policy changes. The right to vote topped the list of priorities of women's groups. The fight for women's suffrage paralleled and became part of the Progressive movement. The suffrage movement grew from its roots in the mid-1800s and gained momentum in Montana in the last decade of the century. With Jeannette Rankin spearheading the final campaign, voting rights for women were finally won in 1914. Two years later, Montanans sent Rankin to Washington as America's first congresswoman.

The Progressive cause fell dormant during World War I, as nationalistic Montanans focused on defeating the international enemy, but the movement reawakened after the war. Joseph Dixon was elected governor in 1920 and achieved tax reform that targeted the Company, which ensured his defeat after a single term. Wheeler captured a Senate seat in 1922 and two years later became the vice presidential nominee on the Progressive Party ticket led by Sen. Robert LaFollette of Wisconsin.

Wheeler would serve in the Senate until 1946. Senator Walsh became a national figure after heading the investigation of the Teapot Dome scandal and served in the Senate until his death in 1933. Murray succeeded Walsh and staunchly supported President Franklin D. Roosevelt's progressive New Deal agenda.

A young Irish-American, Mike Mansfield, was then climbing out of the Butte mineshafts to get a formal education and to develop his own political thoughts, which would lead him to a progressive career in the U.S. Congress from 1940 until 1976. Meanwhile, a boy in the Bitterroot Valley, Lee Metcalf, listened intently on his crystal radio set and read in the newspapers about the Progressive crusades of Wheeler, LaFollette, Nebraska senator George Norris, and others. Metcalf would distinguish himself as a true heir to the Populist-Progressive tradition in his own years in Congress from 1952 until his death in 1978, battling the Montana Power Company in a manner not unlike the campaigns waged by his forebears against the Anaconda Company.

The Company's huge role in Montana politics lasted for decades. It continued to own most of the state's daily newspapers until selling them in 1959 to Lee Enterprises. In 1912 the Company created the Montana Power Company, merging most of the state's energy services with the bulk of its mining operations. In 1915 the Amalgamated parent company was dissolved and the Anaconda Company regained its name. The Company's lobbyists continued to hold sway in the legislature. In 1943 in his acclaimed book *Montana: High, Wide and Handsome*, journalist Joseph Kinsey Howard wrote that "'the Company' has controlled virtually every Montana legislature since it drove Heinze from Montana."

Historians now debate the extent of the Company's dominion in twentieth-century Montana politics. It is a complex historical issue. Some have argued that the Company was a monolithic, omnipotent force that lost only those battles it meant to lose. Others contend that the Company was one of many players in a diverse, pluralistic political community. We do not participate in this debate. It is sufficient for our purposes to note that the Company was a strong, intimidating force in Montana politics and that popular and personal struggles against its domination undoubtedly shaped the ideas of Montana's great political leaders.

Some of our subjects engaged in legendary battles directly with the Company; some did not. Some fought the Company on one issue and accommodated the Company on others. Joseph Toole, for example, initiated the era of Progressive legislation as governor, supporting laws to make workplaces safer and reduce industrial pollution, but reluctantly called the special session of 1903 and signed the change of venue bill into law. Gov. Joseph Dixon, faced with a Company-controlled legislature, took to the people a public initiative to increase the taxation of the state's mines and was driven from politics by the Company as a result. Burton K. Wheeler threatened to "put [the Company] out of politics" for which he was assaulted by a Company thug and smeared by the Company press. Later in his career he was accused, albeit inaccurately, of "selling out" to the Company because of his opposition to certain policies of President Franklin Roosevelt.

Thomas Walsh represented injured workers against the Company for years as a plaintiff's trial lawyer and decried the Company's control of state politics, but bent to Company wishes in 1918 by calling for Wheeler's resignation as U.S. attorney. Lee Metcalf, years later, carried on the fight against the Montana Power Company and was excoriated by its allies in every election cycle. Knowles, Rankin, Murray, and Mansfield had few real conflicts with the Company, not because they acceded to its wishes, but because the issues that occupied them were generally of less interest to the Company.

The nine men and women portrayed in this volume faced myriad foes, some far greater than the Anaconda Company. Most of them carried their progressive, populist principles into a national forum and engaged in battles that extended far beyond the parochial struggles for power in Montana. Each of them displayed courage by challenging ensconced public opinion, major institutions, or mighty special interests.

Joseph Toole confronted the intransigence of a partisan Congress in his quest for statehood. Ella Knowles defied centuries of gender prejudice in her campaigns to win for women the right to practice law, to vote and to run for public office. Joseph Dixon challenged the establishment of the national Republican Party and the captains of American business when he advocated a progressive income tax and when he joined Theodore Roosevelt's third-party drive to break up huge monopolies. Thomas Walsh faced down the presidential administration of Warren G. Harding with his meticulous examination and dispassionate exposure of the Teapot Dome affair.

Jeannette Rankin opposed the international business community, military leaders, two presidents of the United States, and the American people, when she raised a fearless hand against both world wars. Burton K. Wheeler battled the president and his own Democratic Party and alienated much of his constituency in order to preserve the independence of the American judiciary and the constitutional separation of powers. James Murray was bloodied by purveyors of the anti-Communist "red scare" as he fought for national health insurance, federal aid to education, and full-employment programs.

Mike Mansfield, although always diplomatic, vexed military-industrial powers and stood against presidents from both parties, the public opinion of his state, and the will of the nation, by steadfastly opposing America's military activity in Vietnam. He also calmly redressed the most gaping, painful cultural cleavage in American history by successfully shepherding civil rights legislation into the law books. Lee Metcalf attacked the American private power industry on behalf of consumers and braved the anger of timber and mining companies in order to pass legislation to protect forests and wilderness.

The subjects of this book were mavericks in the best sense of the word. The use of that term in the title of the book is not meant to suggest that the profiled subjects were impulsive, erratic, or friendless. In most cases the opposite was true. Instead, the term "mavericks" connotes that these legendary figures were strong individuals with independent minds, willing to stand alone when their consciences demanded it.

The battles of Montana's great political champions teach an important lesson: Monumental public achievements are accomplished only by those willing to face and withstand great opposition. Justice is rarely served without a fight. The men and women whose passions drive them toward that elusive goal must be prepared to endure the enmity and abuse hurled at them when the threatened lash out. Hence, the historic words of Susan B. Anthony: "Cautious, careful people, always casting about to preserve their reputation or social standards, can never bring about reform."

This is not to say that political life should be constantly contentious. Many of the daily affairs of government most effectively are transacted in a climate of cooperation, if not consensus. Too often, in fact, partisan battle lines are drawn in the absence of a true-value conflict, in order to achieve political advantage. Like the boy who cried wolf, politicians mired in petty bickering alienate the governed, and genuine pleas for social justice in threshold issue areas fall on cynical, deaf ears. There is a time for agreement and a time for argument, a time to join hands and time to fight. Each must be nurtured and preserved. The key is to know the difference. More often than not, the men and women profiled in this volume chose their political battles well. They did not always win, but they fought real battles over real issues with real passion and avoided idle rancor.

There is another lesson to be found in the lives of Montana's preeminent politicians: Great movements of conscience, like brilliant entrepreneurial ideas, begin in the hearts and minds of a few. Early on, they are spurned and ridiculed by the skeptical establishment. They prevail when those few, through uncommon fortitude and valor, confront seemingly insuperable forces, transcend the apathy of inertia, and inspire the spirit of the community. Politicians, as a group, have always responded to irresistible, grand, popular movements, but the political giants of Montana marched at the fore of such movements. Their careers contradict those who contend that controversy is inconsistent with electoral success. Indeed, they prove that history looks most fondly upon those special souls who bravely, if deftly, stand for a cause because it is right. They verify that courage is the very essence of distinction in public life.

The authors of this book do not purport to be professional historians or to chronicle novel findings about Montana's past. Rather, this work is the product of two ordinary citizens mindful of our state's remarkable political heritage and hopeful that more people will become at least casually familiar with it. Undeniably, this is also a book with a point of view. It is born of admiration and concern: admiration of the careers and contributions of Montana's distinguished public leaders; concern for the effective conduct of public affairs. In the end, we hope that it will be a prod to those who seek to take the reins of public leadership and an inspiration to citizens who dutifully march to the polls on election day. We hope that prospective leaders, reflecting on the achievements of their political ancestors, will agree that there is nothing better than to fight the good fight— to spend oneself for a worthy cause. We hope that voters will be moved to support candidates who demonstrate courage in their campaigns and public decisions. Finally, we hope this book may also serve as a reminder that spirited argument is the soul of democracy.

True courage will always be precious in political life, but if enough leaders rekindle their commitment to the ideals of candor and boldness, there is a chance to create a new national mood. When that happens, we will bridge the chasm between rhetoric and action, petty partisanship and empty legislation will succumb to honest public debate, and citizens will regain the pride and satisfaction that comes from living in a truly democratic community.

I

Joseph K. Toole,
Champion of Statehood

Do not obstruct the march of American manhood towards the destiny contemplated by the Constitution.

"Mr. Speaker." The lone delegate from the territory of Montana rose and sought recognition.

He was not the only crusader for statehood among the citizens of the Montana Territory, but for ten years he had championed the cause and so had made it his own. The battle had been long and often discouraging. But now, territorial delegate Joseph K. Toole stood in the Congress of the United States with one final chance to plead his case. At thirty-seven years, Joe Toole was among the younger members of Congress, but he hadn't a vote and neither had his territory. Toole confronted his colleagues that January day in 1889 to rectify this injustice and others by securing, once and for all, official statehood for the people of Montana. The moment demanded superior powers of persuasion and political acumen, which Toole possessed in abundance. He came by these qualities naturally, and had refined them as a lawyer and junior statesman in Montana. The delegate from Montana stood six feet four, but the relative stature of his office was diminutive. As Toole rose before the House, its members may not have anticipated the captivating force of his oratory or the resounding national response that would follow. As he prepared to speak, they may not have known that the Union flag was about to gain a new star.

· · ·

Opposite: *Joseph K. Toole, circa 1870. At nineteen, Toole had just arrived in the Montana Territory after making his way up the Missouri River from St. Louis, and was commencing his law practice. Two years later he would be elected district attorney.*

Courtesy of Montana Historical Society, Helena.

He was born Joseph Kemp Toole on May 12, 1851, in Savannah, Missouri. His early youth was absorbed by the unending tasks of daily farm life, but he managed to obtain an education in the public schools as time permitted. When his family moved to the nearby town of St. Joseph, Toole continued his schooling and soon enrolled in the Western Military Institute at Newcastle, Kentucky, where he graduated with honors in 1868.

Joe's older brother, Warren, had packed up his law degree in 1863 and migrated to a part of the Idaho Territory that is now western Montana. Warren first practiced in the miner's courts in Bannack and then moved to Helena, beginning his career as a trial lawyer in the newly created territory of Montana. A short time later, Warren and his colleague, Cornelius Hedges, tried the first lawsuit in the city of Helena.

Inspired by his brother, Joe Toole undertook legal studies himself in the offices of Webb and Barber of Newcastle, Kentucky. Webb and Barber were distinguished members of the Kentucky bar, and Toole could have stayed there and pursued a prosperous career. But the romance of the West lured him, so in the spring of 1869 he embarked from St. Louis up the Missouri River some 3,100 miles to Fort Benton. Traveling by stagecoach, Joe Toole pressed on to Helena where he was reunited with his brother and, in Warren's office, continued to study law. Joe Toole's grandson later remarked, "A more brilliant tutor he could not have had, for Warren Toole was to become, and after his death was acknowledged, the 'Nestor' of the Montana bar in the field of pure legal reasoning."[1]

Joe Toole was only nineteen when he was admitted to the bar in 1870 and became his brother's partner. Two years later, barely having attained the age of majority, Toole was elected district attorney for the Third Judicial District of the Montana Territory. By 1876, the twenty-five-year-old Toole had completed two biennial terms as district attorney. He had proven himself to be a zealous prosecutor, but stepped down in order to devote his entire professional attention to the family law practice.

By 1880 Joe Toole was twenty-nine years old and the political war-horse inside him, if only a colt, began to stomp in its stall. He was elected that year as a Democrat to represent Lewis and Clark County in the Twelfth Territorial Council, predecessor to the modern Montana Senate. The members of that council elected Toole president and presiding officer upon its convocation in January 1881. Toole impressed his fellow members with parliamentary skill, determination, and honorable personal qualities. He did not seek reelection when his term expired, but was elected a year later to the Constitutional Convention, which convened in Helena on January 14, 1884.

The 1884 constitution was not significant in itself, as it was rejected by the United States Congress. Still, it represented the initial effort of Montana people to hammer out the basic principles of government under which they chose to live, and the charter that they created would substantially influence another, later constitution.

Joining Joseph Toole at the Constitutional Convention of 1884 were "copper kings" William A. Clark and Marcus Daly, future governor Robert B. Smith, future senator Thomas C. Power, future federal judge William H. Hunt, successful lawyer William W. Dixon, and prominent editor James H. Mills. While much of the constitution of 1884 was conciliatory, if not sycophantic, it did establish the basic mechanisms of a sovereign government and laid the groundwork for a number of fundamental rights, including religious tolerance and limited voting rights for women.

On February 9, 1884, the attending members signed the completed draft of this constitution after only twenty-eight days of deliberation. Joe Toole was chosen, with four others, to prepare the address to the territorial voters prior to submission for ratification. The constitution contained certain provisions that some people found objectionable, such as the exemption of mines and mining claims from taxation, but the want for statehood prevailed. The constitution was handily ratified 15,506 to 4,266. Toole and others had succeeded in persuading the people that the state's new power to tax the property of the Northern Pacific railroad would permit maintaining state government without any increase in the rate of taxation.

The day that Montanans ratified the 1884 constitution, Democrat Grover Cleveland was elected president, carrying with him a Democratic majority for the House of Representatives. The Senate remained Republican, mostly because fewer members stood for election. Among the new members of the House of Representatives, though lacking the power to vote for his people and their interests, was the young Montana statesman, Joseph K. Toole.

For four years, congressional delegate Joe Toole fought for statehood. In the abstract, the idea seems innocuous enough, but in reality the issue of statehood in the western territories became a political flash point. Republicans sought statehood for Washington and the creation of two Dakota states, all of which were expected to send Republicans to Congress and enhance that party's national political strength. Democrats sought statehood for Montana and New Mexico, where a similarly favorable result for their party was anticipated.

During the first session of the Forty-ninth Congress, Delegate Toole and Sen. D. W. Voorhees of Indiana spearheaded the effort to win Montana statehood. The other Indiana senator was the popular and powerful Republican, Benjamin Harrison, later to become president of the United States. Although Harrison had a son who was a newspaper publisher in Helena and a Montana stockman, he followed strict party lines and opposed Montana statehood. Republicans prevailed and all bills advancing Montana statehood were defeated. A compromise proposal in the second session of the forty-ninth Congress, though ostensibly nonpartisan, met the same fate.

When the Fiftieth Congress convened in December 1887, the bill providing for admission of the territories was renewed. The deadlock continued through both sessions of that Congress. Finally, an opportunity presented itself. In 1888 Senator Harrison captured the White House and carried a flock of Republicans into Congress. Lame duck congressional Democrats, about to lose their bargaining strength, began to consider acceptance of a Republican version of the territorial admission bill. By so doing, they would be the toast of the territories, while leaving to the new Republican regime the burden of nurturing the fledgling states.

On top of the improving political climate, the case for Montana was becoming irresistible. While the 1870s had been characterized by economic depression and lagging population, the 1880s saw the arrival of the Northern Pacific railroad and explosive development of the mining and livestock industries. The population of the territory grew in kind. From a small, migratory population of 38,159 in 1880, the territory swelled to 132,159 people by 1890. By the end of that decade, Montana's treasury boasted a surplus of over $130,000.

Before his own congressional career expired, retiring delegate Joe Toole was determined to make a comprehensive and
exhaustive appeal, grounded in the undeniable facts that
demonstrated statehood was the only appropriate status for
Montana. And so, standing atop this mountain of compelling
evidence, Delegate Toole addressed his colleagues on January
15, 1889. The preceding speeches of the day had lasted into
the evening. Most members had left the floor and the press
crews were packing their papers and pencils.

Joe Toole surveyed the thinning House floor from behind
deep-set blue eyes. Serious in his purpose, he began to speak.
His voice rang with a resonance that commanded attention,
without demanding it. He displayed a natural authority, marshaling facts and skillfully applying the principles of logic and
reasoning. Having served our "Territorial pupilage," Toole proclaimed:

> We have outgrown a system designed only for a weak and
> sparsely inhabited territory. . . . Like a child grown be-
> yond the capacity of its garments, our pride is wounded
> and we are restive under the promise of more suitable ha-
> biliments. We stand in many respects in the same relation
> to the federal government that a child does to its parent,
> or a ward does to its guardian, but unhappily the same
> principles are not applicable or we might go into a court
> of equity and get immediate relief.[2]

As he spoke, heads turned. Congressmen lounging on
benches in the back, enjoying their evening cigars, looked up
from their newspapers. Those chattering about the day's
events fell silent. Members and spectators began filing back
into the chamber and gallery. Reporters unpacked their
notepads. Applause, and then cheers, intervened to punctuate
the delegate's remarks.

Toole rejected the pacifying platitudes of the past: "Professions of sympathy no longer assuage us, and no amount of sincerity will hereafter put us aside." Toole recited the wrongs
that Congress had perpetrated upon territorial citizens
through the continued imposition of territorial status. Among
an even longer list of epithets roughly corresponding to the

grievances set forth in the Declaration of Independence, Toole leveled these criticisms at Congress, crystallizing the plight of the territories:

It has given us a system of courts inherently wrong, and which never can be made suitable to large communities.

It has regulated the number of our judges, which is grossly inadequate in every instance, resulting in the delay, and in many cases the denial, of justice.

It has arbitrarily fixed the time when our local legislature shall meet and adjourn, to our great damage and inconvenience.

It has denied us the authority to call an extra session of our legislature without consent of the President, adding untold burdens to a dependent people.

It has reserved the right to invalidate any law which our legislature may pass, thereby destroying that full faith and credit which our legislation ought to command.

It has bound us hand and foot by a law which restricts these growing and ambitious communities in the expenditure of money for public improvements.

It has declared what we shall teach in our public schools, and manifested a lack of confidence in us in other instances of legislation too numerous to mention.

It has attempted to stifle our industries by prohibiting us from selling our mining properties in foreign markets, thus laying upon us an embargo not borne by the citizens of the states.

It has exempted a railroad and the improvements of its right-of-way for 820 miles in length from taxation, furnishing another evidence of the gross inequality of citizenship in and out of the territories.

It has withheld from us our dowry of lands which belong to our school fund, and refuses to give us any kind of supervision or control over it until we become a state, and then sets deliberately to work to prolong the time when that event shall happen.

It has professed to give us a representative in the lower house of Congress, but denies us a vote, the only element of representation which gives character and influence to a member.

It has left us without any kind of representation in the Senate, and remits us to the beggarly methods of the lobbyist.

It has imposed upon us, with an iron hand, the obligations and burdens of citizenship, while it withholds its corresponding benefits by steadily denying to us participation in the framing of federal legislation and the right of suffrage in national elections.

It has, by a failure to appropriate the necessary money, made it impossible at three successive terms of our court, to summon or procure the attendance of jurors and witnesses in causes arising under the Constitution and laws of the United States, whereby persons accused of crime, invoking the constitutional right to a "speedy trial by an impartial jury," were compelled to be discharged without trial.

It has refused to appropriate the salaries provided by law for the hungry officials whom it has been pleased to send us, and compels them to accept a measly sum in full compensation, notwithstanding an overflowing treasury.

It has refused to appropriate sufficient money to extend the public surveys in the Territory, but it has doled out annually its driblets, which have ofttimes been covered back into the treasury, leaving our boundaries undefined and our titles insecure.

It has, by a false economy in the appropriation and expenditure of the public money, deprived the frontier settlements of proper postal facilities, proceeding upon the unjust and impracticable basis that every office should be self-sustaining.

It has failed to cause to be surveyed, selected, and conveyed to the grantees of the lands falling to railroad grants in the Territories as required by law, whereby millions of acres of land owned by rich corporations escape taxation. . . . [3]

Toole's most virulent attacks were reserved for the custom of carpetbagging, which had aroused great dissension in other parts of the Union. His remarks, though vehement, were not without a caustic wit. Toole continued:

> It has suffered to be fastened upon us the odious system of carpetbag rule and domination which seems to inhere more or less in the territorial form of government. . . . We remember that, "sending hither a swarm of officials," etc., was one of the causes which led to our Declaration of Independence. From that day to this, carpetbaggers have always been odious, and their presence amongst us is and ever will be as poisonous and destructive to good government as the insidious growth of communism.

> Tradition informs us that the wise men all came from the East; and so our Republican friends, unwilling to depart from the teaching of the past, determined that history should repeat itself, and proceeded to treat us in their own good time to a fine assortment of imported political dudes. Some of these hot-house specimens who were too frail to stand transplanting in a northern clime soon gave up their commissions and returned to the genial influences of their own civilization. Others, holding religiously to the doctrine that a federal officer should neither die nor resign, stayed with us, became acclimated, and promise in the years to come to develop into tolerably good and useful citizens. . . . If I could summon a trumpet tongue on this occasion, the proclamation of our protest against carpetbaggism would be so loud that it could be heard all over this broad land.[4]

Toole drew the traits and treasures of the territory to his colleagues' attention in stirring style:

> It was a long overland trip to get to that country. There were many perils to encounter and great difficulties to surmount. Only the courageous dared to start, and only the strong and indomitable survived the hardships of the journey and reached their destination. Their home is a tract of mingled mountains, rolling lands, and expansive prairies. Men who mature in such a land are bound to be patriotic. They are as brave as they are strong, and when

in the years to come the nation may need defenders, it is certain that the contingent from Montana can be counted upon for everything that men can do in the way of toil or bear in the way of danger. . . .

[Here is] a territory which, if measured by the grandeur of its mountains, the fertility of its valleys, the majesty of its rivers, the splendor and utility of its waterfalls, the richness of its mines, the number and value of its herds and flocks, the wealth and destiny of its forests, the health and vigor of its climate, the intelligence, aspiration, and patriotism of its citizens, ought to admonish you that the time is at hand when we should be accorded a political status upon this floor which will no longer be an empty honor and a delusion, but a full realization of the benefits designed by the Constitution, and for the expected coming of which we shall anxiously wait and watch.[5]

Delegate Toole then undertook an exhaustive examination, based upon extensive, objective statistics, of each of the major facets of the Montana territorial society. He addressed the public land, the population, the valuation of property, the public treasury surplus, the value of exports, the mineral resources, the agricultural resources, the rivers, the climate, the livestock, the minerals, the timber, the railroads, the schools, the national banks, the public buildings, the land offices, the cities and towns, the Montana militia, Yellowstone National Park, the labor force, the newspapers, and the badlands.

With insights earned through personal experience, Toole concluded his remarks:

I have no fear of the character of their citizenship; they are faithful and prompt in the discharge of every public duty. No jurisdiction covering the same extent of country and embracing the same number of people can boast of less crime and vice among the citizens. I speak with some means of information and with some feeling upon this question. More than half of my life has been spent among the kind of men who people these territories. I know their stern integrity and rugged honesty, their capacity for local self-government, and their deep devotion to the principles of our institutions. . . .

Upon this important question I beg of you to make no mistake. Do not dam up the river of progress. Do not obstruct the march of American manhood towards the destiny contemplated by the Constitution. Popular development and popular government have made us powerful and great among the nations of the earth, but we have not yet reached the zenith of our power and greatness. Let us remember that delays are dangerous; that now is the time and here is the place to provide the way by which eight new stars may be added to the flag, and two million of our countrymen in the territories shall be enfranchised; and then rest assured that the wisdom and patriotism of our course will be vindicated by the deliberate judgment of mankind.[6]

Young Joe Toole had made his point and the response was magnificent. At the end of Toole's speech, the editors of the *Congressional Record* added simply, "[long, continued applause]." The *New York Sun* proclaimed that Toole "had electrified the House," and reported that "in one speech, Mr. Toole won the reputation of an impassioned orator." One Republican citizen of Massachusetts who had business interests in Montana wrote personally to Toole, "No one of whom I know in Montana can so well, so agreeably, and so ably represent her in the House. Your showing cannot be gainsaid, the logic and the facts are unanswerable."

A Montana Republican and lawyer from Boulder wrote to Toole as follows:

Give me your hand and let us shake, across the continent, over your effort in the House on January 15, 1889. It is the right kind of a nail, driven in the right kind of place, with the right kind of hammer, wielded with sufficient and the right kind of force. If it is democracy, then, to that extent, I am a democrat. Let us shake again.[7]

A young lawyer in Helena who had been associated with Toole wrote, "Men are sometimes elevated to the very pinnacle of fame in a breath. In one short hour you succeeded in creating a national reputation for yourself. . . ."[8]

While members of the national press praised Toole's remarks, the politically partisan newspapers of Montana began to spin the delegate's speech in ways that suited their party's outlook. The Republican papers contended that Toole's scathing indictment of federal transgressions perpetrated on the territories was a well-deserved attack on the Democratic Cleveland administration. This position was apparently espoused without the slightest shame or guilt, although the four-year-old outgoing Cleveland administration had been preceded by twenty-four years of Republican tenure in the White House and although the Republicans of Congress had been those who most vigorously opposed Montana's admission to the Union. Moreover, as the Democratic *Bozeman Weekly Chronicle* pointed out, Montana's Republican legislature quashed a resolution offered by the Democrats to congratulate Toole and affirm his position. Nevertheless, the efforts of the Republican papers to turn Toole's speech to their favor aroused sufficient concern in Democratic circles and with stalwart Democrat Toole himself to provoke a letter to the editor of the *Helena Independent* from the delegate.

> I only regret that the Republican press of Montana, by misrepresentation in giving to my remarks a partisan colouring, should thereby detract from their efficacy at this interesting crisis.
>
> It may not be out of place to say that the record of past Republican administrations upon the question of "home rule" in Montana is strangely at variance with their "righteous indignation" so suddenly and severely expressed concerning the present administration. For 20 consecutive years the Republican party flooded Montana with "non-resident" appointments; during all this time, but five appointments were made from the Territory. I never did, and never will, seek to exculpate the present administration from its just responsibility in that behalf. Neither am I willing to sit silently by in the light of undisputed facts and see our friends (the enemy) flirting in false feathers, proclaiming like the Pharisee, "I am holier than thou," without directing public attention to the masquerade.[9]

When the political dust had settled, it was clear that Toole's effort had appealed widely to both Republicans and Democrats, for as Montanans, they shared a deep longing for statehood.

In the eleventh hour of the Fiftieth Congress and the Cleveland administration, the Omnibus Bill authorizing statehood for the territories of Washington, Montana, North Dakota, and South Dakota was passed. On February 22, 1889, Grover Cleveland signed the Enabling Act, which provided that Montana and the other territories would be admitted as states upon enactment and ratification of constitutions.

In the 1889 May election, the Montana voters chose Joe Toole to be among the delegates to draft the constitution that would become the first supreme law of the state. When the convention opened in July, the collection of delegates included many still-familiar names. Among the twenty-two lawyers at the convention were Hiram Knowles, who would be appointed the first federal judge from Montana, William Dixon, and Joe Toole. William Clark and Marcus Daly associate John R. Toole were among the sixteen delegates whose primary interest was the state's mines. Cattle king Conrad Kohrs and others brought the perspective of the state's stockmen. The bankers included Charles Conrad, and the realtors, Paris Gibson, the "founder" of Great Falls, who would one day find himself in the United States Senate, and J. E. Rickards, the second governor of the state. While Toole was elected temporary president, William Clark was chosen as the permanent president, and the congregation set about the business of devising a constitution.

Much of the constitution of 1884 was adopted and incorporated into the constitution of 1889. Other portions were taken from established states. The delegates moved quickly and, for once, without significant partisan division. The greatest contest pitted rural counties against urban to determine whether representation in the senate would be based upon population. Although Toole argued for a population-based senate on behalf of his Lewis and Clark County and was supported by the other urban counties, the rural counties ultimately prevailed and won equal representation in the state's upper house.

As if his plea for statehood, the passage of the Enabling Act, and the trials of the Constitutional Convention were not enough to occupy his attention, Joe Toole became, at his party's urgent request, a candidate to be the first governor of the state of Montana. The year 1888 had been a Republican year; the election of 1889 was no exception. In a single stroke, Montana voters ratified the new constitution by over 90 percent and sent

Governor Toole, the political father of Montana. As Montana's territorial dele-gate to the United States Congress, Toole issued the successful plea for state-hood. As a two-term governor, beginning at the turn of the century, Toole led the state through the first and busiest phase of the Progressive era.
                    Courtesy of Montana Historical Society, Helena.

Republicans into every statewide office, except one. On November 8, 1889, President Harrison officially declared the birth of the state of Montana. Democrat Joseph Kemp Toole, champion of statehood, was elected the state's first governor.

The constitution had been ratified, but before the ink on the ballots was dry, the new commonwealth found itself entangled in political barbed wire. In Precinct 34, established for the benefit of some 175 workers building branch lines of the Northern Pacific railroad between Butte and Logan, a dispute erupted in the legislative race. Ballots were tallied and the results were sealed and delivered to the county commissioners of Silver Bow County, two Republicans and one Democrat. These Silver Bow county commissioners refused two to one to recognize the results of Precinct 34, on grounds of suspected chicanery. The County Commissioners refused to deliver the ballots from Precinct 34—171 Democratic and 3 Republican—to the State Board of Canvassers, which had charge of determining the results. Silver Bow County went Republican by a margin of less than the Democratic votes from Precinct 34, and the political balance of the state was upset. The state board delivered certificates of election to the five Republican legislative candidates from Silver Bow.

Meanwhile, the Silver Bow county clerk, who was empowered by statute to deliver certificates of election, certified the Democratic candidates for the five contested seats. The stage was set for a partisan showdown. With visions of riots at the legislative convocation, Toole challenged the strict separation of powers and issued a proclamation recognizing the Democratic certificates awarded by the county clerk.

Republicans and Democrats of the State House of Representatives met separately, each claiming for their party the controversial seats and thereby a majority. In the Senate, which was unaffected by Precinct 34, eight Democrats faced eight Republicans and a Republican lieutenant governor who was empowered to break all ties.

In the midst of this partisan standoff and governmental confusion, the first great issues of the new commonwealth demanded attention, not the least of which was sending two senators to the nation's capital.

On December 17, 1889, thirty-eight-year-old Gov. Joe Toole addressed the first Montana State Legislature. Even as the infant state, which he had midwived, faced the historic task of carving its own identity, it seemed bent on self-destruction. The bizarre conflict was undoubtedly an embarrassment to Toole, who had so eloquently celebrated the maturity and patriotism of Montana citizens before his colleagues in Congress. Toole began by directing remarks toward those responsible for the state's inauspicious beginning:

> Constitutional government has been conferred on us, and for the first time we undertake the management and control of our own affairs. The responsibility rests with us. It is our power to make this the great state of the Union, or to hamper and dwarf it for all time. In view of the difficulties which have attended the convening of the first legislative assembly under its state constitution, I yield the opportunity which precedent has established to indulge in the patriotic sentiments which such an occasion under different circumstances might inspire.[10]

With this scolding introduction, Governor Toole outlined the immediate challenges facing the state. With just $5,000 in the treasury, the state confronted maintenance of an asylum for the insane and a state penitentiary, the creation and funding of a Bureau of Labor and Industry, and provisions for the newly elected state officers. Toole placed special emphasis on careful and vigilant management of public lands to maximize funds available for the creation of an educational system. The governor implored legislators to resist those who would have the public lands appropriated to their own benefit at the expense of educational and other institutions.

Unhappily, but understandably, a substantial portion of the governor's message focused on revitalizing the "purity of the ballot." The governor urged ballot reform to eradicate problems such as those which were encountered in the Precinct 34 debacle. He noted that two judges had each claimed official status in the same Silver Bow County district, admonishing that "litigants are without the tribunals for the settlement of their grievances, the estates of deceased persons are jeopardized, business generally is in a state of suspended animation,

and the courts are brought into contempt." The governor acknowledged that two bodies were then sitting, each claiming
to be the legal House of Representatives, and chided:

> Whenever for supposed political advantages the honor,
> welfare, and the glory of the state is prostituted to partisan
> ends, the inevitable penalty will be destruction of popular
> confidence and disaster at the poll. . . . It is high time that
> personal ambition should be subordinated to patriotism
> and the wheels of government permitted to roll.[11]

Toole reasserted his statesmanship in his first gubernatorial
speech. But his efforts were not so promptly rewarded as they
had been in Congress the previous January. The two houses of
representatives continued to meet independently, each unable to transact official business under the constitution. More
dramatic, though, was the situation in the senate. The eight
Democratic members, fearing that the Republicans, with the
vote of Lieutenant Governor Rickards, would control every
measure, first refused to vote and later absented themselves
completely from the proceedings. Meanwhile, Governor Toole
had presented the legislature with the budget necessary to
fund the state in the coming biennium.

A message went out from the senate that a fine, increasing
daily, would be assessed against any member not in attendance. Democratic members, who had been lingering in and
about Helena, took flight! The senators not only fled Helena
but also charged for the state boundaries, where they could escape the jurisdiction of Montana law enforcement altogether.
Sen. W. S. Becker's is perhaps the most colorful and remarkable story of the episode. Becker stopped briefly at his home in
Glendive on his way out of the state; he was arrested there by
the sheriff of Dawson County and placed on a train for Helena.
Word of the arrest traveled quickly along the Democratic
grapevine to all corners of the state. In Miles City, Becker was
taken from the train under writ of habeas corpus, but was
shortly thereafter rearrested by a deputy sheriff of Custer
County, who escorted Becker back to the train, intending to
accompany him all the way to the state capital. At Bozeman
the two were removed from the train and the Custer County
deputy was charged with kidnapping, though he was acquitted

the same day. A special train was sent to Bozeman, which carried the deputy and his prisoner to Helena. The two arrived at 9:30 P.M. Saturday, February 8, and Becker was duly interned in the senate chamber!

That Saturday night, rules were adopted and the appropriation bills proposed by Governor Toole were passed. Becker was released, without fine, on the solemn promise that, patriotism triumphing over partisanship, he would attend the senate's Monday session. Late Sunday night, Becker stole out the back door of his hotel and was driven to a Northern Pacific engine, which was specially reserved for the escape. When the senate reconvened on Monday, Mr. Becker was in Idaho!

The same legislative session was charged with the selection of United States senators. Each party determined to rule, they met separately in joint sessions. The Republicans elected Wilbur F. Sanders and Thomas C. Power (who had just been defeated by Toole for governor), and the Democrats elected William A. Clark and Martin Maginnis. Incredibly, Montana's two legislatures sent four senators to Washington. The selection there was an easy one for the Republican Senate, and the Washington stay of Clark and Maginnis was short and uneventful.

After this nationally embarrassing genesis, the state of Montana began again. In 1890, the entire state house stood for election, as did half of the senate. The Democrats elected five state senators to the Republican's three, giving them a majority of ten to six. Compromises were reached in the house, and the first bicameral legislature finally began the business of state.

Between the first and second legislative sessions, Joe Toole had returned to Washington with romantic intentions. While serving in the Congress, he had become close friends with Gen. William Stark Rosecrans, a Civil War hero who had served as register of the treasury, ambassador to Mexico, and ultimately a congressman from California. In the course of their acquaintance, Joe met General Rosecrans's daughter Lily and was immediately enamored. Toole's granddaughter later reported that the "greatest beauties of Washington" had made their play for the handsome and eligible Mr. Toole, but that his heart first and finally went to Lily, a "quiet, religious girl with the flaming carrot-red hair and soft blue eyes."[12]

After a private wedding and a two-week honeymoon at the

seashore, Governor Toole brought Montana's first lady to her new home. *The Helena Daily Herald* reported that "no young woman in Washington is more beloved for herself, than Miss Rosecrans. . . . She has many accomplishments, being a fine musician and a great linguist. Her charities are proverbial in this city. Her tastes are simple and she dresses without regard to fashion." Lily was described as "tall and slender," and "a woman of rare common sense and of sterling character."[13] Governor and Mrs. Toole took up residence at Joe Toole's house, which still stands at 102 Rodney in Helena, there being no official governor's mansion at the time.

The Second Legislative Assembly, convened in 1891, considered and began to act on Governor Toole's recommendations. The post of Mineral Land commissioner was created to prepare and publish information concerning the millions of acres of gold, silver, and copper lands, which were slated to become the property of the Northern Pacific railroad. The legislature further passed standards to provide for the selection, location, appraisal, sale, and leasing of state lands and to guide the Mineral Land commissioner in his study of realty adjacent to the Northern Pacific right-of-way. The legislature passed other acts delineating the responsibilities of the State Board of Examiners, providing for the election of state and county officers and the canvassing of election returns; moving the tax deadline forward to provide the legislature a clearer picture of available revenue; establishing four regular annual terms of the state supreme court to ensure speedy appeals; placing various public officers on a salary basis to reduce the burden created by ad hoc fees; appointing additional district judges to relieve congestion in the trial courts; providing for prosecution by information rather than indictment of the grand jury, thereby saving costs; continuing the existence of the code commission to ensure that new and existing laws would be harmonized; and providing for the election of presidential electors.

While the measures that preoccupied the second legislature were chiefly ministerial tasks necessary to building the foundation of the state, the agenda was set and orchestrated by Governor Toole. After serving a single term, Toole retired in 1893 to his private law practice.

. . .

In Toole's absence, a tide of greed and self-interest swept over the infant state. Two "copper kings," Marcus Daly and William Clark, rich and powerful as a result of profits from the vast mineral resources of the state, were engaged in a struggle for political dominance. Two communities, Anaconda and Helena, were meanwhile vying for recognition as the permanent capital of the state. The two contests merged as the capital issue became a battleground in the ongoing war of the copper kings.

Clark wanted to be in the United States Senate. Daly's aspiration was situation of the capital in Anaconda, his hometown. Each exercised every power at his disposal to defeat the interest of the other. The state capital issue was to be decided at public election, and the Senate contest was to be decided by the state legislature. Clark used his money and influence to ensure that Helena became the state's capital and thus thwart the Daly effort. Daly marshaled his political influence in the state legislature to defeat Clark and send Lee Mantle and Thomas Carter to the senate. Each victory fueled the fire of determination in the vanquished. The Clark-Daly feud became infamous and cast a dark shadow over the dignity of Montana politics. At the same time, however, it produced a colorful period of political history.

In 1898 Clark undertook to pack the legislature to ensure his election in the senatorial contest of 1899. When the session convened, state senator Fred Whiteside of Flathead County was among its members. Whiteside was convinced that Clark intended to purchase the votes necessary to ensure his election. Whiteside undertook a sting operation to expose the bribers. A joint committee was established to investigate charges of bribery. Whiteside appeared as the first witness and produced $30,000 in cash, which he testified was given to him by Clark agents to bribe certain members. The next day, when balloting for the United States Senate seats began, Clark received only seven votes. A grand jury was called and spent two weeks investigating the charge, finally declining to indict. Meanwhile, the balloting continued, albeit without Whiteside, who was unseated on trumped-up charges of perjury. On the eighteenth ballot, Clark finally received his majority and was declared elected.

A few days later, Clark declared publicly that the charges of bribery had been contrived by his nemesis, Daly, to discredit him. Daly pledged to finance an investigation of Clark by the U.S. Senate, at an estimated cost of $20,000 to $25,000. The United States Senate Committee on Privileges and Elections did review the evidence and charges and, after a controversial investigation, reported that Clark had not been duly and legally elected. The committee's report was issued on April 23, 1900, and on May 11, before the full Senate could act, Clark announced his resignation.

The vacancy created by Clark's resignation would be filled by Gov. Robert B. Smith, who was hostile to Clark. In a scheme of unmitigated gall, Clark instructed his son to deliver the resignation, while Smith was out of state, to Lieutenant and Acting Governor A. E. Spriggs, who promptly appointed Clark to fill the vacancy caused by his own resignation. Smith returned to Montana and revoked the appointment, but, following the death of Marcus Daly in 1900, Clark struck back in 1901 and was elected to Montana's other Senate seat.

On July 4, 1899, the cornerstone of the present capitol was laid. By Governor Smith's invitation, Joe Toole was the principal speaker for the event. During the battle for location of the capital, Toole had campaigned actively for Helena, but escaped the public scorn generated by the Clark-Daly feud. He stepped to the podium with the mantle of statesmanship. Toole seized the opportunity to attack the motto that had been adopted for Montana's official state seal: "Oro y Plata" ("Gold and Silver"). Toole arraigned the selection as "too materialistic to inspire a great thought or encourage a noble deed." He displayed an uncommon vision worthy of modern-day conservationists when he advised:

> If we would establish a higher standard of morals for the coming generation than the mere lust of lucre, we would have our children see something more in the running brook than so many mill sites and water rights, more in the spreading trees than so many cords of wood, more in the setting sun than so many "candle power," more in the "lowing kine" and "sporting lamb" than so many pounds of beef and mutton, more in the landscape than so many "corner lots," more in the performance of official duty than the mere emoluments of office; if, finally, we would endeavor by precept and example to establish and main-

tain a government of which poets have dreamed and prophets spoken, the first important step in that direction admonishes us to obliterate that pernicious phrase, "Oro y Plata," from the Great Seal of our State.[14]

A subcurrent in Montana politics sprang from the agrarian communities in the 1880s and began to swell in this last turbulent decade of the century. Populism had promoted "free silver," a farmer-oriented agricultural policy, labor laws to protect workers, and protection of mineral lands from the Northern Pacific railroad "land grab." The Populist Party reached its zenith in the election of 1896, when it "fused" with the Democrats and elected several of its members to prominent offices. The Populists lost momentum though when economic vitality returned to Montana in some measure.

By 1900 the Populist Party had practically dissolved, but its legacy left an indelible impression on the future of the Democratic Party. In a time when corruption and impropriety had hijacked the ship of state, the foundation of the Progressive agenda was laid. Homesteading immigrants brought progressive sympathies to the state, while Montana citizens, disgusted with the manipulations of Montana politics by unsavory interests in the 1890s, were coming to realize the power of their own vote. Progressive legislation addressing eight-hour workdays, mine safety inspections, child labor protections, the public initiative and referendum, direct election of senators, and women's suffrage, stood at the doorstep of the Democratic Party.

"Free silver" advocate William Jennings Bryan was the Democratic candidate for president in 1900, and Montana cast a large majority vote in his favor. Joe Toole was nominated to return to his role as governor, supported by the populist/progressive arm of the Democratic Party. His opponents included candidates from the Republican Party, the Marcus Daly faction of the Democratic Party, and the "Social Democratic" Party. Toole received an easy plurality and succeeded to office with the entire state and congressional ticket of populist/progressive Democrats.

Toole's imprint is most familiar on the politics of the late nineteenth century. When he took office in 1901, however, he found himself on the cusp of a transition from sporadic populist politics to progressive democratic government. The faith of the Democratic Party's new Progressives in Joe Toole was well placed. As he took office, he articulated the ideals that the Progressives espoused, and his voice refreshingly rose above the din of petty partisanship which characterized the affairs of state in the 1890s.

As the century and the Progressive era opened, the Seventh Legislative Assembly convened in Helena, then the official capital city, in 1901. On Governor Toole's recommendation, the assembly adopted a joint resolution proposing a federal constitutional amendment providing for the election of U.S. senators by a direct vote of the people. The legislature further adopted laws sanctioning the eight-hour workday for laborers and other wage protection measures. Bond issues and special levies were authorized to create sufficient and dependable financing for education. The position of game warden was created, and a system of laws was enacted to regulate and protect game animals.

In 1903 Governor Toole placed before the legislature and the public a series of even bolder Progressive reforms. He proposed that the legislature submit constitutional amendments to the people providing for full women's suffrage, an initiative and referendum process, direct primary elections, and a provision for equalization of the system of taxation of real property. Although many of these proposals would become incorporated into Montana constitutional law, the legislature prevented the submission of these amendments to the people at that time. The legislature also obstructed Toole's efforts to provide for nonpartisan judicial elections and to require smelters to install "scrubber" apparatuses to protect Montanans and Montana from the hazards of air pollution. These Progressive ideas, as well, were ultimately enacted, despite the Seventh Legislative Assembly's reluctance.

The legislature did renew its resolution to Congress urging the direct election of United States senators. In at least one progressive stroke, the body also enacted a series of specific new protections for the safety of Montana mine workers. Further, Toole convinced the assembly to pass restrictions on the dumping of coal dust and screenings in streams. A visionary aspect of the Progressive agenda was the recognition that emission of particulates into the air and water would threaten flora and fauna in a way that would endanger the ecosystem.

Toole gave a forward-thinking eloquence to the cause of women's suffrage, as well. Calling for the political enfranchisement of women, Toole expressed his confidence in their ability to help lift Montana from its recent sordid political events. In his annual address of 1903, he announced, "A new force is demanded in this state to clean out the Augean Stables whose poisonous effluvia ladens the political atmosphere and corrupts the public morals."[15]

Suffrage for women would be delayed until 1914, but Toole can be credited with forcing the state to confront the issue and sanctioning the cause of suffrage with the legitimacy of gubernatorial endorsement.

Not all of Toole's Progressive reforms were delayed. A state board of health was created in 1901 and a pure food and drug law adopted. Two years later, a comprehensive meat and milk inspection act was adopted. Legislation creating the State Bureau of Child and Animal Protection in 1903 was coupled the following year with acts providing a minimum age of sixteen for mine workers and making school to that age compulsory. In 1907 the minimum working age requirement was extended to other areas of labor. A juvenile court system was also established.

If the Progressive reforms initiated by Toole were among the high points of his career, an episode involving the Amalgamated Mining Company must have marked the low point. Though Toole in 1901 denounced before the legislature "the long continued practice of corporate interference in political affairs in this state," he was forced to participate in 1903 in an event that epitomized the subordination of the state's political leaders to corporate power.

Mining magnate F. Augustus Heinze had been engaged for several years in legal disputes with the Standard Oil–Amalgamated Copper Company over ownership of mineral veins. Judge William Clancy of Butte, who adjudicated most of these controversies, ruled consistently in favor of Heinze. Between 1900 and 1903, though mining of controverted veins was illegal, the two mining interests engaged in a literal underground war. In the Minnie Healy mine, miners were attempting to flood each other's shafts until October 22, 1903, when Judge Clancy awarded full title to the mine to Heinze. The same day, Clancy ruled against Amalgamated in another Heinze dispute and declared that the copper trust had no legal standing in Montana and therefore could not operate legally here.

Amalgamated, unwilling to submit to this judicial control, simply slammed shut its doors, leaving 15,000 men, more than half of the wage earners in the state, out of work. Amalgamated refused to reopen the mines until a change of venue law was passed, permitting it to demand trial in another court when it believed the judge to be biased. Toole initially resisted this unvarnished attempt to manipulate the judicial system, but the enormous impact of the closure could not go unaddressed. Toole called a special session of the legislature and the infamous Fair Trials Bill was passed. Unable thereafter to compete with Amalgamated over the many disputed claims, Heinze eventually sold his company's interests and left the state.

Toole was overwhelmingly reelected in 1904, even though Republican Theodore Roosevelt carried with him a strong ticket of Republicans into other offices. In 1907 Governor Toole, in his annual message, recognized the weakness of state government in regulating the conduct of great corporations like Standard Oil and Amalgamated Copper, advising that their conduct could only be regulated by the federal government through effective enactment and implementation of antitrust laws.

In his third term, Toole was chiefly occupied with continuing efforts to enact progressive reforms initiated several years before. Additional laws were passed protecting the interests of workers, consumers, and children. Late in 1907 Governor Toole's health failed and he submitted his resignation on February 1, 1908.

After a brief sojourn to California Toole returned to Helena, where he hoped to reopen his law office but was unable to do so because of his poor health. Toole spent the next twenty years in and out of Montana, and he died in Helena on March 11, 1929, at the age of seventy-seven. On the occasion of his death, the Montana Senate passed a resolution in his honor. In part, the epistle read:

Joseph K. Toole was a pioneer in the truest and best
sense. When this commonwealth was young and pioneer
spirits were blazing the trails which were to lead us to its
present importance and greatness, Montana was favored
with the vision and political wisdom of Joseph K. Toole.
He was not a man of the moment, today in the limelight
and then forgotten. His mark is on the history of Montana
and it is not only one that can never be erased, but one
that will forever resound to his credit. In those early days
he was dynamic with energy, resourceful, vigilant, active,
of great courage and filled with a sense of responsibility
toward his state and the people who were to be its citizens
in the coming years . . . He was a man of great dignity, a
real dignity of the spirit. Through the troublesome days
that came to Montana during his second term, with scandal floating on every wind, no breath of it touched Joseph
K. Toole. He was a valiant statesman, a high-minded citizen, a Chief Executive of noble parts. For what he did for
this state, he has never received adequate reward. . . . He
could not. But he will live in the memories of those who
knew him best as one of those rare souls and charming
personalities, too few indeed of whom walk the painful
paths of this kingdom of time and place.[16]

Joe Toole's public career spanned an extraordinary era in
American and Montana politics. First elected less than ten
years after Montana gained territorial status, Toole served as a
prosecutor, member of the territorial council, framer of two
constitutions, delegate to Congress and three terms as governor. His plea for statehood moved his colleagues, his constituents, and the nation. He articulated the essence of
Montana and eloquently demanded her admission to the
Union. He helped draw the blueprint for the state's new government and set its initial course. Greed and corruption tram-
pled the political process in Toole's absence but were largely
reined in on his return as governor. In his final years of leadership, he breathed life into the progressive political agenda
and renounced the corporate domination of Montana. With
skill, devotion, and courage, Joe Toole launched and captained
Montana on its maiden voyage and thereby distinguished himself as the father of the Treasure State.

Suggested Readings on Joseph K. Toole

No full-length book on Joseph Toole exists. Articles and original source material about Toole have been collected by the Montana Historical Society and can be found there in the Joseph K. Toole vertical file. A twenty-three-page paper, circa 1935, titled "Joseph Kemp Toole" by John B. Ritch, librarian of the Montana Historical Society, was prepared on the basis of a narration by Warren Toole, the son of Joseph K. Toole. Extensive commentary regarding Toole's plea for statehood is carefully collected by Dave Walter in "The Right Kind of Nail," *Montana: The Magazine of Western History* (Autumn 1987).

A detailed tribute to Toole was written by his granddaughter, Patricia Toole Whitehorn, in connection with the American Bicentennial. It was published, along with Toole's first gubernatorial message, in *Then and Now* (1976). Information about the statehood battle, the Constitutional Convention of 1889, the Fair Trials Bill, and early Progressive reforms can be found in M. P. Malone, R. B. Roeder, and W. L. Lang, *Montana: A History of Two Centuries* (Seattle/London, 1991). A thorough account of the antics of the early Montana legislatures is contained in James McClellan Hamilton, *From Wilderness to Statehood* (Portland, 1957). Specific election results can be found in Ellis Waldron and Paul B. Wilson, *Atlas of Montana Elections* (Missoula, 1978).

Ella Knowles Haskell

II

Ella Knowles,
Pioneer of Equality

I believe in justice in all things and if it was unjust for our fathers to be taxed by Great Britain without representation, it is unjust to tax the women of today without representation.

The late-nineteenth-century western frontier drew herds of adventurous souls lured by the promise of vast lands and mountains laced with gold. Most of the new settlers were rugged men seeking fame and wealth. When women joined these men, they often did so reluctantly, sacrificing the comforts and amenities of urban life. Unmarried women who ventured west, leaving home and family willingly and independently, were especially rare. Tested and tempered, the different women of the West shared an irrepressible spirit. As homesteaders, ranchers, or wives, they endured trying hardships at the edge of civilization, emerging as a strong-willed and triumphant class. A precious few embarked on careers and faced perhaps the greatest obstacle of all: the challenge of winning professional respect and recognition in a tough, new, male-dominated society.

Among these women was Ella Knowles, Montana pioneer, lawyer, politician, and activist. Ella merged the resourceful vigor of a New England Yankee with the uncharted possibilities of the western frontier to achieve goals unheard of for women in that time. Tireless in the pursuit of her goals, Ella confronted daunting odds with determination, grace, and wit, dispelling myths that successful women depended on the welfare and generosity of their husbands.

Opposite: *Ella Knowles Haskell, Montana's first woman lawyer. Knowles successfully lobbied for legislation to permit women to practice law, became Montana's first licensed woman lawyer and was the Populist Party candidate for attorney general in 1892. She was a leader in the national suffrage movement and was regarded as the nation's preeminent woman lawyer.*
Courtesy of Montana Historical Society, Helena.

Montana's first woman lawyer, Ella Knowles was also the first American woman to address a state legislature, the first American woman nominated by a major political party for statewide public office, the first American woman to be appointed assistant or deputy state attorney general, and the first American woman to represent a sovereign state before a United States government agency in Washington, D.C. Observers in the first decade of the twentieth century, before she was forty years old, described her as the most prominent woman in the political history of Montana and as the preeminent woman lawyer in America. Although she never served in elected public office, Ella Knowles, by virtue of boundless courage and energy, became a figure of national importance in the struggle to win recognition for women in government.

The Wild West in 1860 was a long way from the settled and civilized town of Northwood, New Hampshire, birthplace of Ella Louise Knowles. She was born that year on July 31, the only child of David and Louisa Knowles. The Knowles's ancestors included early Colonial settlers, who filled positions of responsibility and leadership in their new homeland. From the beginning, Ella showed an aptitude for learning and pursued life with singular focus and drive. Her primary education was provided by her mother. After her mother's death, when Ella was fourteen, she enrolled in the Northwood Seminary and one year later completed the teaching course at Plymouth State Normal School. For the next four years she taught in neighboring schools, saving money to fulfill her dream of attending college.

Higher education in the 1870s was not expected of women, and few schools offered the opportunity. Ella applied to Bates College in Lewiston, Maine, which was one of only two liberal arts institutions experimenting with coeducation. She was accepted and enrolled in 1880, commencing an active and accomplished collegiate career.

As a student, Ella ignored gender barriers and distinguished herself in male-dominated activities. She became the first woman on the varsity debate team, arguing topics like "Resolved: That Circumstances Make Men"; "Was Hamilton's Theory of Government Superior to That of Jefferson?" and "Would the Condition of Great Britain Be Improved by Adopting a Republican Form of Government?" Ella also served as the first woman on the editorial board of the college magazine, *The Bates Student*. These were the first of many challenges that Ella Knowles would raise against the status quo.

Bates afforded Ella a fertile training ground, unavailable to most American women. She gained skills in public speaking, debate, and writing, which contributed immeasurably to her success in later pursuits. Throughout her life she would maintain a close relationship with her alma mater, corresponding regularly with updates on her legal career and private affairs. Ella graduated magna cum laude from Bates in 1884, getting her degree in rhetoric and English literature.

After graduation Ella shunned the more traditional jobs open to educated women of the nineteenth century, and took her first step toward a career in law. She began her studies in the law firm of Burnham and Brown in Manchester, New Hampshire. She was a dedicated and eager law student for three years until 1887 when she was afflicted with the first of myriad health problems that would plague her for the rest of her life. Following the advice of her physician, she decided to move west into drier climes, and Ella's journey to Montana began.

Traveling without family or escort, Ella moved to Iowa to fill the professorship of rhetoric and elocution at Western Normal College. Vexed by persistent ill health, she soon uprooted and pushed farther west, through another teaching job at Utah's Salt Lake Academy, and then north to the bustling gold town of Helena, in the Montana Territory.

Knowles arrived in Helena at the age of twenty-eight, still alone but fortified with ambition, will, and ability. In 1888 Montana was a wild frontier teeming with opportunity for miners, homesteaders, and any free spirit willing to work for a living. Ella took a teaching position at Helena Central School and after only a year was appointed principal of Helena's West Side School. Disregarding the encouragement of friends, she declined the appointment. Ella was determined instead to resume her legal studies, which she did in the Helena law office of Joseph Kinsley, a fellow New Englander. Kinsley was a member of Montana's broad network of transplanted Yankees that Knowles would turn to throughout her professional and personal life.

No woman at that time had ever practiced law in Montana.

The law of the state did not permit it. Knowles was most concerned with passing the bar examination, devised by the newly-formed Montana Bar Association, but a change in the law was necessary before she could sit for the exam. Knowles understood that persuading an entirely male legislature to open the legal profession to women, in a territory that denied women the right to vote, would be a formidable task. Circumstances nationally and in Montana were hardly encouraging. The first woman lawyer in America, Arabelle A. Mansfield, joined the Iowa bar 1869. By the time Ella took her campaign to the Montana territorial legislature, there were perhaps fifty women lawyers in the nation. A few decades earlier the United States Supreme Court had declared that the "natural and proper timidity and delicacy" of women rendered them unfit for the rigorous practice of law. A few months after the 1889 legislative session, the state constitutional convention would reaffirm female non-suffrage by embedding it in Montana's first constitution. None of this, however, intimidated Ella Knowles.

Knowles set about lobbying the legislature and found a supporter in Councilman Walter Bickford. During the final session of the 1889 territorial legislature, Bickford sponsored a bill, drafted principally by Knowles, which would admit women to the bar. Ella addressed the entire assembly on the issue, becoming the first American woman officially to speak to a state legislature. Not surprisingly, debate on the bill was lively and protracted. Seemingly every member of the all-male legislature wanted to express his opinion on the novelty of practicing women lawyers. Several of the more progressive leaders defended the bill as a "matter of principle" and stated that "professional opportunity was a natural right irrespective of sex." The only relevant question, they argued, was whether the mental capacity of women was equal to that of men; if so, women should be admitted to the legal profession. Reactionary members argued that a woman's place was in the home, a place consistent with the woman's physical, emotional, and moral constitution. This band, however, found itself in the minority; progressive reason prevailed and the bill passed both houses. Again, Ella Knowles had broken ground and the doors of the bench and bar were opened to all.

After winning the right to legally practice law in Montana,

Knowles passed the bar exam on December 26, 1889, receiving high praise from the bar examiners. Her victories before the legislators and examiners, though, did not ensure her success. Knowles had yet to prove her worth to the toughest critics, her male colleagues. Her entry into the legal community was met with opposition and little assistance or support. Women had studied law and served as legal assistants in their husbands' offices, but there was no precedent for a practicing female attorney. As she broke tradition and began her professional career, Knowles labored against "the various degrees of ostracism which attend the efforts of women to make their way in fields which the men had been in the habit of considering peculiarly their own."[1]

Ella later delighted in describing the struggle to earn her "first fee" as a practicing lawyer. Following the example of other novice attorneys, Knowles offered herself to business clients as a debt collector. When she approached Helena area merchants, she was all but ignored, as the businessmen told her they had no bad bills. Finally, a merchant admitted to having old debts but doubted that a woman could collect on them. He told Ella, "If you want to collect anything, go and collect some of my umbrellas. I own three of them. Here it is raining and I cannot go to lunch because somebody has borrowed my umbrellas and did not return them."[2] The merchant's obvious hope was that this menial task would discourage the persistent young lawyer. Undaunted, Ella left the store in pursuit of the borrowed umbrellas.

"I straightaway went to the home of the first woman he named, a well-known Helena lady. I rang the front doorbell, and a maid came to the door. I stated my business, and the maid called the woman of the house. To her I explained that I was studying law in a certain lawyer's office in Helena and that Mr. Merchant had asked me to collect some umbrellas for him, one of which had been borrowed some time ago by her. She flared up, but produced the umbrella. . . . I proceeded to the second home. . . . I got the umbrella but it was accompanied by a look that haunted me in my sleep that night."

She delivered the two umbrellas to the merchant:

> He looked shocked and dumbfounded when he realized what I had done and then became angry and started to

storm even worse than the two women had. There were a number of people in the store and I appealed to them to say if I was not entitled to my fee. When they understood the case, they all agreed with me and then the humorous phase of the matter was recognized by my client and he joined in the general laugh.[3]

The merchant paid her twenty-five cents for each umbrella and, with that, Ella Knowles had earned her first fee. She went on to collect other bills for him and later was retained as the firm's attorney. Ella understood the need to be assertive and visible in her pursuits; otherwise, she would have been completely ignored. "When I first began the practice of law," she later recalled, "I was taken as a huge joke and I could have sat in my office to this day and would not have had a case. But I didn't sit in the office: I went out and got my business to start with and soon business came to me in abundance."

Knowles practiced law for one year with Joseph Kinsley. They formed the business partnership of Kinsley and Knowles, Attorneys at Law. Her first lawsuit during this time was a justice court case. The litigation was between a "Chinaman and a Negro." According to Knowles:

> The Chinaman, my client, had been employed by the Negro in a restaurant, and when he quit the employment, there was due him $5 in wages. The Negro refused to pay and I brought suit for the Chinaman. The colored man employed a well-known Helena attorney and at the trial my client told his story and made a statement of the account between himself and his employer . . . [with] a dirty account book showing the entries of credits and debits between himself and the Chinaman. . . . I had no evidence to offset the book and I felt my first case lost, when an inspiration came to me. I procured a magnifying reading glass and examined the colored man's accounts. The glass won the case for me, for it disclosed that some figures had been erased and others marked over them and that the erased figures corresponded with the Chinaman's account.

Knowles later reported, "The $5 case worried me more than many big lawsuits have worried me since, and I had many sleepless nights before the case came to trial."[4]

Knowles was anxious to strike out on her own, and by 1892 was established in a solo practice. Her college magazine that year reported that Ella "has clients in nearly every county of the state, and her income from her profession amounts to thousands of dollars yearly."[5] Despite Ella's multiple clients and a successful track record, her male colleagues expected her to be a weak opponent in the courtroom. She proved otherwise. Winning case after case, Knowles earned a reputation as an able and competent attorney with a gift for oratory and argument.

Ella Knowles was consumed by her passion for the law and achieved high praise and recognition for her work on behalf of the underprivileged across the state. She took a variety of cases, both criminal and civil, pressing her clients' causes and helping to develop a body of common law in the new state. She practiced for two more years before again breaking from the common path by launching a statewide political campaign in a newly formed party.

Throughout the early years of her law practice Knowles attracted widespread attention. Most notably, she won the admiration of the Populist Party, which summoned her to bear its standard. In 1892 she was nominated to run on the Populist ticket for state attorney general. She thus became the first American woman to be nominated by a major party for a statewide public office. It was a risky and dramatic step for the Populists to take, but the party was a leader in the women's rights movement and did not shy from controversy.

The irony of this nomination did not go unnoticed. In 1892 Montana women still did not possess the right of general franchise; women's suffrage was limited to district school elections. Hence, Ella Knowles sought an office through an election in which she could not vote. The law had not contemplated such events, but the dilemma was resolved by Attorney General Henri Haskell, Knowles's Republican opponent. A fellow New England transplant, Haskell issued an opinion that said that Ella could run for the office even though she lacked the power to vote.

Another obstacle had fallen, and Ella Knowles marched on. Fueled by her later-famous drive and energy, she focused first on the organization of her campaign. Recognizing her own political inexperience and the prejudices against a woman running for public office, Knowles studied the national platform of the Populist Party. She became an expert on the free silver issue and concentrated her speeches on this topic.

Ella Knowles entered the political arena with vigor and declared that she was in the fight to win. Although not yet thirty years old, her nomination and the approval of her candidacy by Haskell already had spotlighted Ella as a political figure of national importance. For over five months she was a tireless campaigner. She delivered more than one hundred speeches and canvassed the state's eastern counties with Populist gubernatorial candidate Will Kennedy. Public reactions to a woman "stumping" on the political circuit were mostly positive. Curiosity motivated many people to attend her appearances and more often than not listeners were surprised to discover that her "speeches were replete with reason, gilded with rhetoric and clothed with eloquent passages which stamped them as efforts creditable to the most gifted of Montana's orators."[6] Others criticized her performance, contending that it was improper for a woman to stand up, wave her arms about, and yell.

Detractors notwithstanding, Knowles's eloquence and legal ability earned her the nickname Portia of the People's Party, probably a favorable comparison to the heroine of Shakespeare's *Merchant of Venice*. The novelty of a woman on the hustings assisted the cause of the other Populist candidates. Knowles's presence brought crowds and, as she was often the last speaker on the program, kept the voters assembled throughout each of the new party's rallies.

Despite her dedication and solid efforts, Knowles ran in third place, with 11,464 votes. Incumbent Henri Haskell was reelected with 16,606 ballots. Although not an electoral winner, Ella's performance was solid and significant. Of course, she reserved a place for herself in history as the first woman candidate to run for a statewide political office. Beyond that though, she captured a larger share of votes than any other Populist candidate: 3,671 more than Kennedy and 4,438 more than congressional candidate Caldwell Edwards.

Ella Knowles remained popular within the ranks of the Populist Party and was politically active the rest of her life. In 1896 she was a delegate from Lewis and Clark County to the Populist state convention. She was a also a delegate to the party's national convention in St. Louis; she was named national committeewoman from Montana. At the convention, she was elected to a four-year office on the Populist national committee. There she promoted equal suffrage and was a vocal advocate for Populist presidential candidate William Jennings Bryan.

In January 1893, a year following her defeat, Ella was appointed assistant attorney general by her erstwhile opponent Henri Haskell, conquering another obstacle. No American woman had ever served as an assistant or deputy state attorney general. Ella served capably for four years and distinguished herself in a case of special significance to Montanans, which she argued before the United States Department of the Interior. In 1903 Ella became the first American woman to appear in Washington, D.C., as the legal representative of a sovereign state. She represented the state in the appeal of *Paris Gibson* v. *State of Montana*, which involved the title of school lands near Great Falls worth at least $200,000. She built a reputation in the case as an able and intelligent lawyer. Before she left Washington, D.C., the secretary of the interior rendered a decision in her favor, awarding the disputed lands to the state of Montana. The decision meant that school land could not be taken up for a stone quarry under the Placer Mineral Act.

In addition to her legal responsibilities, Ella Knowles contributed time, energy, and leadership to the cause of women's suffrage. Ella was motivated by a deep commitment to equal justice. Answering an opponent of her progressive position on women's rights, Knowles once declared: "I believe in justice in all things and if it was unjust for our fathers to be taxed by Great Britain without representation, it is unjust to tax the women of today without representation."[7]

The women's suffrage movement in Montana passed through several key stages of development before its eventual success in 1915. The early state organization was dominated by well-educated, often single, older women who had time to devote to a cause. This, however, represented only a small sector of society. The majority of women were preoccupied with the obligations of children and household duties, leaving them with no energy or inclination to support the local suffrage movement. Ella was not encumbered by any such commitments though, and she proved herself a leading force behind the early suffrage organizations in Helena and Butte during the 1890s.

The issue of equal suffrage was debated for many years until the male legislature ultimately threw the question to the voters. In 1884 the leaders of the territory were concentrating on securing statehood. Delegates to the 1884 Constitutional Convention drafted a document that addressed the requirements for admission to statehood, without recommending the expansion of women's suffrage. Anything controversial was omitted from the state's constitution for fear that the partisan Congress might find cause for denial of statehood.

This conservative mood prevailed and persisted as delegates prepared for the 1889 Constitutional Convention. Though Congress had already voted to confer statehood upon Montana, the men of the convention were more interested in preserving the status quo than in advancing novel concepts of justice. The few discussions of equal suffrage focused on who would be empowered to decide the fate of women's right to vote—the legislators or the public.

Walter Bickford, Knowles's proponent on the earlier question of admitting women to the state bar, proposed that the legislature be empowered to grant women equal suffrage. Conservative rhetoric concerning the role of women and the doctrine of "separate spheres" convinced the delegates that no legislative adjustments should be granted. Bickford's proposal failed 34 to 29, and the future of women's suffrage looked bleak. Suffrage now would be achieved only by an amendment to the constitution, a process requiring a two-thirds majority approval in both houses and ratification by the electorate.

In November 1896 the state suffrage organization met in Butte. Local clubs, including both Helena groups, met to elect officers, review past ideology, and shape a philosophy consistent with the needs and realities of Montana women. Ella was elected state president, replacing the influential Harriet Sanders. Ella now faced the monumental task of organizing an effective suffrage lobby. With finely tuned political skills, Knowles was the woman for the job. Her goal: to remove the suffrage issue from the legislature and to "let the people decide."

The 1897 legislature considered a bill that proposed a constitutional amendment for suffrage. Relying on past tactics, the bill's sponsor opted to stress the equity of permitting the state's voters to make the final decision rather than focus on the ideology of suffrage. Knowles was given the floor and reinforced the sponsors' reasoning, stating that if justice did not prevail she would deliver innumerable petitions signed by the people themselves.

The floor debate among opponents degenerated into the tired rhetoric of separate spheres. One representative in particular derided suffragists as "unbecoming models of womanhood." Ella took the floor again and pled for political justice. A strong majority fell in line but the final vote was 41 to 27, five votes short of the necessary two-thirds supermajority.

Despite the narrow defeat, Ella's efforts paved the way for future suffragists. By late 1897 Ella's term as president of the state suffrage organization had expired. The fight for women's equal suffrage in Montana was far from over then, but the organizational structure designed to lead the assault fell into disarray and was unable to mobilize. Whether the success and direction of the organization in its earlier years was attributable solely to Knowles's unusual determination, organizational abilities, and political skills, the leaders of the movement after her resignation were unable to deliver the same results.

During the years following Knowles's stewardship, the suffrage activists began slowly to reorient their philosophies to establish a more politically acceptable rationale for women's suffrage. They reasoned that the best approach was one tempered by political pragmatism. By 1902 the suffragists had abandoned natural rights as the chief argument for suffrage and accepted a modified ideology of separate spheres and women's special moral virtue. However, the shift in perspective did not bring immediate success. The movement struggled through the century's first decade with little progress. It was not until after 1911, when another notable leader emerged in Jeannette Rankin, that the suffrage question would finally be resolved.

Out of the president's chair, Ella remained a visible force in the women's suffrage movement. She traveled the country delivering speeches. In 1896 she lectured at the Atlanta Exposition on the topic "Women in the Professions," pointing to the comparatively large proportion of female lawyers in the West as compared with the established and more populated eastern states. She addressed the convention of the National American Woman Suffrage Association in 1898 on the topic "The Environments of Women as Related to their Progress," reviewing the legal obstacles of previous ages and delineating the advances made by women after achieving only partial freedom. Ella was also recognized by one of her fellow suffragists in 1904 as the woman attorney receiving the largest annual income from her practice. By 1900 Montana temperance activist Mary Long Alderson described Ella Knowles as "by far the most prominent woman in the political history of the state," who "nobly battled for the enlargement of women's legal rights."[8]

As busy a life as Ella Knowles led, she found time to wed. She married her political opponent and boss, Henri Haskell of Glendive, on May 23, 1895, in San Francisco, California. Haskell was also a native New Englander, born and educated in Maine before moving west in 1867. Ella was in California recuperating from broken ribs suffered in a driving accident in Butte when they exchanged wedding vows. Ella Knowles became Ella Knowles Haskell, and the former foes came home to Montana. The newlyweds continued their work in the attorney general's office until 1896, when Henri returned to the private sector, establishing a law practice with Ella in Butte.

Despite shared roots and interests, the Knowles-Haskell union was not permanent. Henri wished to retire to the quiet, rural life of Glendive and Ella preferred the social and business opportunities available in the cities of Helena and Butte. They dissolved both their professional and personal partnerships in 1897, parting childless. Divorce in the late nineteenth century was not common but was demanding acceptance as women realized that marriage and the life of domesticity were not the only alternatives available to able and ambitious females. Ella's independence and determination led her down this path, though such qualities in themselves remained contrary to the traditional feminine values and traits preferred by professional, upper-middle-class men.

Again a single woman, Ella devoted herself to community and social organizations. She was active in the Theosophical Society, Daughters of the American Revolution, Eastern Star, Martha Lodge of the Rebekahs, the Woman's Club, Women's

Relief Corps, Women of Woodcraft, and the New England Society. While living in Butte during her final years she maintained a broad network of friends and acquaintances.

Ella held not only progressive political beliefs but also many unconventional religious and social ideas. She was a student of theosophy and the Asian philosophies. She believed that life is continuous and progressive, that death is merely an incident in life and of no more significance than the act of passing from one room into another.

Sometime after her divorce from Haskell and her presidency of the state suffrage organization, Ella journeyed again to California, to benefit from the mild San Diego climate.

When she returned to Butte, she focused her attention on her law practice in which she won increasing respect and recognition. National suffragist leader Carrie Chapman Catt heralded Ella as "the most successful woman lawyer in America." Ella devoted considerable time to the representation of prominent mining companies and even managed mining properties herself. "That I am interested in mining in several ways is not strange," she once said, "when you consider that I reside in one of the greatest mining states in the Union or even in the world."[9] In 1900, Ella served as a delegate to the International Mining Congress in Milwaukee and was elected a member of the executive committee of the congress.

The urban lifestyle characteristic of early twentieth-century Butte suited Ella's curiosity and ambition. She thrived on her membership activities and busy law practice. But frail health did not support such an active life. In 1910 Ella embarked on a journey around the world to relax and recover from recurring ailments. She returned to Butte with tales and treasures but not restored health. Despite her lingering afflictions, Ella delivered a public lecture, described as one of the best of its kind ever heard in Butte. She also entertained friends and acquaintances in her home, regaling them with the stories of her travels.

Full recovery eluded Ella. In the winter of 1911 tragedy befell Butte when the poor physical condition that Ella had fought valiantly since her youth cut short her life. Neither California sunshine nor world adventures could heal the sickly woman who had left her home in New Hampshire just twenty-five years earlier to cure her failing health. On January 28, the

Butte Miner reported her status as "critical and due to overwork in her office in Butte following a trip around the world . . . the alarming symptoms are evidences of extensive virulent blood-poisoning that sometimes follow a physical breakdown."[10]

Occasionally, in the course of human events, a pioneer emerges who has the potential to bring great changes. Ella Knowles Haskell possessed this potential and fulfilled it. In her brief life she challenged tradition and redefined what it meant to be a western woman of the late nineteenth century. Building from a career that sprouted in a territory on the frontier, Ella rose to national prominence as a model for women who yearned for a meaningful place in government. Too often, Ella Knowles is overlooked by the studies on women who made a difference in the early years of Montana and the American women's movement. Ella Knowles made a great difference. By irresistible will and indomitable commitment to principle, she knocked down age-old walls of prejudice and cleared the path of equality. By so doing, she changed the fortunes of countless women and helped a tough, young state define its new existence.

Suggested Readings on Ella Knowles

Sources on Ella Knowles are limited. The most thorough article on Ella's life is Richard B. Roeder, "Crossing the Gender Line," *Montana: The Magazine of Western History* (Summer 1982). The Montana Historical Society maintains copies of the *Bates Student* (Lewiston, Maine, 1883), which contains information about Ella as a college student. A brief biography of Ella ironically appears in *Progressive Men of the State of Montana* (Chicago, 1902). Bates College produced a documentary video in 1993 titled "Ella Knowles: A Dangerous Woman," which incorporates commentary on Ella from historians.

For a good discussion of the suffrage movement in Montana in the later nineteenth century, see Paula E. Petrick, *No Step Backward: Women and Family on the Rocky Mountain Mining Frontier, Helena, Montana, 1865–1900* (Helena, 1987). The number of votes cast for each candidate in Ella's attorney general race can be found in Ellis Waldron and Paul B. Wilson, *Atlas of Montana Elections* (Missoula, 1978).

An excellent account of the early history of the Montana women's suffrage movement is found in T. A. Larson, "Montana Women and the Battle for the Ballot: Woman Suffrage in the Treasure State," *Montana: The Magazine of Western History* (Winter 1973).

III

Joseph M. Dixon,
the Bull Moose Progressive

Let him who hath no stomach for the fight depart.

He has been called Montana's greatest governor, a rugged individualist, and the leading figure of the Montana progressive movement. In his time, he was known variously as a "stalwart Republican" and a "radical." He was a conciliator and a fighter; popular and controversial. His career passed through local politics, Congress, the Senate, national party leadership, and the governorship, before he was resoundingly denied re-election to that final office. Commentators have postulated that Joseph Dixon's courage and foresight often left him akin to the prophet who was "without honor in his own land." Noted historian K. Ross Toole mused that Dixon had been the victim of an inexplicable "historical eclipse" and suggested that perhaps "the past never really forgives a man who is always ahead of it."[1]

In an era when the mainstream of the Republican party was captive to the great industrial powers, Dixon was among the leaders of a movement that broke free to advocate a progressive agenda for Montana and the nation. Later, when Montana's economy began to crumble and state government plunged into debt, Dixon confronted the omnipotent copper mining interests of Montana and their vitriolic captive press with a call for heavier taxation of the mines. The battle marked his political death but forever changed the state's balance of power.

The young Quaker Joseph Dixon stood poised before the 1887 Earlham College commencement. Although he was still a ju-

Opposite: Congressman Joseph M. Dixon, 1904. As a new congressman, Dixon became a leader of the Progressive Republican movement, culminating in his chairmanship of Theodore Roosevelt's Bull Moose campaign for president in 1912. Courtesy of Montana Historical Society, Helena.

nior, Dixon's peers in the Ionian Debating Society had asked him to deliver the closing oration. Dixon's topics and the forcefulness of his ideas showed a character already well developed, one that would guide this student to the heights of national political leadership. "No more absolute truth was ever uttered, or obtained credence with a civilized people, than the proverb 'Vox Populi, Vox Dei' . . . ," said Dixon. "We, as a nation, having escaped the dogma of the divine right of kings, let us not fall into the equally pernicious error that multitude is divine because it is multitude." Dixon charged that public opinion had become a new tyrant and that there was "hardly a man in public life who dare [sic] confess the honest convictions of his inmost soul." The tyrant of public opinion, said the speaker, had "added a new commandment to the decalogue: cursed be the man who bolts the party nominee."[2]

Dixon's words were not chosen for the faint at heart or the weak of purpose. They were the provocative declarations of a young but thoughtful mind that observed a paralysis in public leadership during times that required courage and resolution. The young student's ideas would prove prophetic as they materialized throughout the course of his Montana political career.

Joseph Moore Dixon was born July 31, 1867, in the Quaker enclave of Snow Camp, North Carolina. His father, Hugh Dixon, was a farmer, teacher, and operator of a foundry, sawmill, and woolen mill. A man with a deep interest in public affairs, Hugh had long opposed the institution of slavery. Though he was forced to use the capital of his mills to produce weapons for the Confederacy during the Civil War, Hugh's heart sided with the Republican North. Joe Dixon's mother, Adaline, was a non-Quaker, which caused a good deal of criticism in the tight Quaker community, but she was as deeply religious as her neighbors and equally devoted to her children.

Joe Dixon began his education at the Sylvan Academy, near Snow Camp. At fifteen, Dixon transferred to the New Garden Quaker Boarding School outside Greensboro to receive a college preparatory education. He was a "chunky lad, with his full face marked by strong, clearly defined features and his bountiful hair escaping down his forehead."[3] Joe Dixon excelled both academically and as a member of New Garden's active debating society. He graduated in 1886.

That same year, Joe left his family and traveled to Indiana to attend Earlham, a well-respected Quaker college. Dixon remained active in debate at Earlham, delivered orations, and wrote articles addressing political issues. In his speech to the commencement of 1887, Dixon not only called for the exercise of independent conscience in the political community but also advocated expenditure of the $500 million federal surplus to establish free educational institutions for "Negro" Americans. This, Dixon argued, would be the first great step in ending the subjugation of this long-enslaved American minority group.

In 1888, before graduating, Dixon left Earlham and returned to Snow Camp. His journey took him through Washington, D.C., where he spent two days observing Congress and touring the capital. When his train pulled away from Union Station, Dixon felt the pride and patriotism that the capital city inspires and wondered whether and when he would return.

Dixon finished his college education at Guilford College, the collegiate arm of the New Garden School. For the next two years, he worked at the family woolen mill, uncertain about his future. He later reported that the uncertainties following college graduation led to "one of the most discouraging times in a young man's career."[4] In 1891 Dixon became restless and dissatisfied. He knew his political ambitions could never be fulfilled in Democratically dominated North Carolina, so he wrote to his father's first cousin, Frank Woody of Missoula, Montana, about the possibility of reading law in Woody's office. Woody acquiesced, and Joe Dixon boarded a train for the Treasure State.

Joe Dixon arrived in Missoula on a westbound Northern Pacific train in the spring of 1891. He reported straight to Frank Woody's office, where he performed odd jobs to earn his keep while reading law. Although Montana ordinarily required two years of legal study prior to admission to the bar, Dixon was admitted in 1892.

Frank Woody was a controversial political activist, and some of this image rubbed off on Joe. Nevertheless, Joe was eventually able to establish a practice with I. G. Denny, then county attorney. Dixon took every opportunity to speak publicly on issues of interest at the time. He took strong positions in favor of the Republican Party and became active in the local central committee. In 1894 he was nominated for the office of county attorney and his partner, Denny, the incumbent Democrat, reluctantly stepped aside. Dixon benefited that year from the emergence of the Populist Party, which drew strength away from the Democrats. He won the county attorney position and separated from Denny. In his personal life, Dixon drew himself closer to social and political prominence by courting and, in 1886, marrying Caroline Worden whose father, a prominent merchant, had been a founder of Missoula and a territorial legislator.

In 1895 the state Republican Party, still gloating over the victory provided by Democratic factionalism, began to divide. The national and state GOP establishment committed itself to the gold standard, which tied the available money supply to gold held by the U.S. government. However, Montanans became widely supportive of the policy to permit free and unlimited coinage of silver at a ratio of sixteen to one. Many local Republicans, including Dixon, sympathized with the free silver movement and became known as Silver Republicans. When the Democratic Party nominated William Jennings Bryan for president in 1896 after his famous Cross of Gold speech, Dixon declared publicly that he believed the people of Montana would choose Bryan for the White House while voting the entire Republican ticket into the state and local offices. In taking this position, the county attorney crossed the Republican establishment and displayed the independence that would increasingly mark his career.

Dixon correctly forecast Bryan's victory in Montana. But the ticket that the Gold Republicans and Silver Republicans attempted to proffer in unity was soundly beaten by the Democrats. The Gold Republicans blamed the electoral disaster on Dixon and his fellow renegades.

Dixon left the county attorney post in 1897, and the following year was selected to be a delegate to the state convention of the Silver Republicans. He was nominated there to represent Missoula County in the state senate. Following the convention, the Silver and Gold Republicans met to develop a unified ticket, and Dixon's nomination was withdrawn. Dixon shrugged off this small setback and returned to his private law practice.

In 1900 with the assistance of an unnamed benefactor, Dixon acquired a controlling interest in *The Missoulian*. The newspaper was not a profitable enterprise, but profit did not motivate the purchase. Dixon had learned that Montana journalism was intensely partisan and that many of the state's newspapers were owned by huge corporate interests that used them to deify the candidates who were beholden to them and to bludgeon challengers. *The Missoulian*, a Republican paper, was likely to side with the Gold Bug conservative Republicans in any political struggle. By his purchase of the paper, Dixon ensured that his views would become well circulated among the people of his area, and hedged against criticism the paper might otherwise direct at him.

That same year, Dixon was nominated by a precariously united Republican Party for a seat in the state legislature. He campaigned vigorously and was elected. During his term he sponsored and campaigned for a crude workers' compensation bill, which was passed handily by the house but later killed in the senate. He met with more success in his efforts to win support for Missoula's Montana State University. Dixon impressed politicians, lobbyists, and reporters with his speaking skills and demeanor and began to assemble a base for statewide election.

In 1902 Dixon resolved to run for the statewide congressional seat as a Republican. The race would be complex in several respects. Montana had become home to a quarter of a million people hailing from many ethnic backgrounds. The state's income was generated largely by mines and timber in the west, wheat farming and other agriculture in the east, and cattle and sheep ranching throughout. The Democratic Party had been successful at all levels in prior elections, but was suffering public scorn in the wake of the wars of the copper kings. At the helm of the Republican Party was Thomas H. Carter, who had served as the territory's last congressional delegate, as the state's first congressman, as the commissioner of the General Land Office under President Benjamin Harrison, as the chairman of the Republican National Committee, and as a United States senator from 1895 to 1901. Carter was a self-proclaimed conservative Republican, sympathetic to Amalgamated (Anaconda) Copper and the railroad companies. Carter was king in the Republican Party, but the stubbornly independent Dixon was unwilling to assume the identity of a mere Carter protégé. Fortunately for Dixon, the Democrats were equally divided. At the Democratic convention in 1902, F. Augustus Heinze, dissatisfied with domination of the party by William Clark and the Amalgamated forces, stormed from the convention to form his own "Labor" party. Complicated by the divisions in both parties, the battle for the congressional nomination chugged forward.

Carter supported a Miles City judge for the congressional seat and announced to the press his prediction that the judge would win the nomination and the election. Carter's opposition unquestionably threatened Dixon's prospects for nomination. But Dixon was lucky. A special train carrying 300 Republican delegates to the state convention was stopped at a burned bridge in Prickly Pear Canyon for twelve hours. The delegates there, outside the influence of Carter and his henchmen, prepared a slate of candidates that included Joe Dixon for Congress. Meanwhile, the secretary of the Republican State Central Committee had invited Dixon to prepare a keynote address for the convention. Dixon accepted and his address was hailed as "an eloquent, rousing speech that fairly electrified the convention."[5]

Dixon left the convention, nomination in hand, and started campaigning vigorously across the state. *The Missoulian*, already paying off as a political investment, charged that the Democratic candidates were mere stooges of the Clark-Amalgamated powers. The Democratic candidate, John M. Evans, was thrown on the defensive and remained there throughout the campaign. The charges of Company control against Evans placed Dixon in a position opposing the powerful copper interests, a conflict that would become a centerpiece in Dixon's long political career.

Dixon won this battle and was elected to Congress. The Republicans picked up seats in the state senate and won a two to one majority in the state house. On hearing the news of Dixon's election, a classmate from Earlham College wrote to him, "I remember well thy declaration—'when I come back I will be a congressman.'"[6]

Montana's congressional delegation to the Fifty-eighth Congress included Senators Paris Gibson and William A. Clark, in addition to Dixon. President Theodore Roosevelt had assumed office following the assassination of President William McKinley, and as Dixon was the lone Republican in the delegation, the benefits of patronage were theoretically his to distribute. Dixon's independence and courage were immediately tested when former senator Carter attempted to dictate the terms of federal patronage. The issue was an important one, given the economic significance of the federal role in Montana. Asserting his political independence again, Dixon publicly announced that the president expected him to be the chief distributor of federal jobs and benefits in Montana.

During Dixon's first congressional term, the Fair Trials Bill made its way into and out of the special session of the state legislature, fueling national criticism that Montana was beholden to the Amalgamated Copper Company. At the same time, Dixon's own *Missoulian* began to ally with the interests of the Amalgamated. Dixon urged *The Missoulian* to publish an article clarifying any confusion and making his position unequivocally clear to the Company. The theme of the proposed editorial: "Let the Amalgamated Keep Hands Off in the Republican Convention."[7] Dixon's profile as an opponent of Company domination continued to grow.

Dixon enjoyed unusual success during his first congressional term. When he returned home at the end of the session, he was met by a thousand well-wishers at the railroad station, decorated store fronts, and a rally of some 5,000 citizens at the Missoula County Courthouse. After another vigorous campaign, Dixon was handily elected to a second term in Congress, and Republicans captured control of the state legislature, permitting them to choose the successor to Democratic senator Paris Gibson. The ever-present Thomas Carter was the only announced candidate for the seat, but it was not until the seventh ballot that he was able to gain the votes necessary for election. When the Fifty-ninth Congress convened in 1905, Dixon found himself in the delegation with his nemesis. Predictably, Dixon and Carter directly locked horns over patronage and other issues. Each was determined to be the voice of the Montana Republican Party in Washington. But Dixon had cultivated a special relationship with Roosevelt and, on the whole, prevailed, enjoying the president's support.

With the Fifty-ninth Congress drawing to a close, Dixon decided to run for the United States senate seat being vacated by William Clark. The senate contest was entirely different from any other race, as office holders were chosen by the state legislature. Consequently, the results of the November legislative elections would largely determine which party would be awarded the Senate seat. During the months preceding the November 1906 election, Dixon campaigned hard for the Republican ticket in Montana. For Dixon's vacated congressional seat, the Republicans nominated Charles N. Pray, and the Democrats, Thomas J. Walsh. For the Senate seat, the Democrats chose Gov. Joseph K. Toole. The Republicans were confronted by the announced candidacies of both Dixon and conservative Republican state party chairman Lee Mantle. An official nomination for the Senate seat did not come from the Republican convention that year, but Dixon was thought to have the advantage based on his respected congressional service. When the Democrats challenged Pray to debate Walsh over salient issues, Pray declined but Dixon accepted the offer. The resulting debate was between Walsh, Democratic candidate for the House of Representatives, and Dixon, Republican candidate for the United States Senate. Each of Montana's various partisan newspapers attempted to spin the debate in its favor. Although each political party claimed victory, the debate helped elevate Dixon above his opponent.

The Republicans won the legislative elections in a landslide, capturing fifty-seven House seats to the Democrats' sixteen and shifting the balance of the Senate to eighteen Republicans and nine Democrats. In January 1907, the legislature rewarded Joe Dixon for his successful congressional terms by electing him to the Senate.

When Dixon reached the Senate he began a course marked by ideological courage that would win him a prominent national identity. The significant events began to unfold after the election of William Howard Taft to the White House in 1908. Dixon had supported Taft, but soon diverged from the new president. The issue that signaled Dixon's departure from the Republican mainstream involved new forms of taxation. Dixon advocated a progressive income tax and an inheritance tax. When fellow Republicans maneuvered to defeat the bill, Dixon went to the White House to enlist Taft's support. Taft was opposed to the tax but, in an effort to appease Dixon's progressive faction, proposed a corporate dividend tax as an alternative. Dixon reluctantly accepted the compromise.

On the inheritance tax Dixon made an impassioned speech urging the senate to tap this source of revenue derived from wealth that was possessed only "by the accident of birth." The inheritance tax met the same temporary ill fate as the income tax, but Dixon's vociferous departure from the party line on tax questions marked him as one of the growing band of insurgents in the Republican Party.

In April of 1909, Dixon took on the railroads. The notion of railroad reform was not an entirely maverick one; the Republican Party platform of 1908 had noted the need for general reform. The inequitable rate structure of the railroad freight lines was a great source of economic hardship for Montana agricultural producers. The railroads often charged more for a short haul in Montana than for a long haul in more populated and competitive markets. Dixon successfully drove through Congress a bill prohibiting the railroads from charging more for a short haul than for a long haul on the same track in the same direction. The measure was enormously popular in Montana, and Dixon was praised for his eloquent advocacy of the measure. At the same time, however, it placed him at odds with President Taft, fellow Senator Carter, and the mainstream of the Republican Party. The most vehement opposition though came from "the Interests," including the Amalgamated, which identified Dixon as one of those intolerable politicians whose votes and words in Washington would be controlled by his conscience.

In 1910 "Uncle Tom" Carter faced reelection. The perennial battle between Carter and Dixon intensified, and the state Republican convention promised to be the focal point for conflict between the progressives and conservatives. Dixon spoke at the Missoula County convention, heralding Roosevelt progressivism and declaring that "I should be humiliated if Montana . . . did not put itself on record with the progressive element."[8] Carter had run an effective campaign, and his confederates were solidly in control of the state convention. Dixon's opportunity to address the convention was postponed until after the conduct of formal business, but Dixon was not dissuaded from his mission. He confronted the ideological schism in the party head-on, imploring delegates to join the "contest between the progressive liberal and the Bourbon reactionary."[9] Dixon warned of dangers posed by monopolies and other huge corporate interests. He urged the delegates to come to terms with themselves as progressives and followers of the principles espoused by Theodore Roosevelt. Dixon's remarks were met with vigorous applause, though the membership of the convention was likely divided over the call to Roosevelt Republicanism.

The convention nominated Carter. And when the postconvention campaigning began, Dixon took to the hustings for Carter, in a show of party unity. Dixon's true dedication to Carter's cause, however, was questionable. He had not been long on the campaign trail before Carter loyalists "were accusing him . . . of really knifing Carter."[10] Carter supporters worked hard to swing enough votes to facilitate the senator's reelection, but it eventually became apparent that a Democrat would be chosen. The Democrats had not officially nominated a candidate at their convention, and the legislature struggled over various potential Democratic candidates. Ultimately, the seat went to Henry L. Myers, a relatively obscure district court judge who hailed from Ravalli County, just south of Dixon's home ground. It became clear that Amalgamated and the Carterites were behind the election of Myers, choosing a noncontroversial candidate from Dixon's part of the state in the hope that Montanans would seek a central or eastern Montana senator for geographic balance in 1912, thus imperiling Dixon. Dixon himself wrote that "[t]he Amalgamated Copper Company and the Carter influence undoubtedly were in league to have the second Senator named in my own back yard to make it embarrassing for me two years from this time."[11]

The legislature of 1911 dealt two additional blows to Dixon. In December, prior to the session, Dixon took a public stand in Washington in favor of a constitutional amendment to establish the direct election of senators. Dixon seized the opportunity to advocate the direct primary and legislative reapportionment as well. The legislature rejected both proposals. After the session, one confidant wrote to Dixon that "Montana is at the present time, corporation controlled. . . . The actions of the 12th Legislative Assembly were dominated completely by the Copper Trust."[12]

When Dixon and Myers arrived in Washington for the new

Congress, the national Progressive movement was proceeding apace. Dixon wrote:

> I am afraid that the trouble with some of our leaders lies in the fact that a revolution is on in this country between the ordinary citizenship and the big interests, and they have not recognized the new condition that has arisen.
>
> I am indeed sorry that the recent session of the Montana Legislature did not enact a primary election law, and am not unaware of the real sources of opposition to the measure. The people of this country have made up their minds that they intend to run their own affairs of government. The great handicap to real representation in governmental affairs by the people themselves is the ease with which the great corporate interests can control conventions and legislatures. . . . [13]

Dixon's senatorial duties did not distance him from domestic Montana politics. Dixon was involved nationally in the development and growth of the National Progressive Republican League. Through his supporters at home, he helped create local chapters of the League to address the direct primary issue, among others. Dixon's relentless advocacy of the direct primary was not completely altruistic: The direct primary represented the best opportunity for Dixon's renomination by the people, who were largely supportive of Dixon's popular stands. Still, Dixon recognized the historical importance of the measure. "Under the present control of legislative assemblies by the big interests," Dixon argued, primary legislation " . . . is the only way to restore representative government to the people themselves. It may be defeated temporarily, but in the end it will come certain as fate."[14]

With growing public sentiment demanding the direct primary, Montana Gov. Edwin Norris developed a draft of a primary election law to be submitted to the legislature. The governor called for a special legislative session to enact the measure. Dixon predicted that " . . . the Amalgamated and railroad interests will be especially exercised to chloroform enough senators and members to prevent a majority of the legislature from supporting the legislation."[15]

Although Dixon encouraged members who favored him to oppose the special session, he undertook a campaign to persuade legislators to support the measure in case a special session were called. Simultaneously, Dixon advocated the circulation of petitions to place the direct primary election proposal on the public ballot. In the end, Dixon was disappointed on both fronts. Legislators were determined not to give the direct primary proposal a chance and the idea of a public initiative failed to gain momentum.

In 1911 Dixon was again up against the Amalgamated forces. When a position opened in September on the United States District Court bench, Dixon submitted the name of veteran state district court judge E. K. Cheatle of Lewistown. Cheatle had stated publicly in 1910 that "the Amalgamated Copper Company should confine its operations to the mining of copper and leave to the voters of the state the electing of legislators and other public servants."[16] It was well known that Cheatle openly favored the direct election of United States senators as well as the direct primary. In an article published in January 1911, Cheatle wrote:

> The convention system is open to much abuse, and is, in fact, often greatly abused. Under the plan of nominating by conventions, a powerful corporation or individual may, and often does, by ingenious combination, secret intrigue or undue influence over the members of the conventions, practically assume to itself or himself sufficient strength to dictate the choice of the convention for any office or offices which such corporation or individual desires to control. . . .
>
> The people of Montana will not be wholly free, politically, until they select the candidates for office as well as elect the officers. It has happened more than once in this state that the people were deprived of any real choice for certain high offices, the candidates therefore on both tickets having been chosen by powerful interests in the state.[17]

In the same article, Cheatle urged adoption of the initiative and referendum law, and a law to permit public recall of officials. Cheatle declared, "There are special interests in Montana far stronger than our state government. This is absurd and dangerous. The government should be stronger than any or all special interests."[18]

Establishment Republicans, beholden to "the Interests," convinced Taft that a Montana delegation would be assembled in his favor at the Republican national convention in 1912 if he saw that Cheatle was not appointed. Taft ultimately sent to the Senate the nomination of George M. Bourquin of Butte and the pervasive power of the Amalgamated again prevailed.

By early 1912 Dixon found himself in an ominous position. The corporate-controlled faction of the Republican Party in Montana had successfully taken control of the state party, and Republican president Taft had paid his allegiance to them rather than Dixon. The fissure in the Republican Party was symbolized by the burgeoning animosities between Carter and Dixon. Helena's *Daily Independent* had written that "Mr. Carter was not favorably inclined to the election of Mr. Dixon to the Senate. From that day to this, their paths have been widening. During the past four years in Washington it has been common talk that the Montana senators were not dwelling in harmony with each other."[19]

Shortly after his defeat in 1910, Carter began indicating publicly that he would challenge Dixon for his seat. Republican newspapers hammered at Senator Dixon. "Once in the Senate," said one such paper of Dixon, "his obligations to the party were forgotten. Even in the first campaign, after taking his seat, he failed to be of any benefit to his friends or his party, and those who had helped him to the Senate, working day and night, went down to defeat."[20]

Carter died in September of 1911, leaving no apparent heir to the Senate seat from his wing of the party, but the rift in the Republican Party remained.

In this setting, Dixon and the Progressive elements of the Republican Party undertook a massive movement to take control of the national and state parties. With Dixon's support and perhaps orchestration, the Progressive Republicans of Montana met in Billings in 1912 to nominate Theodore Roosevelt for president and Joseph Dixon for reelection to the Senate.

Sen. Robert M. LaFollette of Wisconsin had organized the Progressive elements of the Republican Party in 1911 to challenge the Old Guard for control of the national party. As the movement grew, Senator LaFollette suffered health problems and many progressives looked to their champion, Theodore Roosevelt, for leadership. Roosevelt gladly accepted and began a formal, aggressive campaign for the Republican nomination. Roosevelt determined that Joseph Dixon of Montana should manage the effort. Dixon accepted the post in late February of 1912, shortly after his first and only son had died just four days after birth. Perhaps in an attempt to bury his grief, Dixon immersed himself in the national campaign.

When Dixon arrived at Roosevelt headquarters in Washington, the candidate's organization was in disarray. There was scarcely time for organizational improvement, though, as the fight for convention delegates was already under way. The campaign was almost immediately undermined by Progressive ideologues. Moreover, the campaign was dealt an early setback when Roosevelt unsuccessfully challenged LaFollette for the delegates of North Dakota. Laboring under these handicaps, and lacking the necessary campaign finances, Dixon worked feverishly for four months to procure a majority of Republican delegates. It was widely accepted in Montana and across the nation that Roosevelt could win the nomination by popular vote in a direct primary election. The direct presidential primary was unlikely, though. Consequently, Dixon's appeal to the Republican rank and file was thwarted by the Stand-Patters' control of local political machines. In addition, most of the Republican newspapers throughout the country remained loyal to Taft and obstructed Dixon's efforts to publicize Roosevelt's platform. Montana was no exception. Calling attention to anti-Roosevelt editorials, a Great Falls newspaper editor wrote to Dixon that "every effort of the Amalgamated Copper Company is being put forth at this time and will be at the convention against Roosevelt. . . ."[21]

In late March, the state central committee of the Montana Republican Party endorsed Taft and registered its opposition to the presidential primary. In reaction, Montana's progressive Republicans held another mass meeting in April and began publishing a weekly newspaper-style circular with the headline "Put the Amalgamated Out of State Politics."[22]

While Dixon was able to spend little time in Montana during the campaign, he issued a lengthy release to the daily Montana newspapers and circulated the same as a pamphlet, titled "Shall the Amalgamated Company Rule the Republican Party in Montana?"[23] Dixon declared:

> The issue in Montana is clearly defined. Shall the special interests which know no party allegiance, acting in our own state through the Amalgamated Copper Company and its allies, control the Republican as well as the Democratic party, or shall the Republican party be controlled by the people themselves? There can be no compromise in the situation which confronts us. It is a struggle between two diametrically opposed and conflicting ideals and interests. There is and can be no middle ground. The action of the majority of the state committee at Helena has forced the issue. "Let him that hath no stomach for the fight depart."[24]

Not surprisingly, the Amalgamated newspapers refused to print Dixon's remarks, limiting circulation.

Roosevelt came to the June convention of the national Republican Party stridently assailing the Taftite Stand-Patters and their positions. Much of the atmosphere was dominated by the fanaticism of Roosevelt's supporters and detractors. Dixon's role became that of the conciliator, trying to hold the volatile block of Roosevelt votes together. Despite optimistic projections by Dixon, cleavages widened, and the dreams of a Roosevelt victory faded. On June 22, 1912, the convention nominated Taft by a narrow majority. In a tactical move of unusual recalcitrance, and a credit to Dixon's leadership, the Roosevelt bloc held together and abstained from the final vote. Instead, the Rooseveltians bolted the convention and publicly called for the organization of a new party. The new party drew its name from an offhand remark by Roosevelt. Answering an inquiry during the campaign about his health, Roosevelt had exclaimed that he felt "like a bull moose," and the Bull Moose Party was born.

Simultaneously, in Montana, the Democrats rejoiced at the prospect of the split Republican Party. Thomas J. Walsh, whose profile continued to grow, urged the Democrats to adopt a Progressive platform that would equal that of the Bull Moose Republicans. While agents of "the Interests" were present at the Democratic convention, they remained silent as Walsh was nominated for the Senate, preferring anyone to the hostile Joe Dixon. Walsh campaigned actively in Montana and was virtually unopposed there by Dixon, whose national duties continued to keep him away from home.

In the wake of the Republican convention, Dixon's responsibilities revolved around gathering a substantial delegation of progressive Republicans from throughout the country for the national Bull Moose convention. The assignment was complicated by the Democrats' shrewd nomination of Progressive New Jersey governor Woodrow Wilson. The nomination drew into question the reason for the Bull Moose Party's existence, and immediately eroded the popular appeal of Roosevelt's Square Deal. Dixon's political friends at home feared his demise and gave the Roosevelt campaign little chance of victory. Against these odds, Dixon pressed on.

Montana sent sixteen delegates to the Chicago Bull Moose convention. The convention opened on August 5, and Dixon was unanimously elected chairman. Roosevelt and Hiram W. Johnson were ritually nominated as candidates for the presidency and vice presidency.

After a brief stint in New York to christen the national Bull Moose campaign, Dixon returned to Montana to preside over the September convention of the state Bull Moose Party. When the convention opened, Dixon was at the podium and with him, the standard bearer of the party, Roosevelt himself. The convention endorsed Roosevelt and nominated a full slate of candidates for state offices. It ratified the national Progressive platform, which was heralded for its independence from the traditional financial supporters of the Republican Party and its uncompromising appeal to the "common man." In addition to its vote for national Bull Moose principles, the state convention adopted its own platform calling for open legislative caucuses, a public utilities commission, a blue sky law, the long- and short-haul railroad law, public guarantee of bank deposits, equal suffrage for women, public grain inspection, graduated income and inheritance tax laws, arbitration of labor disputes, prohibition of child labor, an employers' liability (workers' compensation) act, investment of state funds in farm mortgages, sanitary laws for mines and mills, a short-form ballot law, a "pure seed" law, support of widows and orphans of convicts, reorganization of state educational institutions, and a full railroad crew law, among other measures.[25]

Cheers for Dixon and Roosevelt filled the air. Delegates stood on their seats. When Roosevelt addressed the convention, he paid high tribute to Senator Dixon. "We could not have gone on with this progressive movement," said the former president, "if Senator Dixon had not, with great cost to himself and with absolute disinterestedness, taken charge of my campaign." Roosevelt challenged the convention to bring the Square Deal to Montana with a victory in November, "true to the heroic past of Montana."[26]

The Montana Bull Moose Party had much in its favor as the November election approached. Its leader, Joseph Dixon, had risen to national prominence through the party. Roosevelt himself had made a moving personal appeal to Montana. Progressive Republicans had cast the establishment Republicans in a dim light, proclaiming that a "Stand-Patter is a friend of the grafters, a friend of the special interests, a friend of the pie counter and an enemy of the common people."[27] The electorate was solidly in favor of the proposals of the Bull Moose platform. None of these advantages was enough, however, to overcome the politically devastating effect of a split Republican Party. The Democrats swept the 1912 election, including Dixon's Senate seat, which went to Thomas Walsh. Nationally, the same result occurred. Woodrow Wilson was, of course, elected president. Roosevelt finished second and the incumbent President Taft, on the only such occasion in history, came in a disappointing third.

In Montana, at least, the 1912 election was not a total loss for those dedicated to the agenda of the Bull Moose Party. In the first place, the Progressives placed twenty members in the Montana legislature, and the Bull Moose Party carried the state, excluding Silver Bow, Cascade, and Deer Lodge Counties, where the Company was most powerful. Second, Democrat Thomas Walsh was himself a Progressive. Of greatest historical significance, though, was the "direct legislation" enacted by Montana voters. Through a series of initiatives, the electorate passed a direct primary system law, a campaign expenditures and corrupt practices act, a presidential preference primary, and a measure clarifying the popular election of senators. By referendum, the voters overturned an act of the 1911 legislature, which had given the governor liberal powers to call out the state militia, presumably for the purpose of crushing labor demonstrations.

The election of 1912 marked a watershed in Montana history. Although Dixon and Roosevelt went down to defeat as candidates for public office, the cause for which Dixon sacrificed himself prevailed. After more than two decades of domination by corporate giants, the people of the state of Montana took a broad step toward self-control. By initiative and referendum, in the stroke of a single election, Montanans eliminated the system of nomination and election that had permitted special interests to exercise undue influence in the selection of public officials.

Dixon's own disappointment was mitigated by the satisfaction of a well-fought battle and an ideological victory. Reflecting over the previous twelve months, Dixon professed pride that he had "participated in the revolution" and asserted that he would not have traded the experience for another term in the Senate. A decade later, Dixon would write to a friend:

> While those months undoubtedly upset the political careers of you and I and many other men, I would not have taken a different course, even though I had known in advance that my action meant inevitable defeat.
>
> In the calm reflection of these after years, my judgment is that we participated in the biggest work of this generation.
>
> Anyway, we raised a whole lot of glorious hell. Since that time I have never been able to feel the old-time thrill of party loyalty and tradition. I know too well the camouflage that covers the temporary actors behind the scenes.[28]

Dixon returned to Missoula in 1913 and directed his attention to *The Missoulian*. From 1913 until 1917, when he finally sold the paper, Dixon used the editorial page of the Missoula daily as his own "bully pulpit." Dixon's epistles concurred with the growing Progressive movement in Montana.

Walsh's victory over Dixon in 1912 had launched the career of a great liberal. Walsh aligned himself with the Wilsonians and their Progressive New Freedom program. A social consciousness and public empowerment were erupting in Montana and across the nation. Political discourse was commonly beginning to address notions such as humanitarianism and a new social and industrial order. Meanwhile, a populist, progressive, anti-Company firebrand orator from Butte named Burton K. Wheeler had been named U.S. attorney after his active promotion of Walsh's senatorial election. Wheeler's virulent attacks on corporate interests over the coming few years would earn him the label Bolshevik Burt.

In 1914 a farmer-labor alliance was loosely formed. Rural concerns enlisted labor support in a successful campaign to secure passage of an initiative providing for the state to invest in farm mortgage loans, although the Company successfully divided farm votes to prevent passage of a workers' compensation program for labor. The Montana Society of Equity was organized in 1914 to campaign for a fair agricultural policy and combat the political influence of the mining interests. By 1917 the society had gained 15,000 members. In the 1914 election, Montana reformers triumphed in their campaign to secure equal women's suffrage and the prohibition of alcoholic beverages. Shortly after that election, the Montana Good Government Association, predecessor to the Montana League of Women Voters, was formed to defend and advance the movement to fully enfranchise women. In 1916 Jeannette Rankin became the first woman elected to Congress. The Non-Partisan League sprang out of North Dakota in 1915 and by 1918 secured a solid foothold in Montana. The league began as a farmers' organization, supporting liberals in both the Republican and Democratic Parties as well as various third-party candidates, who committed themselves to improvement of the general condition of agriculture through government action.

Outside Montana, World War I consumed the civilized world in an international conflagration. American involvement was hotly debated. Wilson was reelected to the White House in 1916 on his pledge to keep the United States out of the war, but in 1917 the U.S. declared war on Germany, Hungary, and Austria, charging into the fray.

World War I had a devastating effect on Montana. Montana sent more men per capita to the war than any other state. A tremendous number of productive men were suddenly extracted from the Montana society and economy. The homestead movement collapsed in 1917, marking the end of the frontier era. The indomitable spirit of Montanans withered as their state's economy buckled at the knees and slumped into postwar depression.

In 1917 Joe Dixon, facing daunting financial pressures, sold *The Missoulian*. He retired to his small ranch on Flathead Lake, where he focused his attention on "farming and philosophy." Dixon extolled the virtues of dairy farming and practiced it himself, but met with financial disappointment in this endeavor as well. Eventually, he traded the better part of his ranch for income-producing property in Missoula. In the meantime, the Non-Partisan League was frequently mentioning Dixon's name, among others, as a potential candidate for office. Dixon began to turn his attention back toward the political arena.

Many Progressive organizations had been spawned during Dixon's absence from politics, but the movement lost steam while Montana rallied around wartime nationalist sentiment. The war ended, however, and the realities of economic depression reverberated through Montana's homes and workplaces; the electorate grew discontented. The Progressive movement picked up a second wind and undertook preparations for a final crusade against "the Interests."

As the elections of 1920 approached, the resurrected Progressive forces circled around a single issue. Since the state constitutional convention in 1889, repeated attempts had been made to increase the tax levied upon mining interests of the state. The postwar depression gave new urgency to the need for additional state revenue and a fair program of taxation. Additionally, events of 1919 catapulted the issue into the public consciousness. A young economics professor at Missoula's Montana State University, Louis Levine, published *The Taxation of Mines in Montana*, which revealed and criticized the failure of current revenue programs to equitably tax the state's mines. The mining interests demanded that the university dismiss Levine, and the school obeyed. This raw exercise of corporate authority and the encroachment upon intellectual freedom created a public uproar, particularly among Progressives. Sufficient sympathy was created by this cause, even in the Republican Party, that Joseph Dixon was urged to seek the nomination for governor. He accepted, pledging to urge tax reform that included an increased levy on the mines. Democrats recognized the same imperative and nominated Burton K. Wheeler, darling of the Non-Partisan League and Labor League. Although chosen by the regulars of his party, Dixon faced a direct primary election against Harry J. Wilson of Billings, who was supported and endorsed by the Company. The public was not fooled by the Company's thinly veiled attempt to protect itself by the nomination and election of Wilson. The electorate chose Dixon as the Republican candidate and Wheeler as the official Democrat. This turn of events presented "the Interests" with a situation to which they were unaccustomed. Not one, but both nominees were hostile to overbearing corporate interests and advocated increased taxation of the mines. While Dixon had been a perennial burr under the Amalgamated saddle, the Company apparently foresaw a greater chance of moderation with Dixon than with the strident Wheeler. In Company newspapers throughout the state, Wheeler was denounced as Bolshevik Burt. The title was especially stigmatic because the Russian Revolution of 1917 had spawned the first wave of public fear and antipathy toward communist revolutionaries.

As the candidates marched through the campaign of 1920, the epithets slung at Wheeler piled up. The state was covered with posters, pamphlets, and company news items labeling Wheeler an advocate of "bloody revolution" and "free love." *The Helena Independent* warned of "dangerous radicals" and charged that the Democratic Party had been overtaken by socialists and bolshevists intent on turning Montana into an "orgy of state socialism."[29] Wheeler, reportedly, was nearly tarred and feathered at Dillon, and at Miles City was forced to speak from a haystack outside town. The Company-controlled press warned that a Wheeler victory would lead to closure of the mines and smelters, bankruptcy of the grain elevators, and ruin of the farms.

Meanwhile, Dixon received a good deal of favorable press. Shortly after his announcement for governor, independent newspapers hailed Dixon. According to one, "He is admitted by his enemies to be a man of ability. He has a record of independence of 'Company' domination. He is too big a man for any 'special interest' to find it easy to handle him."[30] Dixon's opposition to the "two extreme" camps was viewed favorably as a rejection of both Company control and radical insurgency.

Governor Dixon, 1924. As governor, Dixon fought to impose fair taxation on the mining interests. When the Company-controlled legislature blocked his effort, he achieved the measure through public initiative.

Courtesy of Montana Historical Society, Helena.

Another paper reported that "Mr. Dixon's proffered solution of the vital propositions of the present time, are demonstrative not only of capable and careful and unprejudiced thought, but typify the true spirit of 'justice for all the people.'"[31]

Dixon's national profile was cited in his favor, as well. *The Missoulian*, which had passed from Dixon's ownership three years earlier, declared, "Senator Dixon belongs to a group of not more than a half-dozen Montana statesmen and probably less, who since the admission of the territory, have achieved national fame. He is known in Republican councils from the furthermost corner of Maine to the shores of the Pacific."[32]

Dixon was elected comfortably in November, receiving more votes than the Republican presidential candidate Warren G. Harding. The size of Dixon's victory was evidence that he had not only benefited from the Company's effective smear campaign against Wheeler, but that he had appealed to a large bloc of liberals who remembered Dixon's independent, Progressive past. Public support for increased taxation of the mines was unquestionable. Dixon's victory over Wheeler reflected the public's confidence that Dixon would approach the problem with the necessary commitment and vigor. The public's faith in Dixon was well placed.

When Dixon assumed the governor's chair in 1921, the state faced a \$2 million budget deficit in the setting of a comatose economy. Dixon's first address to the legislature, according to historian Joseph Kinsey Howard, "earned rank, in the undistinguished records of that apathetic assembly, as a great state paper. It went to the roots of Montana's economic disorder, yet it was temperate and so scrupulously fair. . . . "[33]

Dixon urged several new sources of revenue, though he applied only a soft touch to the metalliferous mines. Primarily, Dixon promoted stronger inheritance taxes and income levies, a 3 percent tax on the oil yield of the state, a coal severance tax of ten cents per ton, a higher license fee for automobiles, and a one cent per gallon gasoline tax. Although his address to the legislature was met with enthusiastic applause, the assembly failed to adopt the requested revenue measures, leaving the state floundering in financial uncertainty. Disastrous economic developments continued to unfold. Between 1919 and 1925, some 2 million acres of agricultural land passed out of production and 11,000 farms, 20 percent of the state's total, were vacated. Twenty thousand mortgages were foreclosed, and half of the state's farmers lost their land. Agricultural land value fell 50 percent. From 1920 to 1926, over half of the state's commercial banks failed, wiping out thousands of savings accounts. Montana's population began to drain from the state. By the end of the Roaring Twenties, 60,000 more Montanans fled than had arrived, leaving the state with the only net population loss in the country during that period. Ironically, Dixon's victory in 1920, marking his political rebirth, sealed his political doom. Even with a cooperative legislature, Dixon could not have saved the state from the dire conditions largely dictated by national and international events. In a stroke of equally poignant irony, Burton K. Wheeler was elected to the Senate in 1922, christening a career that would become nationally significant in its own right.

In 1923 Governor Dixon's address to the legislature struck hard at the mine taxation issue. He informed the assembly that $20 million in metals had been extracted from Montana mines in 1922, and that the net proceeds tax totaled less than $14,000. The governor compared this ratio to the oil industry, where extraction was valued at less than $3 million and the net proceeds tax totaled $28,000. Further, coal production in the same year was valued at $9 million, while the net proceeds tax on that industry yielded $147,000. Dixon urged the legislature to impose a tax of twelve cents per ton on ore produced in the state.

As expected, "the Interests" invaded the legislature and annihilated the proposed legislation. The legislature did not prove itself completely unfit, though. In a matter unrelated to the pressing problems of taxation, the assembly enacted the nation's first "old-age pension" law. The measure was sponsored by a young Helena attorney, Lester Loble, who would later become a distinguished, longtime state court judge. Loble carried the cause to Montana's legislature from the national convention of the Fraternal Order of Eagles, which had strongly endorsed such a program. While the law was rudimentary, it became the model for the Social Security Act. Loble would later be drafted by President Franklin Roosevelt to help frame that act. Governor Dixon signed the bill and praised the true proponents, saying, "You Eagles have planted this seed and you can no more stop the progress of old-age pensions than you can stem the tide of the Pacific Ocean."[34]

Dixon's primary attention remained focused, however, on

his taxation agenda. In reaction to the 1923 legislature's impotence in addressing the mine taxation problem, the Dixon administration prepared Initiative 28 for direct submission to the electorate in 1924. The Initiative provided a graduated schedule of new taxation for mineral production that exceeded a $100,000 threshold. The major mining interests targeted Dixon and undertook an all-out campaign to defeat him, reasoning that a Dixon loss would spell failure for the initiative as well.

When Governor Dixon addressed the Republican state convention in 1924, he spoke with a tone of political fatalism and a cold determination to bring about an equitable system of taxation. Dixon declared to the convention:

> Gentlemen, these known inequalities of government in Montana are the potent factors that are driving the masses into a state of mind that eventually produces your socialists, your IWW and your red radicals. It is social and economic injustices of this same kind that even threaten the stability of the present order. Men and newspapers in Montana may cry peace, but there can be no peace in Montana until this flagrant discrimination is settled and settled right. . . . Absolute equality of taxation of property is primal essential justice unless it is desired to cultivate a superior class to own the property and a proletariat of peasantry to become their serfs. . . . [35]

Rhetorically, Dixon asked why the public had permitted the inequity to persist. Dixon's own response laid wide open the devices of the corporate interests.

> You think it queer that a half million citizens of Montana would calmly, year after year, go on carrying the burden of government in this state, to the point of confiscation of their own homes, farms and businesses and permit these overlords of the mineral wealth of Montana 99 percent of the dividends which are paid and spent in New York City and the other financial centers of this and foreign countries, to continue this feudal system of taxation. I will tell you, for the time has come to speak plainly.
>
> For years, the larger public affairs of Montana have been administered on the basis of a conquered Roman province, through the control of practically all the chan-

nels of publicity in Montana. Why these great annual expenditures of fabulous sums of money in the ownership
and subsidy of great daily (and some weekly) newspapers
in Montana? Why these great sums invested in the nomination and election of legislative members? . . .

The greatest crime being perpetrated against the people
of a supposedly independent state is the undercover
methods that have for these many years been employed,
at great financial cost, to control the publicity of Montana
for one specific purpose. . . . [36]

Dixon's blunt words were tantamount to a declaration of
war. But then, in a masterful display of diplomacy, Dixon took
the high ground, demanding only a reasonable and just system
that fairly treated the people of his state.

The state administration wages no war on industry. . . .
The fact that they are overwhelmingly owned by nonresi-
dents and that their profits flow into the coffers of absen-
tee owners, who have so grossly abused their Montana
privileges, shall not cause us to deviate one iota from the
program of a square deal. But that same square deal also
contemplates a square deal for those of us who live in and
are residents of Montana, the farmers, the homeowners,
the businessmen, and the rank and file of the citizenship
of this state. . . . [37]

Finally, Dixon invoked the power of the people themselves,
as he challenged the Republican Party to tame the giant special interests once and for all.

. . . If I know anything of the present temper of the people of this state, I have an abiding faith that they do not
longer purpose electing men to the Montana legislature
who will permit themselves to be used as 'rubber stamps'
for the invisible government that knows no politics, no
party lines and no rule of action except that of personal
control of public officials for their own selfish
purposes. . . .

Gentlemen of the convention, the contest is on and will
not be ended until the rule of special privilege in Montana
shall have been driven from the legislative halls and the

corridors of its capital. "LET HIM WHO HATH NO STOM-
ACH FOR THE FIGHT DEPART."[38]

Throughout the campaign of 1924, the Company dedicated every political and economic resource to achieving Dixon's demise. It sponsored a Republican opponent for the primary and John E. "Honest John" Erickson on the Democratic ticket. The Company even sponsored a separate Progressive gubernatorial nominee through the Farm-Labor coalition. Company papers scurrilously attacked Dixon daily. Company agents threatened labor unions that projects would be rolled back and jobs lost if Dixon were reelected. The Company portrayed Dixon to the business community as a threat to capital investment in the state. Dixon the candidate was powerless in the face of this relentless and omnipotent siege. Erickson triumphed in the general election, and Dixon was swept from office by a margin of nearly 15,000 votes. While the sagging Montana economy undoubtedly contributed to Dixon's demise, the Anaconda acted to ensure once again the annihilation of its adversary. But, the Company failed to win the larger war. Despite Dixon's sound defeat, Initiative 28, embracing the graduated net proceeds tax for metal mines, passed by more than 20,000 votes. By their own political miscalculation, the mining interests found themselves bridled by the very tax policy that motivated their political assassination of Dixon. Dixon was no longer governor, but he had sacrificed himself for the greater good. When he returned to Missoula, he took with him that considerable satisfaction.

Dixon's career did not end entirely with the election of 1924. He challenged Wheeler for the Senate seat in 1928, but Wheeler's stature and popularity had grown and Dixon's attempt was foiled. Shortly after the election, President Hoover appointed Dixon assistant secretary of the interior. Dixon moved to Washington and served through the remainder of the Hoover administration. When Hoover left office, Dixon finally retired. On May 22, 1934, Joe Dixon died quietly in Missoula, Montana.

Joseph M. Dixon spent the better part of his political career taking on Goliath with a sling. Though his career was long, Dixon met defeat in most of his great battles. Unfortunately, history tends to distribute fine accolades mainly to the victorious. In the case of Joe Dixon, however, greatness emanated more from his defeats than from his victories. K. Ross Toole summarized the significance of Dixon's contribution:

> It is true that except for one significant tax reform, [Dixon] failed. His enemies prevailed and he was a one-term governor. But as we look backward, the victory of his enemies proves more pyrrhic with every passing year, and we begin to understand how remarkable and dedicated a man he was. In the face of the most concerted, powerful, vitriolic and relentless opposition, he remained coolly rational, steadfast in his integrity and unwavering in his belief that only if the burdens of government were distributed with equity and fairness could democracy survive.
>
> Dixon should not be missed from the list of the finest politicians of his age. He should probably top the list.[39]

For those who fight to ensure that humanitarianism is not lost in the struggle for progress, for those who dream of enlightened approaches to public problems, for those who resist the control of political parties by narrow factions, and for those who refuse to permit a handful of monied special interests to control the government of the people, the cause of Joseph Dixon endures and his crusade goes on.

Suggested Readings on Joseph M. Dixon

The preeminent biography of Joseph Dixon is Jules A. Karlin, *Joseph M. Dixon of Montana* (Missoula, 1974). Professor Karlin has comprehensively compiled and explained nearly all of the known papers about Joseph Dixon, and has woven Dixon's life into the historical context of his times, in this thorough, two-volume work. Much of the general background information in the foregoing chapter is drawn from Professor Karlin's biography of Dixon and sources cited therein. Professor Karlin also authored a pamphlet titled "Joseph Moore Dixon Collection" (Missoula, 1988), published by the Maureen and Mike Mansfield Library of the University of Montana. This fifteen-page document contains a brief biography of Dixon and an index to the extensive Dixon Papers, which were donated to the University of Montana Archives in 1951 and 1975.

Dixon is characterized as the leading figure of the Montana Progressive movement in M. P. Malone, R. B. Roeder, and W. L. Lang, *Montana: A History of Two Centuries* (Seattle/London, 1991). Malone, et al. also discuss Dixon's defeat in 1912, his term as governor, and his later years.

A varied selection of newspaper and magazine articles published during Dixon's career are copied and maintained in the Joseph M. Dixon vertical file at the Montana Historical Society. Copies of Dixon's speeches to the Montana legislature in 1921 can also be found in the Historical Society Archives. A Dixon speech to the Republican State Convention during his term as governor is reprinted in a political newspaper, also contained in the Dixon vertical file. It provides, in Dixon's own words, key insight into Dixon's battle to impose a fair tax on the mining interests.

The distinctive role of Dixon in Montana history is underscored in K. Ross Toole, *Montana: An Uncommon Land* (Norman, Oklahoma, 1959) and Merrill G. Burlingame and K. Ross Toole, *A History of Montana* (New York, 1957). Information about specific election results is found in Ellis Waldron and Paul B. Wilson, *Atlas of Montana Elections* (Missoula, 1978).

IV

Thomas Walsh,
Advocate for the People

The structure of our government rocks upon its very foundations.

You might not have known at first blush that Thomas Walsh was a passionate man. But he was. His jaw was square, his eyes steel blue, his demeanor aloof, and his elocution precise. His heavy mustache drooped walruslike over his mouth, disguising subtle signs of emotion. His voice rarely roared, though it sometimes growled. All in all, Thomas Walsh appeared more of ice and granite than fire and brimstone. Dwelling in the smallish physique of this stern personage, however, was a quiet warrior.

Thomas Walsh did not spend his life in politics. First and always, Walsh was a lawyer. And not just any lawyer. Walsh's career evidenced a profound faith in the American system of justice. Walsh understood that the Constitution and the courts created a diffusion of power in the United States that was unique in human civilization. The halls of the legislature would always be vulnerable to the influence of great monied concerns and the electoral pressure of irrational majorities. But the American bench and bar, armed with the Constitution, permitted the weak and powerless to sit alongside the strong at the table of justice. Thomas Walsh was an instrument of this system and a master of laws and evidence. He was a voice for those who had no voice, a crusader for justice, and an enemy of abused power.

The political career of Tom Walsh came late in his life. In-

Opposite: *Senator Walsh, 1925. Senator Walsh led the investigation that exposed the Teapot Dome scandal, twice chaired the Democratic National Convention, graced the cover of* Time *magazine, was prominently mentioned for both the United States Supreme Court and the presidency, and was President Franklin D. Roosevelt's first appointment for attorney general of the United States.*
Courtesy of Montana Historical Society, Helena.

deed, he held only one political office, but that was enough for a man whose foundation had been solidly grounded in the bedrock of constitutional law. Walsh did not enter the United States Senate until his fifty-third year, but he remained there for nearly a quarter century, and his distinguished service stands out in the annals of American government.

Tom Walsh's parents were immigrants from Ireland. His mother, Bridget Comer, arrived in Canada in 1841. His father, Felix Walsh, emigrated to Canada in 1844. They were married in 1853 in Manitowac Rapids, Wisconsin, later called Two Rivers. Felix worked in the tannery there and, in the spring, rode giant log rafts down the river to the mills. He eventually turned to work in a chair and pail factory as the depleted forests no longer supported the logging and tanning companies. As a fishing industry grew up, Mrs. Walsh took up fishnet making; the children helped by weaving chair seats. Felix Walsh was appointed town clerk and served Two Rivers in that capacity as it grew into a small city over the next twenty-five years. Tom and the other Walsh children were educated by their mother and in the public schools. Their time was divided between their studies, weaving, and the activities of a close-knit Irish family. Of the ten Walsh children, nine survived to adulthood and eight became schoolteachers.

Tom Walsh progressed quickly through the country school system and earned his first teaching certificate at the age of fifteen. He began teaching, and by night he lit and tended the lamps on the public streets of Two Rivers. A friend in Two Rivers later jested, during the celebrated Teapot Dome investigation, that Tom's lamplighting duty marked his beginnings in the oil business.

Young Tom Walsh was known for his love of baseball. In 1876 he and his brother Henry started the Two Rivers Centennials. One commentator later wrote of the Centennials that "[t]hey did not wipe the earth with everything that came before them, but they won considerably more than their share of games, and Tom was a good second base man."[1]

For several years, Tom continued to teach, play baseball, and work in Two Rivers. In 1879 when he was but nineteen years old, Tom earned his lifetime teacher's certificate. He then became the principal of the Sturgeon Bay High School when he was barely old enough to vote. It is said that Walsh developed his meticulous use of the English language during his teaching years to underscore his authority in schools where many of his students were older than he. Walsh gained the equivalent of a college education by studying on his own at night. Unsatisfied, he then developed an interest in the field of law, read extensively on the subject, and resolved to save enough money to attend law school at the University of Wisconsin in Madison.

In 1884, Thomas Walsh received his bachelor of laws from the university. His brother Henry, a lawyer himself, already had moved west to Redfield in the Dakota Territory. So, shingle in hand, Tom moved to Redfield and joined his brother's practice. For five years Tom practiced law in Redfield and watched the territory as it struggled to gain the status of statehood. He rode from county seat to county seat, enduring the rigors of frontier life, but the Walsh brothers' practice hardly yielded a prosperous existence. In 1889 the same year that Redfield became a town in the sovereign state of South Dakota, Tom Walsh married Elinor "Ellen" McClements, whom he had courted periodically since his days in Wisconsin.

Ellen was the daughter of immigrants from the British Isles, but her family enjoyed a respected social status in their adopted town of Sheboygan, Wisconsin. Ellen was well educated, with her own career interests, and had strong opinions on many subjects. Walsh had confided candidly to Ellen, if not romantically, that "I am ambitious beyond anything which fires most young men. . . . I recognize as my greatest need someone who can work with me, who can drive me by argument from untenable positions, and assist me to clothe in convincing language the reasons I can urge for my own views. You cannot drive me from my conviction that you are preeminently fitted for work of this character."[2]

In 1890 Walsh wrote to Ellen's sister Mary that they were considering leaving Redfield. Minneapolis and St. Paul were rejected as a destination because they were "almost at a standstill right now and are crowded with lawyers." Other cities were unappealing for various other reasons. But he wrote, "In about a week I shall go to Helena to look over the ground. . . . It is conceded to be the richest city of its size in the world and we think we may possibly be able to get a little of the wealth."[3]

A month later, Walsh wrote to Ellen from Helena:

I have taken pains to reserve my judgment of the place. The main street is a little wider and a little crookeder than the principal street of Deadwood. Roughness and refinement jostle each other. The great peaks stand like sentries about the town - that is about half way around. To the northwest, north, east and southeast they stand further off. I felt crowded downtown, but on taking a short walk, I found quite extensive plats suitable for residences, where the houses didn't seem engaged in a perpetual struggle to push their neighbors off a small piece of ground. The business houses are costly and some of them grand. The banks suggest ponderous wealth but there are no other startling indicia of its existence in super-abundance. . . . They have a magnificent court-house, used temporarily as the statehouse too. If my courage . . . does not all ooze out, I'll go in and pay my respects to the governor.[4]

Before the end of the year, thirty-one-year-old Thomas Walsh settled in Helena with his wife and opened the doors of his own law office. Tom and Ellen worked together to establish a law practice, he as the attorney and she as the paralegal, secretary, and assistant. The two worked together day and night mastering the cases that were shaping early Montana law. The Walshes brought with them to Montana their infant daughter, who would later recall that she hardly saw her mother from breakfast until night and that, when her parents returned home from their office, the work would continue there.

When the Walshes made their start, Helena and the entire mountain West was in the midst of an economic slump that would climax in 1893. The chances for a young lawyer seemed grim. Most of Walsh's colleagues made their start in the profession through representation of the mining interests that dominated the state. Walsh chose a less traveled route. Tom was closely related on his mother's side to Michael Davitt, an Irish member of the British House of Commons and founder of the Irish Land League, an organization created to advance the interests of the Irish working class. It seemed to Walsh that the great opportunity for doing justice lay in the representation of the state's working men, so he became a trial lawyer. While he represented businesses as well as people and handled mining claims, among other types of cases, the focus of Walsh's practice became plaintiffs' work.

The course that Walsh chose astounded many of his peers. He not only declined to hitch his practice to the business operations of the mining interests but in case after case, he began to sue the great companies on behalf of injured people! For the most part, his clients carried no power or influence, but in Walsh's eyes, they deserved an equal portion of justice. Several of his cases survive as colorful stories for his biographers.

In 1895, 350 cases of dynamite illegally stored in a warehouse in Butte exploded while a nearby building-fire raged. The explosion sent steel, rock, wood, and glass flying for blocks. More than 60 Butte citizens were killed and 300 permanently crippled. Many of the families who lost loved ones and wage earners came to Walsh seeking redress. Nearly all the assets of the company, which illegally stored the dynamite, had been destroyed by the explosion, but Walsh was not deterred. He prosecuted an action to hold the wealthy directors of the company personally liable, on the theory that they knew or should have known of the dangerous illegal stash. With this theory, creative at the time, Walsh was able to achieve compensation for many of the devastated Butte families.

In 1896, Walsh represented Charles Krohne in another widely celebrated case. Krohne was an employee of the Northern Pacific railroad, his legs were cut off by a switch engine. Walsh took Krohne's case and recovered a substantial compensation award, but by the time the judgment was rendered, the Northern Pacific had gone into receivership. It had been bought by a new corporation that repudiated the debt to Krohne.

In the 1890s such developments would have discouraged and defeated most lawyers, but Walsh pressed on. He filed another suit contending that the foreclosure proceedings on the Northern Pacific had been flawed and that in any case the new company was bound to pay the personal injury debt. The lawyer opposing Walsh in the case was Thomas Carter, whom Walsh would later face in the 1910 race for the United States Senate. Carter and his client, facing the ongoing litigation tactics of Walsh, compromised and settled Krohne's claim. Krohne went on to establish himself in Livingston and became a lifelong friend of Walsh.

Also in the 1890s, Walsh undertook the cause of Pat Mullins, who, twenty years earlier, had acquired a lease to the Comanche Mining Claim adjacent to properties being worked by the Boston and Montana Copper Mining Company. The superintendent of this company became partner to Mullins, agreeing to finance the mining of his claim in return for Mullins's daily labor. Mullins worked the claim diligently, digging a shaft 600 feet deep, following a vein of copper. The copper company superintendent discovered that Mullins was following this vein. He convinced Mullins that the vein would no longer be profitable and cut off Mullins's financing. In truth, the mother lode of the claim lay just 100 feet farther in the direction that Mullins was digging.

Shortly after Mullins was driven from his project empty handed, the Boston and Montana Company procured the lease to the claim and uncovered the treasure. Mullins went to Walsh, pleading for relief from the fraud. The action was filed and Walsh convinced the trial court to issue an order compelling the mining company to produce its entire store of records, correspondence, and maps. Rather than face the evidence of their wrongdoing in the public courtroom, the company settled and Mullins regained at least a portion of the wealth he had earned. Pat Mullins entered politics himself and a few years later became one of Butte's most flamboyant and celebrated mayors. In 1903 Mullins hosted President Theodore Roosevelt on behalf of the people of Butte.

Walsh's fame as a litigator continued to spread. The rich and powerful Amalgamated Copper Mining Company was formed in 1899 when Marcus Daly sold his Anaconda Company to Standard Oil. The Amalgamated became nervous at the prospect of facing Walsh in court. In a strategic effort that would prove typical of Amalgamated's business conduct, the Company in 1900 urged Walsh to accept a position as general counsel for the Company. Walsh declined, asserting that while he would represent the Company in cases of his own choosing, he refused to be beholden to it. He told the Company he cheerfully would represent them according to his own discretion, but he would much rather sue them. One journalist later explained that "Old Montanans will tell you, chuckling, that two of the Amalgamated officials died of heart failure at the cold-blooded impudence of this still young lawyer daring to refuse a retainer from one of the corporations that claimed to own the state."[5]

Later, Walsh represented a miner named Kelly who worked for the Fourth of July Mining Company. Kelly suffered an accident that broke his back and left him a paraplegic. Walsh achieved a judgment for his client, but again found the defendant bankrupt. He discovered, though, that the company's assets had been sold to the Amalgamated to the great benefit of Fourth of July stockholders. Walsh sued to force the stockholders, including Joseph Clark, brother of copper king Sen. William Clark, to satisfy the judgment. The opposing counsel was hired for his renowned eloquence, and the two took the case to the jury. Kelly, incapacitated, was not able to attend the trial. The corporation's lawyer pointed to the empty chair and charged that Kelly's absence proved his lack of interest in the lawsuit. Walsh responded quietly but dramatically, "Counsel asks why my client is not here. I'll tell you, gentlemen of the jury, why he is not here. My client is at the moment in a plaster cast on a hospital bed in a distant city where he is destined to remain for so long as life lasts, forlorn, forsaken by everyone but his fighting lawyer."[6] Walsh again prevailed, and the judgment was paid.

Years later, as a candidate for the United States Senate, Walsh reflected on his legal representations. His opponent, Tom Carter, argued that Walsh was a "contingent fee lawyer," which was somehow less worthy of public respect. Undaunted, Walsh replied:

> It is a matter of great gratification to me that in my professional career my services were at the command of any man who had a just cause, whether he was rich enough to fee me in advance of the trial of his case or not. I have secured justice for many deserving men injured in the services of railroad and mining corporations who would have failed, perhaps, to secure a dollar had they not been able to secure my services or the services of some lawyer of more or less eminence upon a contingent-fee basis.[7]

Walsh then turned the accusation against Carter, recalling the famous Krohne case, saying:

The only time I ever met Senator Carter professionally was when he appeared against me in a proceeding I had instituted to enforce payment of judgment for a poor fellow who had lost both legs in the Northern Pacific Railway yards at Livingston, Montana. I am glad to say that out of the little money I got for him, he has been able to establish himself in the city of Livingston and is as good a friend as I have in the state. If this kind of campaign persists, Walsh concluded, I propose to take Charley Krohne along with me, and wheel him onto the platform as Exhibit "A."[8]

In spite of his diligent dedication to his law practice, Walsh did not isolate himself entirely during those years from the affairs of politics. Tom had participated in the political movement to gain statehood for the Dakota Territory and the debate over division of the territory into two states. Not long after he arrived in Montana, the political waters began to churn with the battle for the state's official capital. The final contestants were Helena and Anaconda.

Walsh entered the fight on behalf of Helena. He traveled widely and spoke out for his adopted hometown. In the process, he saw much of the state and learned about its people and resources. In 1896, Walsh was unanimously offered the Democratic nomination for judge of the district court in Helena. Although his election would have been virtually certain, he declined the nomination to continue the development of his law practice.

By 1906 Walsh had clearly established himself among the most eminent members of the bar. In that year, he made his first venture into electoral politics. Walsh ran for and received the Democratic nomination for Congress. The Republicans nominated Charles Pray, who eventually would win in an election that handed the Republicans a veritable landslide.

In the course of the campaign, however, Walsh began to develop and articulate his Progressive political profile. In a speech before the Montana Federation of Labor, he argued in favor of the initiative and referendum as well as the direct primary, and he urged legislative action to improve safety for railroad workers. He was called the dominant figure at a convention of Montana railroad shippers who met to address rail-

Thomas J. Walsh's law office in Helena's Penwell Block, 1911. Walsh was a cele-brated plaintiff's personal injury trial lawyer who did not hold public office un-til he was fifty-three years old. His commitment to American jurisprudence substantially influenced his twenty-five years in the United States Senate.
Courtesy of Montana Historical Society, Helena.

road injustices, which were gaining the attention and reproba-tion of the public. During the coming legislative session, though not a member of that body, he would become a promi-nent figure in the creation and passage of the state's Compre-hensive Railroad Act.

Walsh was made temporary chairman of the Democratic State Convention in 1906, urging the party toward the Progres-sive agenda. In his speech to the convention, Walsh spoke of "the rising tide of democracy," and the genesis of a powerful "public conscience." Though the party was still heavily in-fluenced by those tied to the state's great corporate interests, Walsh condemned "those faithless public servants who, though chosen as the people's representatives, have shown themselves . . . the mere instruments of great corporate inter-ests which they serve. . . . " Walsh scorned the Republican Party as inextricably tied to the financial resources of the great trusts and argued, accordingly, that the Democratic Party carried the only true hope for reform.[9]

During the 1906 campaign, the Democrats challenged Charles Pray to debate Thomas Walsh. Pray declined the offer, but Joseph Dixon, then a candidate for the United States Senate, accepted. The odd result was a debate between Walsh, candidate for the House, and Dixon, the would-be senator. Both were devout Progressives and the debate likely elevated the causes of the embryonic Progressive movement.

After his defeat by Pray, Walsh entered into partnership with attorney C. B. Nolan. They continued to represent injured workmen in personal injury claims, in addition to handling various other legal causes. James E. Murray, who would later become a United States senator, knew Walsh at the time. He later recalled that "Walsh was a thin man, but wiry, pale looking, and very efficient. He never fumbled with papers. He knew just where everything was. In court he was very austere, clear, cold, precise, inspiring confidence. I guess I never saw a more earnest man. . . . His eyes were piercing, almost hypnotic in their effect. . . . He had life, vigor; he was alert and quick."[10]

Walsh's continued success as a trial lawyer did not quell his political ambitions, though. Once the political bug had bitten, Walsh looked for another opportunity for election. In 1908 Walsh was elected to the Democratic National Convention. The convention met in Denver in July. William Jennings Bryan, who led the Free Silver movement in 1896, had become the party's undisputed standard bearer. In the ten years since his famous Cross of Gold speech, Bryan had distinguished himself as an early progressive who advocated popular reforms and decried boss rule of the Democratic Party.

During the preconvention campaign, Bryan argued to his fellow Democrats, "We cannot hope to rival the Republican Party in securing the support of the corporations that have been controlling politics. We must secure the support of the voters, of the rank and file—of the producing class; and this cannot be done by imitating Republican methods."[11] Walsh allied himself with this philosophy by vigorously supporting Bryan at the convention. Of Bryan, Walsh said, "The eminent Democrat is a man whose character and career have always held my profoundest admiration. I am in hardy accord with Bryan's political views."[12]

Walsh succeeded in marshaling Montana's delegation for Bryan's nomination. Walsh served on the convention's platform committee and helped draft a declaration of principles that renewed the party's commitment to the preservation of a government "of the people, by the people and for the people," which would "ensure, as far as human wisdom can, that each citizen shall draw from society a reward commensurate with his contribution to the welfare of society."[13]

After the convention, Walsh contributed substantially to the Bryan campaign fund and spoke at political functions throughout the state in favor of Bryan and progressive Democratic principles. Walsh carried with him on the political circuit Bryan's admonition that, "[t]here is a difference between corporate man and natural man. There is a difference in creation. God made man and placed him on His footstool to carry out a divine decree. Man made the corporation for material purposes."[14] In the end, Republican William Howard Taft prevailed and was elected president. Nonetheless, the campaign was significant for Walsh. He became acquainted with many of the state's political leaders during his service at the Democratic convention and was provided another opportunity to refine his own progressive views and espouse them throughout the state.

Walsh remained alert to political opportunities, and the next one presented itself in 1910 when Republican senator Thomas Carter stood for reelection. Democrats Walsh and W. G. Conrad challenged Carter.

The senatorial election of 1910 would be decided in the 1911 legislature. Carter had been Montana's last territorial delegate and her first congressman. He served as United States senator from 1895 to 1901 and was elected again in 1905. Carter was a former chairman of the Republican National Committee and former commissioner of the General Land Office under President Benjamin Harrison. His roots were deeply planted in Republican soil and spread throughout the country. When not occupied with politics, Tom Carter had served as legal counsel to many of Montana's largest corporations. Carter was generally regarded as a dependable representative of big business in government. He personified the opposition to Progressivism, and the campaign fight of 1910 became a clash of causes.

In the early Democratic rustlings of the 1910 election, two Democrats emerged as opponents to Walsh. The most conspicuous was millionaire W. G. Conrad. Copper king William Clark also tested the waters. He secretly harbored a desire to return to the Senate after a somewhat less than illustrious or honorable tenure, which he served from 1901 to 1907, after exerting years of questionable influence over the legislature.

Walsh failed to win the party's nomination at the Democratic State Convention, which was captive to the influence of his two millionaire opponents as well as the omnipresent copper company. The convention's result did not exclude Walsh from the race, however, and the election would ultimately be decided in the legislature. Walsh campaigned vigorously throughout the election season to help send a Democratic majority to the state assembly. He argued throughout the state that "the corporate interests controlling great industrial enterprises, and operating railroads and other public utilities have cozened from the people the substance of self-government."[15] At an Independence Day rally in Missoula, Walsh proclaimed,

> What a world this would be, had the men whose thoughts and deeds this day recalls been content to acquiesce in the abuses of their times lest immediate pecuniary interest might suffer! Every age has them. Every generation must meet them. They clog the wheels of progress. They hold the toilers in subjugation to favored classes. But, however formidable they may be, those that afflict us must succumb if we shall but revere the memory and emulate the virtues of the men who made glorious the fourth day of July.[16]

Not surprisingly, the Amalgamated and its business allies saw Walsh as a maverick who would be difficult to control. Walsh's strong Progressive message stood in contrast to the lackluster efforts of Carter. Sen. Joseph Dixon spoke widely during the 1910 campaign season, but offered little support to his fellow Republican Carter. Instead, Dixon traveled the state espousing his own Progressive ideals, which aligned him more closely with Walsh. When the votes were counted, the Democrats won a seven-seat majority in the legislature. Clark had faded, and Conrad and Walsh began to jockey for the legislative votes necessary to capture the Senate seat.

By virtue of his effective campaigning and widespread support, Walsh should have been the natural choice for the Senate. The continued influence of corporate interests, though, bore upon the legislature to Walsh's detriment. Burton K. Wheeler, then a member of the legislative delegation from Butte, reported of the assembly that "the Democrats controlled the House, the Republicans controlled the Senate, and the Company controlled the leaders of both."[17]

Bowing to the Company, twelve Democratic members of the legislature, chiefly from Butte, refused to caucus on a candidate for senator. The principal recalcitrant was Wheeler, who pled vehemently for Progressive principles and the election of Walsh. Although Walsh led Conrad among the remaining Democrats, he was unable to gather a majority. In a final compromise effort to prevent the election of Carter and to send a Democrat to the Senate, Walsh withdrew and handed his votes to the little-known Hamilton judge Henry L. Myers.

Myers proved acceptable to the various factions and was elected. Walsh later described the political affairs of the legislative session as corrupted by a "plain, undisguised effort, partially successful, to throttle self-government in an American commonwealth." Nonetheless, Walsh was pleased with the election of Myers. He considered Myers a good man and was delighted at the defeat of Carter, who "had voted consistently against every reform demanded by the people. . . . "[18]

Walsh had barely rested from the campaign of 1910 when he undertook a challenge to incumbent Senator Dixon whose seat would be up in 1912.

The election of 1912 cannot be explained without reference to Sen. Joe Dixon and his national political involvement. Dixon, raised a Quaker and distinguished in the Progressive movement, was a longtime ally and confidant of Theodore Roosevelt. Dixon was drawn into the Bull Moose campaign in 1912 and became Roosevelt's principal national leader. Dixon devoted very little time to his own candidacy in Montana, where he ran as a Bull Moose under the banner, "Put the Amalgamated Out of Montana Politics."

When the state Democratic convention met in 1912, Walsh argued, to the benefit of his own candidacy, that the Democrats would need to elect a Progressive to win. He maintained that such a move by the Democrats would deny the Bull Moose Party its reason for existence and the split Republican Party would not be able to muster a majority.

Walsh delivered the keynote address to the Democrats in Billings on September 24. He advocated the direct primary to end the corruption of the convention system, and he urged reform of the campaign contribution laws to alleviate the obligation of candidates to later perform government favors for special interests. Walsh argued that the convention system "has been found easy to manipulate and is manipulated by those who make a trade of politics—the bosses—with money furnished by the favor- and privilege-seeking interests. Under this system, the latter become the real sovereigns, the bosses making nominations at their dictation."[19] Walsh also advocated the progressive income tax, the direct election of United States senators, the publication of campaign finances, and the admission of Arizona to statehood, all issues dear to the Progressives.

In spite of the continued corporate influence of the Democratic state convention process, Walsh was easily nominated. The Republican candidate posed only a nominal threat, and the election resolved itself into a contest between Walsh and Dixon. Befuddled by a choice between Progressives, the corporate interests, for the most part, remained in the wings. The Democrats swept the 1912, election which, for the first time, included a meaningful vote for the United States Senate. Walsh easily captured Dixon's seat. Under the rules of this transitional period, some of the legislators were bound by the popular vote and others were not. Those who were permitted to maintain their discretion, though, recognized that a vote against Walsh after his commanding victory would put them squarely at odds with a determined electorate. When the legislature met in 1913, they officially sanctioned Walsh's election and inaugurated what would become one of the nation's great senatorial careers.

The election of 1912 had other repercussions as well. Perhaps as a result of the combined Progressive campaigns of Walsh and Dixon, the voters passed initiatives that created a direct primary system, a campaign expenditures and corrupt practices act, a presidential preference primary, and a measure further clarifying the popular election of senators. For the first time in Montana's history, the people of Montana asserted themselves effectively against the corporate interests, signifying the beginning of the end of Company tyranny.

At the national level, Democrats had reaped the same

benefits from a split Republican Party. New Jersey governor Woodrow Wilson defeated President Taft and achieved an electoral mandate for his program, which was espoused as the New Freedom. Walsh pledged himself to the New Freedom before a joint session of the state legislature, explaining that "this legislation will be incidental to the main object of the movement—the abolition of privilege through which an unjust share of the prodigious wealth our prolific country produces finds its way into the hands of the relatively few where it accumulates in menacing magnitude."[20]

When Walsh arrived in Washington, he quickly took up the cause of Wilson's New Freedom program. In many ways, the relationship between Walsh and Wilson paralleled the one that had developed between Dixon and Roosevelt. Wilson recognized that many of the proposals incorporated in his program, designed as they were for the betterment of common men and women, would be viewed as radical. Nonetheless, Wilson and his supporters, including Walsh, were determined to "play for the verdict of mankind."[21] Walsh was appointed to the prestigious Senate Judiciary Committee as well as the Committee on Territories. He soon became known as the chief senatorial spokesman for the Wilson administration, backing nearly every one of Wilson's proposed reforms. Walsh advocated passage of the Federal Reserve Act and fought successfully for the Federal Farm Loan Act, the latter enabling American farmers to secure mortgage loans at low interest rates. As a member of the judiciary committee, he helped draft the women's suffrage amendment and carefully honed it to ensure constitutionality. He spoke with equal commitment in favor of the child labor laws. He successfully campaigned for the provision of the Clayton Act of 1914, which protected farm organizations and trade unions from suit under the Sherman Antitrust Act.

In 1913 Walsh was given the opportunity to reward Burton K. Wheeler for his courageous espousal of Walsh's candidacy and progressive principles in the 1910 legislature. On Walsh's recommendation, President Wilson appointed Wheeler United States district attorney for Montana. The appointment not only repaid a debt to Wheeler but also put the firebrand liberal in a position where he could monitor the ever-suspect activities of the copper interests.

Perhaps Walsh's only significant difference with the Wilson agenda came over the tariff issue. Wilson advocated the Underwood Tariff Bill, which promised to remove the tariff on commodities important to Montana, including wool, sugar, meat, and lumber. While Sen. Henry Myers supported the president and the Underwood bill, Walsh dissented, saying, "The people of Montana scarcely expect me to stand idly by and voiceless when its interests are discriminated against by this proposed legislation. Practically everything we produce in Montana is on the free list. Wool, sugar, meats, lumber, coal, copper. Materials we buy are on the dutiable list pending the passage of this bill. Therefore, it condemns us to selling what we produce on a free-trade basis and buying what we use in a protective market. . . . "[22] Walsh succeeded in achieving certain changes to the legislation, eventually becoming a supporter of the compromise measure, and the Underwood Tariff Bill was passed.

In 1916 President Wilson nominated Louis Brandeis to become the first Jewish associate justice of the United States Supreme Court. Anti-Semitics from coast to coast organized to defeat the nomination. Walsh was a member of the subcommittee that initially reviewed the nomination, and he conducted extensive examinations of the witnesses who appeared for and against Brandeis. At the conclusion of the hearing process, Walsh delivered a courageous statement in favor of Brandeis, revealing the philosophy he had developed in the course of his own legal career:

> It is clear that Judge Brandeis has been a vigorous, aggressive, relentless antagonist in all of his legal battles. Moreover, he has been successful. . . . The real crime of which this man is guilty is that he has exposed the inequities of men in high places of our financial systems. He has not stood in awe of the majesty of wealth. . . . He seems to have been sought after in causes directed against the most shining marks in that class. . . . He has written about, and expressed his views on, "social justice," to which vague term are referred movements and measures to obtain greater security, greater comfort, and better health for the industrial workers—significant safety devices, factory inspections, sanitary provisions, reasonable working hours,

abolition of child labor—all of which threaten a reduction of dividends. They all contemplate that a man's a man, not a machine. . . . It is to be regretted that such a controversy as this in which we are involved should arise over a nomination of a justice to the Supreme Court. . . . It is easy for a brilliant lawyer to conduct himself as to escape calumny and vilification. All he needs to do is drift with the tide. If he never assail the doer of evil who stands high in the market-place, either in the court or before the public, he will have no enemies or detractors or none that he need heed. The man who never represents the public or the impecunious citizen in any great forensic contest, but always the cause of corporate wealth never has these troubles. It is always the other fellow whose professional character is a little below par. . . .

The bar is still the bulwark of the liberties of the people. To it they must look in the future as they have looked in all our history for fearless champions. Discouragements enough beset the ambitious youth who resolutely sets out upon the path of devotion to duty and to the cause of justice; who strives to render some real public service. I do not care to warn him to abandon the hope of reaching the summit of his profession by that route.

My vote is for the confirmation of the nomination of Louis D. Brandeis for Associate Justice of the Supreme Court.[23]

Walsh's eloquent endorsement was instrumental in the confirmation of Brandeis by the Senate. While Brandeis's service on the United States Supreme Court would, over time, significantly shape the character of American society, a more immediate upheaval was developing on the world stage.

In 1914 the heir to the Austrian throne and his wife were assassinated in Sarajevo, Yugoslavia. The ensuing international imbroglio became World War I. Soon all of Europe was at war. Germany, allied with Austria and Hungary, pitted itself against France, England, and Russia in an explosive confrontation. Serbia, Montenegro, Belgium, Turkey, East Prussia, and Poland were drawn into the chaos before the end of the year. American financial markets trembled, fearing the worst. Nevertheless, the American military remained at home. At the White House,

Commander-in-Chief Woodrow Wilson was convinced that the forces of reason would prevail and bring aggressive dictatorships to their knees. The policy of isolationism, though, soon began to appear obsolete. American commercial interests throughout the world were jeopardized, and the anti-German alliance was rapidly demanding production support from the United States.

In 1915 the British liner *Lusitania* was sunk by a German submarine off the Irish coast. Among the 1,200 who drowned were 128 Americans. Despite the resulting national fury, America's neutrality continued through 1915 and 1916, and the issue became a major source of debate in Wilson's reelection campaign. During these years, Thomas Walsh stood beside the determined president. Walsh defined issues of neutrality in Senate speeches and papers that were widely read and respected for their legal incisiveness. Montana and the entire country divided over the question of America's participation in the war. But the alignment of factions was such that Wilson succeeded in his bid for reelection, promising to keep America out of war. In spite of the pledge, only weeks after Wilson was inaugurated to his second term, the United States declared war on Germany. The foreign European war suddenly became our war.

Senator Walsh continued to employ his sharp skills of legal analysis to support the president's position. Walsh reasoned that it must have been the intention of those who "took from the states the power to make war and lodged it in the national government, to endow that government with all the authority necessary to bring a war in which it might engage to a successful conclusion. . . ."[24]

America was placed in another awkward position in 1917 when Communist insurgents seized the government of war ally Russia. Congress passed the Red Law, supposedly to guard against Communist espionage, but the law became a tool for the harassment of pacifists and labor activists. Attorney General A. Mitchell Palmer relied upon the law to justify his Red Raids.

Thomas Walsh rose up against a growing tide of anti-Communist sentiment to condemn the encroachment upon constitutional rights. He denounced the raids as "unconstitutional methods of warfare," saying, "I do not think it is any answer at all to the charge that illegal things have been done to say that there are bolshevists and anarchists in this country. If there are, they are entitled to whatever protection the law affords." Walsh continued, "It is only in times such as these that the guarantees of the Constitution as to personal rights are of practical use or value. In seasoned calm no one thinks of denying them. They are accorded as a matter of course."[25]

Walsh's beloved wife, Ellen, died in 1917 and Walsh, stricken with grief, took a brief leave of absence to recover. The heat of international events and his own approaching reelection campaign, however, shortly drew him back into the fray. Walsh took a tough stand against the German enemy in his home state, but did not lose faith in the vision of a new and better world. "It does not satisfy me to say, 'there have always been wars and always will be,'" Walsh declared, "I shall not confess in advance that the statesmanship of the world is unequal to the task before it. The first condition, of course, is to whip the Kaiser. . . ."[26]

Though Montana and the country were consumed by war and awash in the patriotism that invariably accompanies such struggles, Walsh admonished his constituents that a better way of addressing international disputes must supplant the status quo. Walsh advocated Wilson's plan for a League of Nations to enforce peace in the international community in the years ahead. Walsh was convinced that this "general association of nations" would afford "mutual guarantees of political independence and territorial integrity to great and small states alike."

Walsh contrasted this idealistic vision with the old customs. "There are two ways of attempting to preserve peace in the future," Walsh explained. "The one has been outlined [League of Nations]. The other is the way of the past, by building up and maintaining a huge military establishment so formidable that no nation will be likely to attack us. With that must go universal military training. But if we pursue that policy, every other first-class power will do the same, to the limit of its ability, and thus we would be forced to engage in a race involving expenditures for war, staggering in amount."

In the climax of this ominous and prescient declaration, Walsh noted that "the policy of allowing every nation at will to make itself a menace to the world through the magnitude and perfection to its own military system precipitated a series of wars involving all of Europe. . . . Will the next one come out of the regenerated Russia 100 years hence, or out of China, when that drowsy giant shall have aroused itself."[27]

Walsh's reelection bid in 1918 did not hang, however, on the nuances of his positions on international affairs. The most pressing political problem for the senator involved the question of reappointment of Burton K. Wheeler as United States attorney. During his term in office, Wheeler had made more enemies than friends. The mining interests were, of course, solidly aligned against him. In addition to long-standing ideological feuds, the Company charged Wheeler with being remiss for not prosecuting unruly labor leaders whom Gov. Samuel Stewart accused of being tied to "surreptitious German influences" and whom "the Company" said were influenced by socialists.[28]

Wheeler had managed, with Company help, to incur the wrath of German haters and Communist haters alike! Conservative Democrats joined with Republicans in attacking Wheeler, but the U.S. attorney refused to surrender his post. In early October before the election, Walsh painfully succumbed to the pressure and asked Wheeler to resign. The Company had again prevailed, but Walsh's premier biographer, Leonard Bates, later argued: "Walsh did not become a corporate tool when he yielded on Wheeler and secured Company backing in this election; his subsequent career proves that. He did surrender temporarily on Wheeler, so that once again the big interests of Montana showed their power."[29]

When the 1918 election arrived, Walsh won against a Republican conservative stalwart, Dr. Oscar Lanstrom, and against Jeannette Rankin, who ran as a Progressive. Walsh garnered 46,160 votes to Landstrom's 40,229 and Rankin's 26,013.

Peace negotiations had already begun in Paris in 1918 and on November 11, the armistice was signed. Early in 1919 President Wilson presided over the first League of Nations meeting in Paris. That same year, the United States Senate took up consideration of the League's covenant. Walsh argued fervently in favor of ratification of the covenant and America's participation in the League because "it is the only system the statesmanship of the world has been able to present as a substitute for the horrible arbitrament of war." Walsh was confident that if the members of the Senate and the American people would "be impartial in their judgment while remembering the tortures our boys suffered and the enormous expense to which the citizens of this country have been put," the covenant would be ratified.

Opponents to the League of Nations were equally determined. Many objected to the idea of a body vested with the powers to enact, interpret, and enforce world law. Public opinion sided with the League's opponents. The nation that had brought home the laurels of victory from "over there" was not of a mind to submit itself to the authority of the new international sovereign. The defeat of the League of Nations covenant in the United States Senate sounded the death knell for the Wilson administration and the dreams of the New Freedom.

In 1920 the divided Democratic convention ultimately nominated former Ohio governor James Cox, with thirty-eight-year-old Franklin Delano Roosevelt aboard as the vice presidential candidate. Tom Walsh was again a member of the Platform Committee of the Democratic National Convention. Walsh's platform urged "cooperation with the states for the protection of child life through infancy and maternity care; the prohibition of child labor, and adequate appropriations for the Children's Bureau and the Women's Bureau in the Department of Labor."[30] The Republicans threw their support to Sen. Warren G. Harding and Calvin Coolidge. The Republicans prevailed in the general election, sending Harding to the White House. There, the seeds of scandal were planted, which grew into a fiasco that would cripple the confidence of Americans in their government and catapult the legal talents of Thomas Walsh into the spotlight of world attention.

During his presidency, Theodore Roosevelt advocated setting aside certain oil reserves for the use of the navy in a time of national emergency. One such reserve, because of its proximity to a certain Wyoming geological formation, became known as the Teapot Dome.

The explosive growth of the automobile industry in the teens created a new enormous demand for oil. The oil industry became the new frontier for robber barons of the twentieth century. Those who had made millions in the business hungered for more, and eyes were covetously set upon the naval oil reserves of California and Wyoming.

Three leaders of the Harding administration became principal protagonists in the Teapot Dome drama. Secretary of the Interior Albert Fall had served with Harding and Walsh in the Senate. Assuming the lead role in this perfidious scheme, Fall was supported by Secretary of the Navy Edwin Denby and Attorney General Harry Daugherty. Fall, like Walsh, was a respected lawyer in the Senate. Harding readily looked to him for legal advice, trusting not only his professional judgment but also his commitment to the public. Harding's faith was misplaced.

Among the nation's biggest oil magnates were Harry F. Sinclair, Edward L. Doheny, and Col. Robert W. Stuart, chairman of the board of the Standard Oil Company of Indiana. Doheny had been a friend of Fall's since the 1880s when they were prospecting for gold and other precious metals in New Mexico. Doheny had moved on to southern California, where he parlayed a single small oil lease into a $100 million oil empire that stretched from California to Mexico.

Doheny and the others had pushed aggressively but unsuccessfully during the Wilson administration for release of the naval oil reserves. Albert Fall, however, was of the philosophy that the nation's natural resources should be placed entirely in private hands for development. Fall's appointment as secretary of the interior represented a great opportunity for Doheny and his cohorts. Immediately after his appointment, Fall set about persuading Harding to transfer control of the naval petroleum reserves from secretary of the navy Denby to the Department of the Interior. In less that three months, the transfer was accomplished, and Fall began courting suitors from the great oil concerns.

As negotiations proceeded, Walsh's interest in the oil industry began to grow. In 1920 Congress had passed an act to ensure that oil leases would be distributed widely throughout the country to enhance competition in the production of crude oil. The following year a Federal Trade Commission report concluded that the Midwest Oil Company controlled 93 to 97 percent of the oil production in Wyoming. Walsh persuaded his Senate colleagues to pass a resolution authorizing the Public Lands and Surveys Committee to undertake an investigation. While the conclusions of this investigation were not especially significant in themselves, the information that turned up convinced Walsh that scandal was brewing in the Wyoming Teapot.

In April 1922, Secretary Fall executed a lease transferring Wyoming's Teapot Dome reserve into the hands of Harry Sinclair's Mammoth Oil Company. Sinclair paid competitors not to participate in the bidding, and the lease was secured without competition. Sinclair then bought up surrounding wells in Wyoming to guarantee his monopoly. The lease to Sinclair left no room for conservation in the interests of national security. The lease was for twenty years or "for so long as oil can be taken in commercial quantities from the ground."

Within three weeks of the Wyoming lease, the California Naval Reserves were leased to Doheny, doing business as the Pan-American Oil Company. The stock of Doheny's and Sinclair's companies soared on Wall Street. Days later, Sen. Robert LaFollette of Wisconsin introduced and successfully engineered passage of the resolution directing Walsh's Public Lands and Surveys Committee to investigate the leasing of the reserves.

Though Walsh was not the chairman of the Public Lands and Surveys Committee, his interest in oil and mineral production, combined with his keen legal skills, ensured his recognition as the de facto leader of the investigation. Walsh was not motivated by any great moral commitment to conservation or environmental preservation. Generally, he believed in aggressive development of natural resources. But Walsh knew that the naval oil reserves had fallen into private hands illicitly and that American taxpayers and consumers had been denied the benefits of a competitive bidding process.

Walsh was also concerned about national security interests that were compromised in the release of the reserves. Walsh's respect for the law, for the voiceless American consumer, and for the security of the country inspired his efforts to scrutinize every detail of the deals and confront the wrongdoers with their transgressions. Walsh undertook this task in spite of his longtime personal friendships with both Fall and Doheny.

Commencing the investigation in 1923, Walsh declared, "Many years ago, it was recognized by the government of the United States that it was an unwise practice to authorize any of the departmental officials to contract or make enormous contracts binding the government to pay tremendous sums without competitive bidding."

Albert Fall was called as the first witness before the committee. Fall was confident in his position, and "bore himself with somewhat more than his usual touch of quiet arrogance."[31] Fall argued that the transfer of the naval oil leases into private hands was unquestionably within the scope of his legal authority as the secretary of the interior. He also argued that the transfer was in the interest of the United States, as the oil reserves were "draining," which would result in a tremendous loss of oil and wealth to the country. Walsh questioned Fall on his financial connections with certain oil barons and at the end of the interrogation posed the ultimate, candid question: "Did you get any compensation at all?" Fall would later regret his untruthful answer, "I have never even suggested any compensation and have received none."[32]

The second witness called by Walsh was Edwin Denby, secretary of the navy. The testimony of Denby made clear that he was woefully ignorant of the terms and implications of the oil reserve leases. Department of the Interior experts representing Secretary Fall had convinced Denby that drainage in the Teapot Dome was a real danger and that the leasing of the reserves was in the best interests of the public. By the end of Walsh's questioning, Denby's negligence and naiveté had been revealed, although he did not appear to be involved in the criminal activity that swirled around Secretary Fall.

Edward Doheny was the next key witness. The cross-examination of Doheny was not a task that Walsh relished. The two had known each other since their early days as young men in Wisconsin. When Ellen died in 1917 and Walsh traveled to southern California to recover from his grief, Doheny acted as his host and caretaker. Walsh's obvious affection for Doheny did not soften his inquiry, though.

Doheny argued that the loss of oil from the naval reserves through drainage was a very real threat. He insisted that good government policy required that the naval leases be transferred to private hands for development. Notwithstanding Doheny's adherence to these platitudes, Walsh elicited the admission that Doheny had received preference in one of his contracts with Fall giving him the lease to the Elk Hills Naval Reserve. Walsh also presented strong evidence that the arguments about drainage of the reserves were inconsistent with geological estimates.

Late in 1923, information surfaced suggesting that Secretary

Fall had mysteriously come into a substantial amount of wealth. Walsh learned that Fall, who left the Senate in 1920 broke and in debt, had suddenly found sufficient capital to satisfy his financial obligations and invest in an array of businesses. Walsh sent a letter of inquiry to Secretary Fall at his New Mexico ranch. Fall did not answer. When Fall returned to Washington, Walsh summoned him to reappear before the committee. Fall refused, claiming illness. Eventually, Fall wrote to the committee, explaining he had received a $100,000 cash loan from the "honorable" Edward B. McClain of Palm Beach, Florida. McClain verified the story. Skeptics pronounced that Walsh's investigation had arrived at a dead end, demonstrating no impropriety.

Walsh's conviction in the justness of his cause, however, did not wane. Instead, he boarded a train for Palm Beach to take the deposition of Edward McClain personally! McClain admitted under oath that the story was a fabrication. The investigation went forward.

On January 21, 1924, Walsh called Archibald Roosevelt, son of Theodore. Archie Roosevelt had read reports of McClain's admission that he had not actually lent Fall the $100,000. Roosevelt was serving on the board of directors of various Sinclair corporations. Knowing that Harry Sinclair planned a sudden departure for Europe, Roosevelt began to suspect Sinclair's complicity in the scandal. Roosevelt spoke with Sinclair's secretary, who, according to Archie, reported that a payment of $68,000 had been made by Sinclair to Fall. Roosevelt resigned his position on all boards of directors in Sinclair's companies and then related the story in his testimony to the committee.

Edward Doheny was summoned back to the committee. This time he admitted that he had lent Fall $100,000 in January 1924. Doheny claimed that the $100,000 was insignificant to him in light of his great personal wealth, but Walsh pointed out that the question of bribery revolved around the significance to Fall of the loan, which was tremendous.

When Walsh's investigation was completed, the pieces of the puzzle came together. President Harding had illegally transferred jurisdiction over the naval oil reserves to the Department of the Interior. Secretary of the Interior Fall, with the acquiescence of Secretary of the Navy Denby, leased the Elk

Reprint from Hearst's International Magazine, 1924.

Courtesy of Montana Historical Society, Helena.

Hill Reserve in California to Doheny's company and the Teapot Dome Reserve in Wyoming to Sinclair's. In return, the government obtained some oil storage tanks in Pearl Harbor, Hawaii, and Fall received at least $100,000 from Doheny and $68,000 from Sinclair. The cash "loan" from Doheny had been delivered to Fall by Doheny's son in a black leather satchel. The amount received from Sinclair was eventually shown to be upward of $300,000.

Walsh's investigation forced the resignation of Secretaries Denby and Fall, and civil actions in the federal courts were brought to cancel the oil leases. Criminal prosecutions, which continued throughout the 1920s, eventually sent Fall and Sinclair to prison. In a speech to his colleagues in the Senate on February 9, 1924, Walsh scrupulously reported many of the facts uncovered and declared:

> Mr. President, this is no time for hair-splitting contentions. . . . A great crime has been committed. The structure of our government rocks upon its very foundations. The only way to restore to the government the confidence of the people—confidence so essential to its perpetuity—is to follow every guilty man with the utmost rigor of the law and to drive from public office every man who by connivance or supineness allowed this crime to be committed.[33]

A Texas newspaper reported of Walsh's investigation:

> He had been on the trail for months before he bagged the game. He cornered Fall, he asked McClain where Fall got the money, he chased Sinclair out of the country, he forced young Roosevelt to resign, he asked for the resignations of Daugherty and Denby and he dragged the Doheny secret from the heart of the California petroleum king who made millions in Mexico, millions in California, and who hoped to make $100 million according to his own testimony by working a Naval oil reserve which he had leased from the not overly fastidious Fall of New Mexico.[34]

In spite of the opportunity for turning the investigation to political advantage, Walsh remained analytical and adherent to legal burdens of proof. While Walsh had met with accusations of groundless mudraking early in his efforts, by the time the investigation was complete, reviews of his performance were glowing. When the final written report of the committee was published, *The New York World* opined that Walsh "writes like a man more interested in recovering the nation's property than in attacking the administration."[35] The *Cincinnati Times Star* said that Walsh had "dealt in a spirit of fairness, no matter to what extent others may have sought to turn the incident to political advantage."[36]

"No man in Washington was better fitted to the task," said the *Times Star*. "Others might tire; Walsh was tireless. Others might change, Walsh was unchanging. Others might quit, Walsh stuck doggedly to his task."[37] An Illinois paper wrote, "The Montana Senator has emerged from this chapter of history with a greatly enhanced fame. He has displayed solid qualities that fitted him perfectly for the job that came to him—persistence, patience, a hound-like scent, and as well a certain equipoise and sobriety that commanded general respect and confidence."[38] And the *World* declared, "If the country today is aroused to a demand for vigilant honesty in public life, it is to Thomas J. Walsh of Montana that the initial credit belongs. He was the pioneer, and a very lonely pioneer at first, in the return to decency."[39]

When the Democratic National Convention assembled in the summer of 1924, Thomas Walsh was made the permanent chairman. The Republican convention nominated Calvin Coolidge, who succeeded to the presidency on the death of Warren Harding. The chief factions competing for the Democratic nomination were represented by Al Smith and William McAdoo. The convention was tumultuous and divided. Walsh himself received as many as 123 votes, and that on the 102nd ballot. Ultimately, John W. Davis was chosen on the 103rd ballot as a compromise candidate. The next item of business before the convention was the selection of a vice president. The assembled delegates rose to their feet, roaring "We Want Walsh! WE WANT WALSH!" Walsh rose unmoved above the clamor and, recognizing a motion from "the delegate from Montana"— none other than himself—adjourned the convention. The next day Walsh declined the vice presidential nomination in a letter to the nominating committee, which in turn chose Charles W. Byran, brother of William Jennings, for the post.[40]

A New York newspaper lauded the unanimous voice of the convention to offer the nomination to Walsh:

> It was a tribute to the scrupulous fairness with which, through more than two trying weeks of turbulence and passion, he presided over the convention's deliberations.
>
> It was a tribute to a great mind which is capable of grappling with the most intricate of public problems.
>
> It was a tribute to the superb courage with which, throughout his life, he has fought the battle for progressive principles and bearded reaction in its den, whether it be at Washington or Helena.
>
> But, most of all, it was a tribute, swelling out from the homes and hearts of America, to the man whose keen intellect, inquisitorial genius, unbounded energy, and limitless patience uncovered corruption in the public service, exposed the culprits in high places and turned them over to the prosecution of the courts.[41]

In his own election campaign back home, Walsh faced immense sums of money being poured into the state by western oil interests to defeat their nemesis. Nonetheless, Walsh was reelected easily with a margin of 16,000 votes, although Republican Calvin Coolidge carried the state by about 14,000.

Walsh continued to show independence and courage in his Senate activity after the Teapot Dome affair and the election of 1924. He voted against the McNary-Haugen Bill to provide an equalization fee for farm products, believing the bill to be unconstitutional, though it was very popular among Walsh's constituents. He voted to submit repeal of the Eighteenth Amendment to the states, though he had been a consistent Prohibitionist for many years. He opposed confirmation of the appointment of Judge John J. Parker to the Supreme Court because of Parker's conspicuous record upholding yellow dog contracts. He voted to bring the issue of Irish independence before the League of Nations for an international public debate. Meanwhile, civil and criminal actions engendered by the Teapot Dome affair dragged on through nearly the end of the decade.

Walsh had become a truly national figure. In May of 1925,

Thomas Walsh's image graced the cover of *Time* magazine. Rustlings began to suggest the possibility of a Walsh presidency. In 1928, the *St. Louis Post-Dispatch* wrote:

> The White House certainly has had less than a dozen occupants with Walsh's intellectual gifts. He has courage so fixed and habitual that it requires virtually no effort for him to be firm. He understands the business of government thoroughly, not only in its functional aspects, but in its fundamental purposes.
>
> All these qualities undoubtedly would contribute to a successful administration of the most powerful office in the world. But Walsh has that which, it seems to me, is even more important—he has that general, inclusive thing we call "character," and he has it to a degree almost unparalleled in the public life in the nation.[42]

Walsh allowed the discussion of his candidacy to develop, although his prospects for the nomination were uncertain. Walsh's candidacy was hindered by two highly divisive characteristics. The tide of prejudice rose powerfully against the notion of a Catholic president. Moreover, Walsh was considered a "dry" as the public mood increasingly favored repeal of Prohibition. Walsh and Al Smith, who were "wet," were the leading contenders as the Democratic convention in Houston, Texas, approached. Having lost the California primary to Smith, Walsh determined that his candidacy would not likely prevail but would prove a divisive influence; he therefore withdrew his name from consideration for the nomination prior to the convention.

Governor Smith became the Democratic candidate and faced Republican Herbert Hoover in the general election. Smith, too, was a Catholic and spent much of the campaign defending against the usual anti-Catholic epithets. The Prohibition issue also remained divisive, and Hoover benefited from the country's strong economic climate during the 1920s. The Democratic Party was defeated, in Walsh's words, by "the Three P's—prejudice, prosperity, prohibition."[43]

Less than one year after Hoover was elected, Wall Street crashed and the nation plunged into the Great Depression.

Walsh rode his Senate seat through these stormy waters and into the Senate election of 1930. Oil interests, still vindictive about Walsh's prosecution of the Teapot Dome offenses, again poured tremendous sums of money into Montana to effect the national leader's defeat. To the chagrin of these special interests, the Republican Party nominated Judge Albert J. Galen, who would only criticize Walsh's opposition to President Hoover and publicly stated his friendship with and respect for the senator. Despite a forceful negative campaign instituted directly by outside financial interests, Walsh was reelected by the greatest margin in his career.

The onset of the Great Depression dealt the new Hoover administration a crushing blow from which it never recovered. By October 1931, the Hoover White House still had failed to advance a strategy for overcoming the nation's economic collapse. Walsh was among thirty Congressional leaders called to the White House to confer with the president on possible solutions. A solid bridge between the White House and the Democratically controlled Congress was not formed, though, and piecemeal attempts to address symptoms of the Depression offered little hope of a financial turnaround.

As the election of 1932 approached, Democrats were justifiably optimistic. Al Smith lingered in the wings, but the likely party leader was Franklin Delano Roosevelt, Smith's successor as governor of New York. Walsh argued energetically on Roosevelt's behalf in Montana and other states, and was Roosevelt's choice for chairman of the Democratic convention in 1932. After defeating an opponent for chairmanship proffered by the Smith forces, Thomas Walsh, "the Montana Ringmaster," ascended to the speaker's stand as the convention organist played "Springtime in the Rockies."

The chairman declared, "These are indeed times that try men's souls. Reflecting minds have speculated on whether we are not passing through one of the great crises in the history of mankind." Walsh recited the startling facts and numbers that illustrated the gravity of the country's financial woes. While specific solutions proposed by Walsh and other Rooseveltians were vague, Walsh pointed the convention toward the ideals that would be the guiding stars in the nation's journey toward recovery. "The theory that national well being is to be looked for by giving free rein to the captains of industry and magnates in the field of finance and accommodating government to their desires," Walsh declared, "has come through the logic of events to a tragic refutation."

Walsh proposed international involvement and commitment to the common man. In conclusion, he said, "A great opportunity as well as a great responsibility is before us, an opportunity as rare as the occasion is extraordinary. Let us proceed to the task to which we are called in an accommodating spirit, so far as principal will permit, mindful always of the truth that he serves his party best, who serves his country best."[44]

Pledged to a New Deal for the American people, Roosevelt swept through the convention and marched past Hoover in November, ushering in a significant new chapter of American history. During the transitional period, seventy-three-year-old Thomas Walsh was notified that President Roosevelt had selected him to be the nation's attorney general. Roosevelt's choice of Walsh was praised widely in the press and one newspaper said, "No wise Democratic politician is likely to go to him in his new job looking for special favors. It would be like asking the Statue of Civil Virtue for a chew of tobacco."[45]

On February 25, 1933, Senator Walsh was married in Havana, Cuba, to Señora Maria Nieves Perez Chaumont de Truffin, widow of a wealthy Havana businessman. The newlyweds started for Washington to attend the inauguration, but Senator Walsh fell ill in Florida. Early in the morning of March 2, Walsh died in his sleep aboard an Atlantic Coast Line train.

The circumstances surrounding Senator Walsh's death have long been the subject of speculation. Some say the senator died "in the arms" of his new wife and others have suggested that he was murdered. At the time of Walsh's death, the Cuban government was unstable and various forces were vying for power. The family of the new Mrs. Walsh was conspicuously affiliated with the incumbent party, and some argued that Walsh was poisoned on his journey to Washington by undercover sympathizers with the opposition movement. The true cause of death was never determined.

Members of Congress and other dignitaries lined up to pay tribute to Senator Walsh at his memorial services in Washington. Among those eulogizing the great Montanan was his longtime protégé, Burton K. Wheeler. According to Wheeler:

Thomas J. Walsh wanted to be a lawyer, a philosopher, a statesman, a character in American annals—and he was; a man of intense ideals, capable of righteous indignation against iniquity—he proved it, and the nation will come to appreciate it. He had an intuition for progressive movements and a quick and keen apprehension of the character and location of reactionary forces. Even his friends did not realize what he was doing, working ceaselessly. His equipoise was splendid. With tireless patience he pursued the even tenor of his way with open-minded frankness, moral and intellectual integrity, courage, sound judgment, and levelheadedness. His advice and opinions were highly esteemed and accorded sincere weight. He was conscientious in thought and action; gentle of spirit, his heart beat in unison with his fellow man, and it was not o'erleaping ambition or crass love of power or gain that caused him to devote the best part of his life to the services of his country and state.[46]

The forces paying tribute to the late Walsh also included Rep. Joseph P. Monaghan of Montana. In his final words, the congressman declared this wish: "When his inscription shall have been written upon the pages of American history may it place these words upon his lips, 'I have fought the good fight; I have run my course; and I have kept the faith.'"[47] For Thomas J. Walsh of Montana, that epitaph would have been just right.

Suggested Readings on Thomas Walsh

The most complete single biography of Thomas Walsh is *Thomas J. Walsh, a Senator from Montana* (Francestown, New Hampshire, 1955), by Josephine O'Keane, Walsh's cousin. O'Keane's book is relied upon extensively in the foregoing chapter for background information.

The leading biographer of Thomas Walsh is J. Leonard Bates. His Ph.D. dissertation, *Senator Walsh of Montana, 1918–1924, a Liberal Under Pressure* (Chapel Hill, North Carolina, 1952), contains a thorough examination of Walsh's second Senate term, in which the Teapot Dome investigation occurred. Walsh's early career is well treated by Bates in "T. J.

Walsh: Foundations of a Senatorial Career," *The Montana Magazine of History* (October 1951). Walsh's courtship with Elinor McClements and life in the Dakota Territory is brought to life by Bates in *Tom Walsh in Dakota Territory* (Urbana/London, 1966), which compiles correspondence to and from Walsh before he moved to Montana.

For a discussion of Walsh's Senate career in the context of Montana's Progressive movement, see Merrill G. Burlingame and K. Ross Toole, *A History of Montana* (New York, 1957). A good book length history of the Teapot Dome scandal and investigation is Robert M. Werner and John Starr, *Teapot Dome* (New York, 1959).

The Montana Historical Society's Thomas Walsh vertical file contains extensive copies of newspaper and magazine articles published during Walsh's career. The vertical file also includes a paper by former Helena judge Lester Loble, "Senator Thomas J. Walsh: Was He Murdered?" This article and its addendum contain fascinating information about Senator Walsh's marriage to Maria Perez Chaumont. A good discussion of Walsh's election to the Senate appears in M. P. Malone, R. B. Roeder, and W. L. Lang, *Montana: A History of Two Centuries* (Seattle/London, 1991). Particular election results are documented in Ellis Waldron and Paul B. Wilson, *Atlas of Montana Elections* (Missoula, 1978).

Jeannette Rankin,
Warrior for Peace

I want to stand by my country but I cannot vote for war.

Alone . . . again. As she sat in her congressional office on the afternoon of December 8, 1941, composing a letter to her constituents, Jeannette Rankin pondered the lonely task of explaining her uncompromising and unpopular opposition to war. She had been there before. In 1917 she had raised her voice against war as the first and only woman member of Congress and suffered the backlash of public outrage. Now, decades later, she had stood up again, facing into a gale of patriotic fury, to denounce war as an instrument of international policy. That is the way Jeannette Rankin was. With courage and perseverance she challenged popular assumptions and demanded reason. Jeannette Rankin was a Republican—and a Progressive—who cared more about results than reprisals; more about equity than expediency; more about peace than politics.

A lifetime of nearly one hundred years spans myriad social, political, and economic changes that bring new directions and values to a nation. In Jeannette Rankin's ninety-three years she did more than witness such changes; she prodded, cajoled, and provoked the people of her time toward them. Guided by steadfast devotion to the principles of peace and equality for women, she raised the flag of conscience in battles typically driven by the forces of monied power.

. . .

Opposite: *Jeannette Rankin, 1917. The nation's first congresswoman. Representative Rankin was among a small group of members of Congress to vote against America's entry into World War I. In her second term, more than twenty years later, she was the only member of Congress to vote against America's entry into World War II.*

Courtesy of Montana Historical Society, Helena.

Jeannette Rankin's father, John Rankin, born in Canada, had heard the tales of cheap land and quick riches in the Montana Territory, and so ventured to the northern Rockies with his brother in 1869. Trained as a carpenter, he settled in Missoula and established himself as a builder. He invested in ranching and built one of the town's first sawmills. Before long, he won reputation as a respected civic leader and accumulated a small fortune. Meanwhile, another adventurer, Olive Pickering was teaching lessons in a one-room schoolhouse near Missoula after leaving her native state of New Hampshire.

John and Olive married in August 1879. At Grant Creek Ranch outside Missoula, they started their family the following year. Jeannette Rankin was born June 11, 1880, the oldest of seven children. Her only brother, Wellington, was four years her junior and the pride of their admiring mother. He would later establish himself as a prominent member of Montana's legal, business, and political communities.

The Rankin family was considered prosperous and the children enjoyed a privileged upbringing, spending winters in their town home and summers working and playing on the ranch. As the oldest child, Jeannette was often treated more like a son. She learned the value of hard work and compassion for those less fortunate. "It was only natural for the girls to learn to clean, bake, sew, cook, and care for the animals," Jeannette later recalled. "I remember making a bandage for Chep's foot after he got caught in a trap, sewing up a horse torn up by barbed wired, and learning how to operate the saw mill."[1] Being the oldest also meant she was responsible for much of the care of her younger siblings. In her role as caretaker, Jeannette learned and excelled at the domestic skills so praised in Victorian women.

The rigid structure of formal education frustrated Jeannette and left her academically discouraged. An average student harboring an above-average intellect, her mind was sparked more by discussions of pressing social issues than by routine drills and instructions. Perhaps partly because of her formal education, Jeannette graduated from high school uncertain of her future and without clear goals or direction. John Rankin, however, placed a high value on education and therefore encouraged his daughter to attend the newly established state university at Missoula.

Jeannette enrolled and began her studies, but college did little to define her goals. Tempted to quit school before she had completed her degree, she endured the academic programs more out of a sense of obligation than a desire to serve any personal ambition. During her senior year at the university, she wrote in her diary: "Go! Go! Go! It makes no difference where, just so you Go! Go! Go!"[2] Jeannette graduated in 1902 with a bachelor of science degree in biology.

At the turn of the century a woman's life choices were limited. Marriage and family was the path most traveled. For those women who remained single, employment options were scarce, even for those armed with a college degree. Jeannette first tried teaching in a rural school, but found little satisfaction there. She quit teaching and tested her skills as a seamstress apprentice in Missoula. This, too, failed to hold her interest. She longed to contribute on a larger scale.

In the midst of her job changing, Jeannette's father died of Rocky Mountain spotted fever in 1904. Jeannette was devastated by his sudden and premature death. The void in her life left her even more confused and indecisive. Olive Rankin was also shaken by the loss of her husband. Jeannette returned home to Grant Creek and spent several years helping her mother with housework, cooking for the ranch hands, and assisting with child care, becoming a surrogate mother to her younger sisters. During these years, reading fueled her imagination and piqued a growing curiosity.

Jeannette also managed, in 1904, to visit her brother Wellington while he was a student at Harvard. She enjoyed mingling in high brow society but was dismayed by the squalor and bleak conditions of Boston's poor and destitute communities. Growing up on the frontier, Jeannette knew little of the social stratification and strife of the newly industrialized eastern cities. As a child, she learned the importance of human compassion from her father, and the reality of Boston's slums awakened her sense of social justice.

At age twenty-six, Jeannette embarked on a course that would help to shape her future. She traveled to San Francisco to visit relatives, where a chance encounter triggered her decision to study social work. In the city of San Francisco, settlement houses sprang up to provide a refuge for the burgeoning immigrant population. Beds and food and medical care were made available there to the newcomers. Jeannette wandered into one such facility and met Elizabeth Ash, a leader in the Progressive movement. She would become a significant influence on Jeannette's future outlook and adherence to the ideals of the reform movement and progressivism.

Jeannette threw herself into volunteer work at a settlement house and was convinced she had discovered her calling. Her tendency toward indecisiveness was replaced by a drive and determination to contribute to the cause of reform. This, she thought, was finally her opportunity to make a meaningful contribution to the public welfare.

Despite Jeannette's early antipathy for school, she decided to pursue professional training in the field of social work. Money from John Rankin's estate was specially earmarked for graduate education and Jeannette used these funds to finance her enrollment in a year-long program at the New York School of Philanthropy. In the fall of 1908, Jeannette arrived in New York to attend the country's foremost institution of social work. She studied under an impressive list of faculty members, including Louis Brandeis and Booker T. Washington.

The doctrine of social Darwinism, also known as survival of the fittest, was a popular social philosophy of the day. The New York School of Philanthropy, however, preached something different. The faculty generally opposed social Darwinism and promoted the philosophy of the growing Progressive movement. The Progressives argued that correcting social inequities would strengthen democracy while advancing constitutional ideals of fairness and equality. Progressives worked to expose the bias of public laws and prove that there was an imbalance. They considered the judicial system unfair and not beneficial for all Americans.

Under the tutelage of the school's faculty, Jeannette was able to explore the writings of an array of alternative thinkers and to develop some of her own ideas more fully. The philosopher Simon N. Patten had a particularly profound impact on Jeannette. In his *New Basis of Civilization* he stressed that poverty and misery were not inevitable conditions of life and could be eliminated through greater efficiency and social reform. Jeannette supplemented her academic regimen by gaining valuable practical experience working in the night police courts and counseling children on the city's lower East Side.

Upon graduation in the spring of 1909, Jeannette was eager to apply the theories she had learned and the knowledge she had gained to real-life problems. Neither the Salvation Army nor the temperance movement, though, both popular causes of the day, captured her interest. The option of settling down to a private life of marriage and family remained equally unappealing. Jeannette's adventurous and independent spirit yearned for its own crusade.

She returned West, landing in Seattle, where she rotated through several different positions working with and protecting the welfare of orphans. Again, Jeannette became disillusioned. The reality of a heartless bureaucratic system that seemed to ignore the well-being of society's children discouraged her. Finally, Jeannette determined that the most effective approach to reform was to shape the laws that governed social welfare institutions.

Before women could directly influence any legislation they first had to win the right to vote. Suffrage campaigns had sprung up across the country. Such efforts in Washington State were active and organized in 1910. Jeannette joined their ranks, first as a volunteer and later as a member of the Washington Equal Suffrage Association. After two months of arduous campaigning, the suffrage measure was easily approved in a popular vote. For Jeannette it was a sweet victory indeed. The women of Washington State had won their franchise, and Jeannette's humanitarian outlook and quest for social change took root in the fertile ground of the American suffrage movement.

Jeannette returned home to Montana for a holiday respite where she learned of a suffrage bill pending in the Montana House of Representatives. Following the example of Ella Knowles and the other early Montana social activists, Jeannette volunteered to speak before the state assembly on behalf of the Equal Franchise Society. The legislature extended the invitation, and on February 11, 1911, Jeannette stepped forward. Nervous, but well prepared, she delivered an impassioned plea to the assembled audience of male lawmakers and onlookers:

> It is not for myself that I am making this appeal, but for the six million women who are suffering for better condi-

tions, women who should be working in more sanitary
conditions, under better moral conditions, at equal wages
with men for equal work performed. For those women
and their children I ask that you support this measure.[3]

Jeannette reassured them that women were not aiming to
enter the male domain, but wanted only to enjoy representation with taxation. She urged the representatives to vote to
submit the suffrage question to Montana voters at the next
election, but her efforts were not sufficient to topple the an-
cient walls of gender division. The house debated and narrowly defeated the bill.

Although the suffrage question in Montana remained unre-
solved, Jeannette earned a statewide constituency of suffrage
supporters and national recognition through her role in the
campaign. Nor did the defeat in Montana distract her from her
larger goal. Many other battles remained to be fought.

Packing her bags, Jeannette moved East again to work on
suffrage campaigns in New York, Ohio, Florida, and Michigan.
For three years she was a tireless campaigner, working long
hours with little compensation. Her leadership qualities, high
energy, determination, and interest in promoting the greater
good of the movement distinguished her from other workers.
She quickly earned the respect of colleagues and established
herself among the leaders of the national organization. In 1913
she was appointed field secretary for the National American
Woman Suffrage Association (NAWSA).

Meanwhile, back in Montana the demand for universal voting rights swelled and the legislature resumed consideration
of the suffrage referendum. Gov. Samuel Stewart was actively
involved, persuading the legislature to support the proposal as
part of the Democratic Party's reform package. He and others
were successful in convincing the lawmakers; with only two
dissenting votes in the house and in the senate, the amendment was passed and finally placed on the ballot for a public
vote.

The legislative victory was critical, but marked only the beginning of a greater contest. The daunting task now fell to the
women of the state to rally and persuade the men to grant
them the right to vote. An experienced organizer and persua-
sive speaker was needed to mobilize the far-flung and dis-

parate groups of the state. If anyone could meet the challenge, it was Montana's own Jeannette Rankin who by now was a seasoned veteran in the struggle for women's suffrage. At the behest of her hopeful sisters in the Montana suffrage movement, Jeannette quit her job as field secretary of NAWSA and returned to Montana in early 1914.

Armed with a card file of women's suffrage supporters compiled during the efforts of 1911, thirty-four-year-old Jeannette began developing a powerful grassroots organization from a headquarters in Butte. For the previous thirty years, the fight for equal suffrage in Montana had been characterized at times by both victories and failures, while popular interest had swung from ambivalence to widespread concern. National leaders had already spent considerable time and money to organize and empower the women of Montana. Their efforts met with varying degrees of success. With Jeannette officially on board as the permanent chairman of the revived Montana Equal Suffrage Association, there were high hopes at the national and state level for a long-overdue victory in Montana.

Montana in 1914 was, as it is today, a rural state with pockets of urban population in the towns of Butte, Missoula, Great Falls, Billings, Kalispell, Helena, and Bozeman. Voters were scattered across a geographical expanse of nearly 150,000 square miles. During the course of the campaign, Jeannette traveled 9,000 miles within Montana and once made twenty-five speeches in twenty-five days, often relying on the generosity of strangers for her evening meal. She went to all lengths to win even a single vote. Her dedication and sacrifice earned her widespread recognition, while the combination of her commitment, charm, and personable style made her a formidable and highly effective political figure.

Suffrage clubs were established throughout the state. In each of the forty counties, a representative was appointed to lobby the local politicians and publicize the issue. Other grassroots campaign techniques included massive letter-writing campaigns to legislators, the governor, and the other opinion leaders.

Due to a constitutional amendment, voters had a year to consider the referendum before it was placed on the ballot. Consequently even though the legislature had passed the measure in January 1913, it was not until November 1914 that the suffrage question was finally placed before the male voters of Montana.

Jeannette brought to the Montana campaign the same single-mindedness and energy she had displayed throughout the other state suffrage movements. Mary O'Neill, press secretary of the Montana Equal Suffrage Association, described Jeannette as "a whirlwind worker, a young woman with the temperament of those who suffer and conquer, who inspires trust with her sincerity and unselfish work."[4]

At a time when most women preferred not to be political or take a public stand, Jeannette thrust herself into the fray with singular passion, tempered by savvy public relations skills. She managed to deliver her message without offending men or alienating uncommitted women. She fine-tuned her arguments with moderate reasoning, which appealed to a broad sector. When speaking to women, for example, Jeannette commonly lamented their inability to control political prejudices affecting their home lives. She brought women together by emphasizing the problems of caring for a family without the protection of political representation and living under laws passed by men they had no power to elect or replace.

Such a long and active campaign needed significant funding. The national suffrage organization was well financed by eastern money. Secret New York benefactors, James and Harriet Laidlaw, contributed substantial amounts of cash to the Montana cause. Without such economic support, Jeannette's full-time commitment and personal sacrifices would have been impossible.

After many years of groundwork and a populist inclination toward fairness, Montana was finally on the brink of a successful suffrage campaign. Nevertheless, dissension and strong opposition existed, especially within three specific interest groups. The National Anti-Suffrage Association was a powerful group whose central platform claimed that suffrage would disrupt home life and force women and children into the streets to be "political." They often relied on moral and religious arguments to win public support. The liquor wholesalers and bar owners feared the enhanced power of the Women's Christian Temperance Union and the increased likelihood of passage of a Prohibition amendment if women won the vote. Finally, the powerful Anaconda Copper Mining Company in Butte opposed the suffrage amendment because of the industrial reforms enfranchised women were expected to support.

But public opinion was stronger than all the forces of opposition. On November 3, 1914, by a close vote of 41,302 to 37,588, the amendment was approved. Montana became the tenth state to grant women suffrage, and Jeannette Rankin added another victory to her growing list of political achievements.

For three long years Jeannette had devoted herself to the women's suffrage movement. Finally in June 1915, she took a break from her nonstop schedule. Ever the adventurer, she traveled to New Zealand for relaxation, but ended up studying the working conditions of New Zealand women while earning a stipend as a seamstress. Now well familiar with the power and potential of grassroots politics, she talked about women's suffrage and encouraged her coworkers to think about improving their status. Jeannette returned to the States in mid-1916 as World War I raged in Europe and as Americans pondered the propriety of American involvement. In this charged atmosphere, Jeannette Rankin contemplated a campaign to become the nation's first congresswoman.

By 1917 many of the causes championed by the Progressives during the previous twenty years either had been enacted into law or were gaining momentum as part of a growing movement. Women were winning the vote across the country and to some the time seemed right for a woman to enter the arena of electoral politics. Jeannette weighed the sentiment of the times and her personal background. She thought herself a likely candidate for Congress, but many of her loyal friends disagreed and thought she was premature in running. It was still too soon, they said. Montana was not yet ready for a woman to hold such high public office.

Jeannette ignored the naysayers and announced her candidacy in July 1916, with a platform that called for an eight-hour workday for women, Prohibition, revision of the tariff, child welfare, more publicity of the business and issue positions of congressmen and, most important, suffrage by federal amendment. She proclaimed her primary reason for seeking election "is to further the suffrage work and to aid in every possible way the movement for nation-wide suffrage which will not cease until it is won."[5]

At the time, Jeannette's selection of party affiliation was motivated in large part by practical considerations rather than a belief in ideology, although she would remain a Republican throughout her life. Despite her support of Progressive policy she ran as a Republican because she calculated the difficulty of winning the primary against a Democratic incumbent and determined she stood a better chance as an opposition candidate.

Jeannette did not find overwhelming support for her candidacy, especially among friends and fellow suffragettes. Many approached her brother, Wellington, to persuade him to change her mind. Her detractors suggested she start her political career in a lower-level office and then, if rejected by the voters, she could still recover for future races. They argued that if she aimed too high and missed, her political career would be finished.

Jeannette remained convinced that the time was right and she embarked upon the campaign for Congress with the invaluable assistance of two supporters who would remain loyal throughout her life. Her brother, Wellington, managed her campaign; and Belle Fligelman, former fellow suffrage worker and editor and manager of *The Montana Progressive*, supervised the daily operation of the organization from its Helena headquarters.

As a suffrage leader Jeannette had learned the benefits of grassroots campaigning. She built on these same principles and activated much of the same network to develop a formidable congressional campaign. She was not afraid to get out and meet the voter face to face, which she did throughout the campaign. A gifted politician, she had a remarkable ability to move from drawing rooms to railroad yards with charm and ease. The creativity that often comes with a first-time experience fostered clever ideas. For instance, postcards were mailed to voters and on election day her volunteers conducted a phone bank with the greeting "Good morning, have you voted for Jeannette Rankin?" At the end of the day, perseverance and political savvy prevailed, and Jeannette emerged from the field of eight Republicans a winner in the June primary.

Her strong victory put Jeannette ahead of the other general election candidates, two Democrats, one Republican, and two Socialists, in the race for the state's two at-large congressional seats. Her base expanded to include the unlikely support of Prohibitionists and many anti-suffragists. Jeannette brought into her camp newly enfranchised women from all backgrounds, including many who crossed party lines, by emphasizing issues of particular concern to women. Near the top of this list was the welfare of children. Jeannette criticized the federal government for failing to protect the rights of children, noting that Congress had appropriated $300,000 to study feed for hogs while only $30,000 was set aside to study the needs of children. "If the hogs of the nation are ten times more important than the children," Jeannette argued, "it is high time that women should make their influence felt."[6]

Another important element of Jeannette's continued success was the intense public interest generated from a woman's congressional campaign. Growing public attention was especially important because her candidacy was all but ignored by the state's major newspapers, most of which were owned by the powerful Anaconda Copper Mining Company. Also critical to her viability was the assistance of her large family; several members volunteered their time and effort to campaign across the state.

As the campaign drew to a close, Belle Fligelman, in a brief article in *Sunset* magazine, wrote:

> When the role is called in the House of Representatives in Congress next winter, it is possible that a low, vibrant feminine voice may respond to the call for one of the congressmen at large from Montana. There will follow a craning of masculine necks over starched white collars, and the accruing discomfiture will be rewarded by the sight of a splendid young woman with a wealth of soft curly hair, a pair of dark eyes that flash fire, and an expression that radiates the joy of living. . . .
>
> Miss Rankin is the first woman in the United States to be nominated for Congress by one of the big political parties, and her candidacy has created a unique political situation in the Treasure State. Because to her, more than any one woman in the state, is due the credit for having won the right of suffrage for Montana women two years ago, the women believe they owe her their support. As a result,

> Democratic woman as well as Republican and Progressive women are laying aside party lines and are openly supporting Miss Rankin.[7]

On the eve of the election, Jeannette returned home and spoke to an overflowing crowd of supporters at the Missoula Theater. *The Daily Missoulian* reported the event:

> Miss Rankin's address last evening ended her brilliant campaign. Because of that fact and because she had not previously spoken in Missoula since the primary election she drew an audience which packed the theater, seats and standing room. . . .

> For the sake of the nation's children, whose needs women best understand, Miss Rankin called upon Montana to give women a representative in the national legislative body.[8]

Jeannette told the assembly at Missoula that, "no matter what I do, nothing can take from Missoula, Montana and the Republican party the honor of having sent the first woman to Congress."[9]

Prospects for Jeannette in the general election were promising. She had run strongly in the primary, finishing well ahead of her primary opponent. Moreover, she was supported by three broad voting groups that carried great weight in Montana elections. Having endorsed the Equity Farmer's political program, she had the hardy support of most of the state's farmers. As a known champion as the rights of workers, she was widely supported by members of organized labor. Finally, and most important, her successful work on behalf of women's rights and child protection had endeared Jeannette to the women of Montana.[10]

Election day, November 7, 1916, finally arrived. But it would be two more long days until the outcome was determined. Votes were counted manually and, thus, slowly. On the morning of November 8, the headlines declared that Democrats John Evans and George Farr had captured the two seats. "The day after the election," Jeannette said a few days later in her acceptance speech, "it looked very much as if I had not been elected, but it seemed to me that the campaign had been nevertheless worthwhile because the women had stood together, the women had learned solidarity. . . . That one thing had been alone worth striving for."[11]

Although disheartened, the thirty-six-year-old suffragette waited to concede the election until all the votes were counted. Votes from eastern Montana trickled into Helena and the electoral picture began to change. The Rankin candidacy, declared dead by the Company press, rose from the ashes and surged ahead of Farr. Three days after the polls closed, the results were final. A new milestone appeared on the horizon of American history. A young, progressive, crusading woman from Montana had burst through the invisible barrier that insulated the all-male Congress and the face of the nation was changed forever.

By this single, collective act of political will, Montana and Jeannette Rankin were thrust into the national spotlight. Overnight, Jeannette became not only a spokeswoman for her Montana constituents but also a national symbol of hope for all the women of the country. How could anyone be prepared for the deluge of publicity that follows such a historic event? The press surrounded Jeannette's house and congratulatory letters and telegrams poured in.

Jeannette was not eager to cooperate with the press, and the sudden notoriety surprised her. Her reticence and desire for privacy unwittingly led to many inaccurate reports of her demeanor, personality, and appearance. The eastern press portrayed her as a rough-and-ready Montana cowgirl who "packed a .44 caliber six-shooter and trimmed her skirt with chaps fur."[12] In reality, the new congresswoman was more "East Coast society" than "Rocky Mountain rancher," but it was no wonder when Jeannette finally arrived in Washington that her colleagues were surprised to see this slender woman in fashionable clothes.

Jeannette had a sophisticated sense of style and insisted that her outfits be well made of quality materials, attractive and appropriate for her new position. *The New York Times Magazine* commented by poem on the novelty of Rankin's election:

We have so many congressmen
Whose ways are dark and shady

How joyfully we welcome then
The coming congresslady!

I wonder is she old and stout
Or is she young and pretty?
How long the members will stay out
Who are on her committee.

We'll hear no more of shabbiness
Among our legislators
She'll make them formal in their dress,
They'll wear boiled shirts and gators.

Her maiden speeches will be known
For charm and grace and manner.
But who on earth will chaperon
The member from Montana?[13]

Meanwhile, a prominent suffrage leader quoted in the *Washington Times* said that "Jeannette is one of the best stump speakers, can dance like a boarding school girl and, believe me, she will lead those congressmen a merry two step when she comes to Washington."[14] Another former colleague said of Jeannette in the postelection press: "She is a good fellow, a corking good fellow, just a normal American girl, who sat beside her brothers at college and studied sociology and economics and psychology and is therefore pretty much the same. . . . She is young, attractive, quick, bright, mighty intelligent looking and has a fine, sharp, well balanced mind."[15]

Before heading to Washington, D.C., to take her seat in the Seventieth Congress, Jeannette signed a contract with the Lee/Keedrick speaking bureau. She was offered $500 per speech, a considerable amount for someone who until then had devoted herself to social causes for little or no compensation. Within a few weeks, she earned $10,000, but her contract contained this important clause: The appearances would cease if the war resolution came before Congress, and Jeannette voted against it. For a time the condition remained satisfied, but the debate over the "war question" intensified and Congress faced pressure to act.

Jeannette Rankin, the suffragette and peace advocate, was not ready to have her deepest ideals tested so soon in her con-

*Congresswoman Rankin addressing the National American Woman Suffrage
Association, 1917. Jeannette Rankin was a major figure in the national
women's suffrage movement and led the final successful campaign in 1914 that
gave Montana women the right to vote.*

Courtesy of Montana Historical Society, Helena.

gressional career. In theory, Jeannette knew she opposed
American intervention in overseas conflicts; she believed force
should be used only when U.S. territory is threatened. But now
as an elected official, she had to reevaluate the question, figur-
ing in the swelling popular fervor for entry into the war.

Congress convened earlier than usual when President
Woodrow Wilson called an emergency session to begin April 2.
Early that morning, national suffrage groups sponsored a
breakfast in Jeannette's honor. Jeannette understood that the
expectations of these women rested on her success in Congress and was therefore especially aware of the responsibility
she had to make wise decisions and thoughtful statements.
This diverse gathering of feminists represented the polar ex-
tremes of the women's movement on the war issue. Pacifists
and interventionists alike vocalized their positions and each
faction clamored for her support and loyalty. She recognized
the inevitability of alienating some large section of the
women's rights community.

Along the way to the Capitol, Jeannette stopped at the national suffrage headquarters to deliver a brief speech. Then, in an open-air car, she joined a procession of suffragists, waving to cheering onlookers along the crowded streets. Once at her office building, she was surrounded by people extending good wishes, requesting autographs, and bestowing flowers.

At last the moment for her long-awaited appearance in Congress had arrived. Accompanied by her Montana colleague, John Evans, Jeannette entered the House chamber. Ellen Maury Slayden, wife of a Texas representative, recorded her impressions of the historical moment when Jeannette entered the floor of the United States House of Representatives:

> She wore a well made dark blue silk and chiffon suit, with open neck, and wide white crepe collar and cuffs; her skirt was a modest walking length, and she walked well and unself consciously. . . . She didn't look to right or left until she reached her seat, . . . but before she could sit down she was surrounded by men shaking hands with her. I rejoiced to see that she met each one with a . . . frank smile and shook hands cordially and unaffectedly. It would have been sickening if she smirked or giggled or been coquettish; worse still if she had been masculine and hale fellowish. She was just a sensible young woman going about her business. When her name was called the House cheered and rose, so that she had to rise and bow . . . which she did with entire self possession.[16]

After House business was concluded, members of the Senate joined the representatives in joint session to receive the president's war message. At 8:00 P.M., President Wilson entered the chamber and made his way to the rostrum. As he spoke, he condemned Germany's aggression in Europe and called upon the Congress to make the world "safe for democracy."

As soon as the president's speech concluded, Jeannette was approached by war lobbyists, including her brother, Wellington. She retreated to her office to contemplate the clash of her ideals against the reality of American involvement in a foreign war. She asked herself if America could wage war for peace, and for the next few days she struggled to find an answer.

Before the vote, Jeannette consulted with many different groups to help her clarify her own thinking and reach a satisfactory decision. The women's groups argued that Jeannette should keep a low profile on the war issue so as not to jeopardize her future congressional agenda, especially introduction and passage of the federal suffrage amendment. Even Wellington urged her to "vote a man's vote." All agreed that a "no" vote would destroy the credibility of women in public office before a real foothold had even been secured.

An uncomfortable mix of solemnity and urgency pervaded the House chamber during debate on the war resolution. Jeannette chose to wait in her office until the vote was near. Finally, she walked down the long halls and into the chamber. Once seated, she quietly concentrated on her personal convictions and campaign pledge to keep Montana's boys out of war. As the debate tapered, a silence fell over the members and they began to vote. Jeannette sat, waiting anxiously, but failed to answer on the first roll call. Her colleagues turned and stared, wondering if she was unfamiliar with House procedure.

Finally the second roll call came to "Rankin." The gallery was packed with reporters, pacifists, and war advocates. The legislators and onlookers waited for her vote. Jeannette stood, gathered her breath, and softly stated, "I want to stand by my country but I cannot vote for war. I vote no."[17] The short explanation violated a House rule against uttering more than the vote, but the concise rationale was perfect. Jeannette voted her conscience and was instantly, indelibly labeled a pacifist. Years later, Jeannette reflected on the importance of that moment:

> I knew it would be a popular war. I knew I would not be reelected. I had been told that a "no" vote might set back the cause of suffrage. But this was not a question of personalities or self interest in any narrow sense. One does not make a moral decision on the basis of expediency: you do what is right, not because of foreseeable consequences, but because it is right. I voted my conscience. And as I did so, I was conscious of my position: this was the first time in the history of civilization that a woman had been elected to a major legislative body in a free country—I was a symbol and a representative, not only of women in Montana or in the United States, but of women of all nations and ages."[18]

From this moment forward, Jeannette Rankin's identity was inextricably tied to her vote against war. She was now a peace-keeper to her supporters and a traitor to her detractors. It was a defining moment in her political career and she was keenly aware of her place in history.

The next several days were long and sad for the "Lady from Montana." She was subjected to inaccurate and highly critical newspaper accounts of her vote and there was much discussion of her emotional state when she cast her vote. News reporters, most of whom did not witness the moment firsthand, claimed she openly wept and therefore was clearly unfit for the rigors of such a high position. Critics charged that Jeannette's conduct confirmed the warnings of skeptics: A woman was not capable of making important decisions of national consequence. *The New York Times* opined that Jeannette's vote "was almost final proof of feminine incapacity for straight reasoning."[19]

Mail poured into the Rankin office for days following the vote. It was a mixed bag of support and criticism. At least Jeannette could take comfort in knowing that the American people were also divided on the war question. Back home, however, in her own district, Jeannette's opponents far outnumbered her fans. *The Missoulian*, her hometown newspaper, lampooned her in a political cartoon. Throughout the country, in fact, Jeannette was the subject of merciless cartoons, editorials, and commentary. It was not just her vote against entry into war; fifty-five other congressmen had joined her in dissent. Indeed the attention seemed to turn to the broader question of whether women were fit to govern in the public sphere at all.

During the remaining two years of her term, Jeannette never softened her position on war, and her resolve became legendary. On the floor of the House, in December 1917, she stood firm:

> I still believe war is a stupid, futile way of attempting to settle international difficulties . . . I believe war can be avoided and will be avoided when the people . . . have the controlling voice in their government.[20]

Jeannette also struggled to achieve national women's suffrage legislation and generally to fulfill her campaign pledge to improve conditions for women and children. Responding to suffrage opponents who maintained that women should stay in the home, Jeannette said:

> It is beautiful and right that a mother should nurse her child through typhoid fever, but it is also beautiful and right that she should have a voice in regulating the milk supply from which the typhoid resulted.[21]

On January 10, 1918, Jeannette addressed the House of Representatives on the joint resolution proposing an amendment to the Constitution of the United States extending the rights of suffrage to women. In the midst of World War I, Jeannette believed the enfranchisement of all American women was never more urgent. She told her colleagues that the nation was then mobilizing all its resources for the ideals of democracy but that something was lacking in this national effort:

> With all our abundance of coal, with our great stretches of idle, fertile land, babies are dying from cold and hunger; soldiers have died for lack of woolen shirt. Might it not be that the men who have spent their lives thinking in terms of commercial profit find it hard to adjust themselves to thinking in terms of human needs; might it not be that a great force that has always been thinking in terms of human needs, and that always will think in terms of human needs, has not been mobilized? Is it not possible that the women of the country have something of value to give to the nation at this time? . . .

> Today as never before the nation needs its women—needs the work of their hands and their hearts and their minds. Their energy must be utilized in the most effective service they can give. Are we now going to refuse these women the opportunity to serve in the face of their plea—in the face of the nation's great need? . . .

> How can people in other countries who are trying to grasp our plan of democracy avoid stumbling over our logic when we deny the first steps in democracy to our women? . . .

> Can we afford to allow these men and women to doubt for a single instant the sincerity of our protestations of

democracy? How shall we answer their challenge, gentlemen; how shall we explain to them the meaning of democracy if the same congress that voted for war to make the world safe for democracy refuses to give this small measure of democracy to the women of our country?[22]

Jeannette's early attempts to introduce other socially conscious legislation were largely thwarted by a war-obsessed Congress. One effort, the Rankin-Robertson bill, actively promoted women's health, proposing instruction on venereal disease and birth control. Although the bill had strong support among the public, it was defeated by an uninterested Congress.

Despite the indifference of her colleagues to progressive reform, Jeannette slowly regained popularity among Americans who appreciated her tireless efforts to fight the bureaucracy and to restore dignity to working men and women. Her liberal battles were waged on many fronts. After fighting for better working conditions for Butte miners and arguing for equality in government loans for farmers, she introduced a resolution advocating American recognition of the independence of Ireland. Such boldness earned her favor among her Irish-American constituents in Butte but further alienated her from the conservative vote.

With her political base eroded and no longer able to run in a state-wide election, since the legislature had split the congressman-at-large seat into western and eastern districts, Jeannette soberly evaluated her chances for reelection. The *Washington Star* described Jeannette's dilemma this way:

> The nation at large sat up and took considerable notice when from Missoula, Montana, came the news that a woman had been elected to the House, but all signs point to a finish fight, now that Miss Rankin has thrown the gauntlet into the ring and evidently intends to make a new political battle under entirely new conditions.

> When she ran for the present Congress she and three men [contended] for two places "at large." Representative Evans, Democrat, beat her, heading the list, and Miss Rankin came second. Therefore, she and her Democratic opponent received the two places.

Now the state legislature has divided the State of Montana into two congressional districts and if Miss Rankin wants to return she must receive the nomination at the primaries a year from September and must run against Representative Evans, who is accredited here with having the Democratic nomination in his vest pocket.

If she does not want to run for a seat in the House, she may try to wrest a senatorial toga from Senator Walsh. In fact, friends of Miss Rankin have already seen to it that Montana papers should carry dispatches from Washington intimating that Miss Rankin should run for the Senate. Her friends say that the same voters who placed her in the House from the state at large would vote for her in an attempt to make the Senate.[23]

Jeannette did indeed choose the Senate race, adopting a new approach, but one that she reconciled with her commitment to peace. She promised to vote for every war measure to encourage victory and hasten the end of the war.

Her opponent in the Republican primary was Oscar M. Lanstrum, publisher of the *Montana Record-Herald*. Despite negative reports in the Company press and her weak and unpopular congressional record, Jeannette ran well in the primary, but lost to Lanstrum by a margin less than 5 percent of the vote: 18,805 to 17,091.

After seeking advice from Wellington, Jeannette decided to run in the general election as a third-party candidate. Her Democratic opponent was Montana's senior senator, Thomas Walsh. Although Walsh considered himself "safe," Jeannette's alliance with the Nationalist Party worried him. This independent party was a loose coalition of Non-Partisan League farmers, pro-war Socialists, antiwar Progressives, Prohibitionists, and others dissatisfied with two-party politics. Walsh was depending on these liberal voting blocs to defeat Lanstrum and he was concerned that Jeannette could drain his support. He appealed to Wellington to persuade Jeannette to drop out of the race, but Wellington refused.

Jeannette's presence in the race was likely a significant factor in Walsh's reluctant and painful decision to call for the resignation of U.S. Attorney Burton K. Wheeler, a friend whose appointment Walsh had secured less than six years earlier. Wheeler was a vocal antagonist of the Anaconda Company. By ousting him, Walsh gained the support of the Company and strengthened his base. Meanwhile, Jeannette lost the backing of leading suffragist Carrie Chapman Catt, who was a strong advocate of American entry into WWI and disapproved of Jeannette's dovish approach to foreign policy.

Jeannette finished third in the general election, winning only 26,013 votes to Walsh's 46,160 and Lanstrum's 40,229. Thus ended the early political career of the nation's first congresswoman. Only two years earlier, she had entered the House of Representatives with high hopes of leading the fight to pass the federal suffrage amendment and instead found herself a part of an assembly preoccupied by a world war. In the process, her own agenda changed and she bravely commenced a lifelong commitment to world peace.

Although no longer able to effect change as a legislator Jeannette continued to work for the public good throughout the next twenty-four years. From 1918 through 1923 she remained in Washington and dedicated herself chiefly to the advancement of women's and children's rights. In 1924 she abandoned the capital altogether and moved to rural Georgia. During her congressional term she became acquainted with southern congressmen and developed a personal and political kinship with them. In the South she envisioned strengthening the peace movement because the southern congressmen and southern press had been vocally opposed to American involvement in a European war.

In Georgia, Jeannette sought a quiet, rustic surrounding where she could live independently, contemplating and developing her ideas. She settled in rural Bogart, partly because of its proximity to the University of Georgia at Athens. She purchased a sixty-four-acre farm and designed and built a house without electricity, running water, or a telephone. Jeannette supported herself with an allowance from her father's estate and help from her brother who by now was a prominent Montana attorney and large landowner.

For the next four years she lived and worked on her small farm, occasionally traveling to give speeches, to lobby and to serve a year as field secretary for the Women's International

League for Peace and Freedom. By 1928 she had forged many relationships and contacts with her Georgia neighbors, which eventually led to the establishment of the Georgia Peace Society, one of the first peace action groups in the country. The organization continued to serve as her base for pacifist operations from the late 1920s until it faltered due to lack of funds on the eve of World War II.

In late 1929, Jeannette began a turbulent collaboration with the National Council for the Prevention of War (NCPW). Throughout her tenure as a lobbyist, she was dissatisfied with her inadequate salary and frequent conflicts with the organization's national leaders over policy positions. Furthermore, she disliked being unable to work at her own intense pace and complained of the lack of commitment among her colleagues. Despite these difficulties and disagreements, she remained with the council for ten years, a relatively long affiliation for Jeannette.

The NCPW executive director, Frederick Libby, bolstered the group's image by promoting his connection with former congresswoman Rankin, though she was just one of eighteen field workers. Meanwhile Jeannette used her position as lobbyist to further her own peace agenda and thereby enjoyed some mutual benefit from the association. As an NCPW agent, Jeannette testified before congressional committees on disarmament, profiteering, and military appropriations. Her constant presence on Capitol Hill earned her the reputation of an elder stateswoman. At times, Jeannette seemingly took on the military-industrial complex single-handedly. She fought military buildup and argued that being prepared for war was equal to preparing to go to war. She unflinchingly advocated total disarmament and supported all amendments outlawing war.

Pacifists saw their greatest victory in the mid-1930s with the passage of arms-embargo legislation. Any measure that adversely impacted the munitions industry was regarded by Jeannette and her comrades as significant and supportive of the cause for peace.

In the late 1930s, Rankin set a frantic pace for antiwar activity. In 1937 she published a national magazine article reflecting on her vote against war and reasserting her pacifist philosophy. She wrote:

I knew that no war could ever "make the world safe for democracy," however lofty our ideals in the matter. I had been *thinking* peace and I knew war was a futile method of adjusting human relationships. . . .

Have the two decades that have gone by since that historic moment changed my mind? *They have not!* I still feel no good was accomplished by our participating in the war that could not have been accomplished by peaceful means.

A militant crusade against the whole war system, beginning here in America and taken up by the peace-loving nations, might easily spread in time to restrain the warlords from the mad acts they plan.

So long as we have the "war system," we'll have war. It is time to establish the fact that war has no place in modern life.[24]

Jeannette testified against further naval appropriations, against recision of the nondiscretionary portions of the neutrality legislation, against the occupation of Greenland and Iceland, against the fortification of Guam, against lend-lease, against the use of convoy patrols to protect lend-lease goods, against the Atlantic Charter, and finally against the extension of the draft. Exhausted and frustrated by defeats on many of these issues, Jeannette resigned from her position as lobbyist in 1939 and turned her attention back to Montana where the political landscape was in flux.

Finished with her lobbying responsibilities, Rankin embarked on a new but familiar challenge. On June 5, 1940, she launched her campaign for the congressional seat in the western Montana district. Throughout her absence from her home state, she had maintained her residency and voter and car registrations in Montana. For the first time since 1916, the moment seemed right for a woman like Jeannette to run for Congress. But the reasons were different this time. She decided to throw her hat in the ring because of a strong peace sentiment in Montana that could propel her back into the national forum with a mandate for her pacifist ideals.

She ran on the slogan "Prepare to the Limit for Defense, Keep Our Men Out of Europe." Her influential and wealthy family connections and endorsements from prominent liberal political leaders, such as New York mayor Fiorella La Guardia and Frances Perkins, gave her a secure base from which to launch her campaign. La Guardia had said of Jeannette: "This woman has more courage and packs a harder punch than a regiment of regular-line politicians."[25]

Repeating the successful tactics she developed twenty-four years earlier, Jeannette took her arguments directly to the voters, applying her winning grassroots campaign style. She talked to schoolchildren, who went home to their parents and told stories about Jeannette Rankin in their classrooms. She preached the power of the vote and encouraged women to use it to prevent war. She won a close primary over Republican incumbent Jacob Thorkelson and defeated Democrat Jerry O'Connell by a vote of 56,616 to 47,352 in the general election. The woman who was practically run out of Washington, D.C., in 1918 was returned to Congress by a new generation of voters eager to prevent U.S. involvement in another world war.

Congress had changed since 1920. First, Jeannette was no longer the only congresswoman and therefore was not so distracted by media attention or the burdens of representing a gender. She could concentrate on her objectives for antiwar legislation. Second, perceptions also were altered. Now, the peace movement was considered the bastion of reactionary, isolationist Republicans instead of a plank in the Progressive platform.

Jeannette wasted little time. Her first crusade was against the pending Lend-Lease Bill, which authorized armaments to be sent to our allies in Europe. She introduced her own legislation that authorized unlimited expenditures for a national defense perimeter. It was defeated. She then attached an amendment to the Lend-Lease Bill prohibiting the president from sending any soldiers overseas without congressional authorization. Finally, she proposed legislation against mandatory conscription.

In the months preceding the bombing of Pearl Harbor, Jeannette remained optimistic about preventing U.S. entry into the European war. Even after the Japanese bombed U.S. ships, Jeannette thought there would be a lengthy debate to consider U.S. options. But Congress could see no options; there was but one choice. Jeannette underestimated the national outrage at the attack on U.S. soil and left town to deliver a speech in Detroit. En route she heard Roosevelt call for a joint session of Congress and turned back to D.C. Gripped by the urgency of this national moment and torn between her patriotism and pacifist ideals, Jeannette pondered her course of action as the train chugged eastward through the rolling countryside.

Back in Washington, she remained undecided. She searched for quiet and solitude by driving around town considering her fate and the fate of her causes if she voted against a U.S. declaration of war. In later years, Jeannette would describe the hours before the vote as some of the most agonizing in her life. She avoided the crowds and did not seek advice as she had done in 1917. Wellington, nevertheless, volunteered his opinion. He strongly recommended that Jeannette vote for the war resolution. He knew her position but tried to reassure her she could justify a "yes" vote on the grounds of national self-defense. As she had done in 1917 she waited in her office, away from the mounting frenzy, until the session bell rang. Roosevelt's speech was short and pointed: the United States should declare a state of war with Japan.

Debate on the war resolution was limited to wild calls for an aggressive assault on the Japanese—nothing short of the destruction of her war machine was satisfactory. Sentiment in the Congress was seemingly unanimous, and an immediate vote was called for. Within this atmosphere Jeannette attempted to get the floor to present her own opposition argument for peace. She was ignored by Speaker Sam Rayburn. As she tried again for recognition, she was told a roll-call vote could not be interrupted. And with that rejection, the roll call proceeded. Quickly the names were called and a steady sequence of yeas were recorded. When the clerk read "Rankin," the pattern was interrupted. The eyes of Congress, and perhaps figuratively the eyes of the world, turned to the lady from Montana in that instant, and she resolutely declared her position: "As a woman, I can't go to war and I refuse to send anyone else."[26] For the second time Jeannette bolted convention and voted her conscience. This time, however, she was the *only* member of Congress to vote against the war resolution. Others abstained from a vote but no one else stood up and risked his or her future career for the cause of peace.

She was alone in her opposition. The backlash was furious.

After the vote Jeannette took refuge in a phone booth and dialed the Capitol switchboard for an escort back to her office. Once safely there she collected her thoughts for a letter to her constituents explaining her vote: "While I believed the stories were probably true," she wrote, "still I believed that such a momentous vote, on which could mean peace or war for our country, should be based on more authentic evidence. . . ."[27]

Jeannette also reminded western Montanans of her campaign pledge to make every effort to keep the United States out of war. She later called Wellington, who sternly rebuffed her and reported that "Montana is 110% against you."[28] Most likely aware that she had sacrificed any chance for reelection Jeannette stated, "I have nothing left but my integrity."[29]

Letters poured into her office, most of them condemning her position. She was accused of treason and called a "traitor nazi." The letters were searing in their disapproval. For example, one antagonist wrote: "I sincerely hope that your failure to stand by the people of Montana, and the U.S., will cause you to send in your resignation immediately and drop out of public life, where it is apparent that you never belonged."[30] The anti-Rankin sentiment was both vicious and widespread. In her public release, Jeannette explained:

> When I cast the only vote against war, I remembered the promises I had made during my campaign for election to do everything possible to keep this country out of war. I was thinking of the pledges that I had made to the mothers and fathers of Montana that I would do all in my power to prevent their sons from being slaughtered on foreign battle fields.
>
> . . . But now we are sending American men and boys into a war to "protect" the United States, and doing it based only on a few brief, incomplete radio reports, which do not pretend to give the entire story.
>
> It may be that it is right for us to enter the conflict with Japan. If so, it is my belief that all the facts surrounding the present situation should be brought into the open and given to the Congress and the American people.

> So in casting my vote today, I voted my convictions and redeemed my campaign pledges. I feel I voted as the mothers would have had me vote.[31]

The explanation did little to assuage the hometown press. The *Harlowton Times* said Rankin's vote was "in accord with the views of Hitler, Bonito, Hirohito and Company. We trust she will call on these gentlemen for her December check and further wages . . . we think Western Montana should recall Miss Rankin from Washington."[32]

The editor of the *Cambridge Hot Springs Exchange* suggested that Jeannette resign and donate her 1942 salary of $10,000 to the War Department, "as a down payment on a new bomber."[33]

Tendering perhaps the most shamelessly chauvinistic criticism, the editor of the *Choteau Acantha* wrote:

> For Jeannette Rankin—an order that she be publicly spanked on the floor of the House. That an old fashioned hairbrush be used as per the good old days, and be it specifically stipulated that there be no silk, rayon, or any other fabric between the backside of the hairbrush and the point of contact with Jeannette's anatomy.[34]

She was called "pig-Rankin," and told to pack her bags and go to Japan. She was accused of ignoring the murder of her own people. She prepared more than 3,000 form letters to reply to everyone who wrote.

Still, not everyone was against her. A substantial number of sympathetic Montanans conveyed their support for her courage if not her vote, while letters from other states, Canada, and South America were ten to one in favor of her stand against the war. A few newspapers extolled Jeannette's courage. The reliably liberal *People's Voice* of Helena said:

> Republican Rep. Jeannette Rankin of Montana was booed in the House of Representatives Monday; Americans should instead thank God that they have before them her splendid example of courage and conviction.

> Had the vote been 389 to 0, we should have had no prominent reminder, no simple expression of the values for which we fight. Miss Rankin, in doing her duty to her country as she saw fit, has truly made a great contribution to America and the cause upon which we embark.[35]

The *Emporia* (Kansas) *Gazette* mused:

> Probably a hundred men in Congress would have liked to
> do what she did. Not one of them had the courage to do it.
> The *Gazette* entirely disagrees with the wisdom of her po-
> sition, but, Lord, it was a brave thing.[36]

A Missoula County High School student wrote this letter to
the editor of the *Daily Missoulian* on December 17, 1941:

> ... Whether we agree with that woman or not, she had
> the given right to stand up and claim her right of free
> speech, without a mob of panic-stricken people forgetting
> what democracy means, and demanding her job.

> The people must agree that, when this woman was
> elected, everyone knew her platform. Hats off to this
> woman who has the strength of her convictions.[37]

Secure in those personal convictions, Jeannette managed to
endure the pain and condemnation. But she was resentful that
the cause she had dedicated herself to for the past twenty-five
years was so resoundingly rejected by the majority of the
American people. She pinned her last hopes on the women of
America, encouraging them to use their voting power to deny
Roosevelt a fourth term, hoping that another president might
bring a faster end to the conflict.

After the fateful vote of December 8, 1941, Jeannette faced
a full year remaining in her congressional term. Several days
after the war resolution vote, another resolution declaring war
on Germany and Italy breezed through the Congress. During
the roll call Jeannette simply said "present" and made no effort to speak. For the next several months, the stubborn
woman from Montana was ostracized and viewed as an eccen-
tric, out of step with the national conscience.

Jeannette spent much of 1942 researching and building a
case against what she saw as the Roosevelt administration's
back-door approach to war. A year to the day after her unpopular antiwar vote, she inserted into the *Congressional Record* a
detailed defense of her stand, titled "Some Questions about
Pearl Harbor." She accused British imperialists of conspiring to
bring the United States into the war by convincing Roosevelt to
impose economic sanctions of ever-increasing severity upon
Japan. At the Atlantic Conference, Churchill persuaded Roo-

sevelt to enforce embargo provisions against Japan to impede their military aggression in Asia. Britain felt challenged by the Japanese. The severe restriction angered Japan. It retaliated by bombing Pearl Harbor.

Jeannette theorized that Roosevelt suspected an attack by the Japanese but had no definitive knowledge of it. "Astounding as the Pearl Harbor attack was to the American public as a whole," Rankin said, "if it was anticipated by the administration why did the President permit our forces at Pearl Harbor to be taken by surprise?"[38] Others agreed with her investigation and resulting findings but were reluctant to reveal what might be considered treasonous. Jeannette ignored such warnings, but won little public attention as the nation focused on war.

Three weeks later Jeannette Rankin was again a former congresswoman. It was 1943 and the grand dame of the struggling American peace movement was sixty-two years old. Beaten and discouraged, she languidly returned to Georgia to rebuild her house, which had burned in a fire, and to ruminate about her future.

During the election of 1944, Jeannette stepped up her appeal to women voters to reject Franklin Roosevelt for a fourth term, with the hope of sending a strong antiwar message. But American women did not mobilize and unite to protest the war; nor did they turn out to defeat Roosevelt. The president's reelection made Jeannette even more pessimistic. She wrote on November 30, 1944: "A little longer to wait for a saner attitude of the people. The 'little longer' may be 'too long' for me."[39]

As she became increasingly disillusioned with wartime politics and the American/European style of conflict resolution, Jeannette turned to the Far East for a role model. In particular she was captivated by India and Mohandas Gandhi's passive resistance tactics. In 1946 she embarked on a world tour that included the first of seven visits to India. She returned in 1949, 1951, 1956, 1959–60, 1962, and for a last time in 1970–71. On her first trip she planned to meet and learn from Gandhi but he was a thousand miles north of Delhi trying to calm a riot. She decided to wait, but before she could meet him, Gandhi was assassinated. Nevertheless, Jeannette concluded that India, with its stable democracy and desire for independence could become a model for world peace.

During her first visit to India, Jeannette witnessed the essence of Gandhi's theories at a school for self-sufficiency. Gandhi emphasized the idea that self-knowledge and proficiency at a productive skill led to control of one's destiny and thwarted authoritarianism. Jeannette found this notion compelling and uplifting. It supported her belief that if society controlled its future it could prepare for peace and avoid war.

Jeannette was inspired enough that she considered writing a book about Gandhi. She drafted an outline of chapters in which she planned to discuss the reasons and causes of war, the importance of public opinion in creating a state of neutrality, and a lesson on how to organize a peace plan, using Gandhi's protest tactics. Unfortunately, the project never reached fruition.

During her years of world travel and reclusive lifestyle in rural Georgia, Jeannette faded from the public eye. But another war, with growing discontentment and antiwar demonstrations, returned her to the forefront of the ever-evolving American peace movement. In 1967 the idea of a peace march in her name was proposed. She was captivated by the thought of thousands of women, representing the national desire for an end to the Vietnam War, marching for peace. A Washington peace march would be more than a protest of war to Jeannette; the marchers embodied the very spirit of the peace movement for they represented her hope that American women in nonviolent demonstration could end war forever.

Jeannette's ideas, spawned by the writings of Benjamin Kidd, were now being embraced by a new generation of social activists. She continued to believe that women had the power to save the world because women were more attached to and concerned about the well-being of the social and political environment. After a half century of advocating peace, Jeannette witnessed a groundswell of support for her beliefs. At last the nation was catching up with Jeannette Rankin. By October 1967 women from across the country were gathering around the banner of the Jeannette Rankin Peace Brigade.

On January 15, 1968, 5,000 women convened in Washington, D.C., to protest what they saw as the disgraceful human and capital waste of the Vietnam War. The throng marched through the capital, raising a national call to end the conflict. At the front of the brigade, banner in hand, was Jeannette

Rankin of Montana. At age eighty-eight, she marched with women who were not yet born when she cast her last congressional vote against war. With years of disappointments and rejection behind her, Jeannette was finally at the forefront of a revitalized peace movement.

Demonstrations on the Capitol grounds then were still prohibited by an 1882 law. Jeannette later explained her fear that any militant actions might lead to violence, but she had publicly announced an invitation to her sisters: "They told us we couldn't demonstrate on the Capitol grounds, but I am going to the Capitol and I expect many women—all dressed in black— to go with me."[40]

When the army of determined women reached the grounds, Jeannette and sixteen others climbed the Capitol steps to present a petition to House Speaker John McCormack. The petition demanded, among other things, that Congress end the Vietnam War and immediately withdraw American troops. Jeannette later met with Montana senator Mike Mansfield, telling him "we must bring the boys home from Vietnam."[41] Mansfield agreed.

The peace brigade was Jeannette Rankin's final public crusade. In the waning years of her life, though, she remained a sage in the timeless debate over war and peace. In 1969 she told a reporter for the *San Francisco Examiner*, "War is nonsense. Bring the boys back forthwith. Surrender is a military idea. When you're doing something wrong, you stop." Her bold style raised Jeannette to the status of an icon among members of the antiwar counterculture.

As the 1970s began, Jeannette was ninety years old, but not finished yet. She spread her message of peace and equality through national television talk-show appearances and meetings with women's political caucuses throughout the country. She impressed upon women their special responsibility to end war and particularly to bring about the end of the war in Vietnam. "We raise the sons and have them shot. But women don't work hard enough, don't think hard enough, so we are still lacking. . . ."[42]

In 1972, ninety-two-year-old Jeannette Rankin addressed the Constitutional Convention of Montana on her philosophy of "people power." The same year, *Life* magazine wrote that Jeannette's "political experience and phenomenal energy are helping to make her one of the most popular—and surprising—figureheads of the women's movement." The National Organization of Women called her "the world's outstanding living feminist" and chose Jeannette as the inaugural member of the Susan B. Anthony Hall of Fame.

On May 18, 1973, Jeannette Rankin died in her sleep at her apartment in Carmel, California. Twelve years later, her statue was selected to be one of the two Montana figures enshrined in the United States Capitol. At the dedication ceremony, Congresswoman Claudine Schneider of Rhode Island called Jeannette "one of the greatest women this country has ever known . . . a woman of strong conviction and strong words. Articulate, witty and quick on her feet," said Congresswoman Schneider, "she was never afraid to speak her mind." Historian Joan Hoff Wilson called Jeannette a "gallant warrior for peace" and noted that she was the first woman ever elected to a legislative body in a Western democracy.

"You don't do the right thing because of the consequences," Jeannette Rankin once said. "If you are wise, you do it regardless of the consequences." By this creed Jeannette Rankin lived and labored, shaping the ideas and pricking the conscience of her country for six decades. For Congresswoman Rankin, the devotion to principle was everything. Courage was her signature, and that is why Jeannette Rankin will never be forgotten.

Suggested Readings on Jeannette Rankin

The most thorough biography of Jeannette Rankin is *Flight of the Dove: The Story of Jeannette Rankin,* by Kevin S. Giles (Beaverton, Oregon, 1980). Giles covers Jeannette's entire life and career. Although the book includes no footnotes, it appends a useful, comprehensive bibliography. Much of the background information about Jeannette in this chapter is taken from Giles. Other books about Jeannette Rankin are Hannah Josephson, *Jeannette Rankin: First Lady in Congress* (Indianapolis/New York, 1974) and Mary Barmeyer O'Brien, *Jeannette Rankin: Bright Star in the Big Sky* (Helena, 1995). O'Brien's book is an especially good treatment of the subject for young adult readers. Jeannette's Montana suffrage activity and elections to Congress are covered by M. P. Malone, R. B. Roeder, and W. L. Lang, *Montana: A History of Two Centuries* (Seattle/London, 1991).

Among the many articles about Jeannette, Joan Hoff Wilson's articles from *Montana: The Magazine of Western History* stand out as thoughtfully analytical and well documented. See "Peace Is a Woman's Job, Jeannette Rankin and American Foreign Policy" (Winter and Spring 1980). The Montana Historical Society's Jeannette Rankin vertical files include copies of a broad selection of articles discussing Jeannette's life, her anti-war votes, her early suffrage work, and her commitment to world peace. The vertical files also contain extensive newspaper clippings, which are useful as primary-source material. Specific election results can be found in Ellis Waldron and Paul B. Wilson, *Atlas of Montana Elections* (Missoula, 1978). A useful compendium of testimonials regarding the life of Jeannette Rankin is contained in a work produced to honor the unveiling of her statue in the Capitol on May 1, 1985; *Statue of Jeannette Rankin, 1880–1973, Presented in the Rotunda, U.S. Capitol* (Washington, D.C., 1987).

Burton K. Wheeler,
Montana's Yankee Maverick

Create now a political court to echo the ideas of the Executive and you have created a weapon, . . . which in the hands of another president could well be the instrument of destruction.

A rugged Butte man stood at the mouth of an Anaconda mining shaft distributing the *Daily Worker*. It was the summer of 1937 and Senator "B.K." Wheeler had just handed Franklin Roosevelt the only real defeat of his fourteen-year presidency, blocking a bill designed to pack the Supreme Court with FDR supporters. "I passed out Wheeler's campaign brochures in 1934," the paper man told a national reporter, "but I'd roast in hell before I'd do it again!" A mud-spattered miner, toting his lunch pail and waiting for a streetcar outside the M&M Cigar Store, registered the same complaint. "No, by gosh, I wouldn't vote for Wheeler for dog catcher. He's sold out Labor and gone over to the A.C.M. I'm through with him for good, and I've voted for him every time."[1]

As the workers spoke, a conservative newspaper editor sat behind his desk and praised Wheeler as a "truly big and great-souled statesman." Asked whether he would vote for Wheeler next time around, the editor replied, "Nope. He's too darn radical."[2]

Such was the paradox and dilemma of Burton K. Wheeler. During more than thirty-five years of public life in Montana, he thrived in the clamor of politics. Years after leaving the United States Senate, Wheeler began his autobiography with

Opposite: *Senator Wheeler, 1924. Progressive candidate for vice president. Senator Wheeler ran on the Progressive Party ticket with Wisconsin senator Robert LaFollette. He had recently led an investigation that uncovered graft in the Harding justice department. The Progressive campaign championed the interests of workers and farmers while decrying the exploits of "profiteers."*

Courtesy of Montana Historical Society, Helena.

these words: "Controversy has sparked my public life from start to finish. My opponents have ranged from the giant Anaconda Mining Company to the leaders of both my own Democratic Party and the Republican Party. The names I've been called run the gamut from Communist to Fascist and include a great many other derogatory terms besides. I've been accused of almost everything but timidity."[3]

Indeed, although Wheeler spent an unprecedented four terms as Montana's U.S. senator, he picked up enemies at every turn in his career. Wheeler's professional life knew little tranquillity, but he would not have had it be otherwise. For him, the alternative to conflict was the swelling of concentrated power—the kind of power that could crush the democratic government of the people—and for Wheeler, that was reason enough to fight.

Burton K. Wheeler was born February 27, 1882, at Hudson, Massachusetts, reportedly the product of 300-year-old American stock. He was the youngest of ten children. Wheeler's father, Asa, was a cobbler by trade and a Quaker by faith. From him Burt acquired an abhorrence of war, a tolerance for those with whom he disagreed, and a familiarity with progressive ideas. Burt's mother, Mary Elizabeth Wheeler, was "an aggressive, ambitious, disciplined woman, fiercely loyal to the strict moral standards of her 19th-Century Methodist faith. . . . "[4]

From the beginning, Mary urged Burt to study law and become the first member of his family to enter that profession. Burt respected his mother and sought to fulfill that dream, but his early academic career was less than auspicious. While he performed quite well in certain classes, Wheeler was a troublemaker in high school. "The trouble with you, Wheeler," the principal scolded, "is that you have no respect for your superiors." Later in life, Wheeler acknowledged that charge to be true "to the extent that I have always pointedly avoided kowtowing to people of wealth, social position, or power."[5]

During Wheeler's high school years, his mother died and Burt suffered a devastating emotional blow. He gave up on certain classes required for the regular high school diploma and received it only by promising the principal that he would go on to study law.

After high school, Wheeler began to commute to Boston to

earn money toward his legal education. Over the next couple years he bargained his way from job to job as a stenographer, raising his salary from $6 a week to $13 a week. In 1902 Wheeler demanded his employer raise his wage to $18 a week. The employer refused. Making good on his ultimatum, Wheeler left the firm and headed west for the University of Michigan Law School.

Wheeler got his first taste of politics during his three years at Ann Arbor. He was nominated during his second year for class president and ran against the candidate sponsored by the fraternity houses. Because he had worked for the law school dean during his first two years, he was labeled the "dean's candidate," but managed to overcome that stigma to defeat his opponent by a narrow margin. The race taught Burt some early lessons about the importance of hard work and organization, but represented only a minor distraction for him. Wheeler later wrote, "What I was interested in was the study of law. What excited me most was the verbal cut and thrust in the arena of the courtroom."[6]

The summer before his third year in law school, Wheeler peddled books door to door in the countryside around Ann Arbor. At one house, the door was opened by a young woman named Lulu White, who would become Wheeler's wife. Although he never sold a book to the family, Wheeler talked his way into the White home for lunch and courted Lulu throughout the summer of 1904.

Near the end of Wheeler's law school years, the dean of the school of law suggested that Wheeler go east to New York in search of money and opportunity. Wheeler was determined instead to go west. Wheeler kissed Lulu good-bye on the banks of the Mississippi and traveled toward Eureka, California, where an elderly lawyer was selling his practice. Wheeler got as far as San Francisco and realized that Eureka could only be accessed by boat, which made it a little more isolated than even this adventurous new lawyer had in mind. The great western job hunt took Wheeler to Los Angeles, Portland, Tucson; the cluster of southwest Colorado towns known as Telluride, Montrose, and Ouray as well as Pueblo and Denver; Salt Lake City and Ogden, Utah; and Pocatello, Idaho. In Telluride, Wheeler stopped for a couple of months to work as a stenographer, financing further job-hunt travels.

Finally, on a bitterly cold Sunday morning in October 1905, twenty-three-year-old Burton Wheeler stepped off a Northern Pacific passenger car in Butte, Montana. He made his way to a boardinghouse where he conducted his own survey of the mining city's practicing lawyers. In the coming days, Wheeler strolled around the town displaying his Michigan law degree and offering his services. The search revealed a single opportunity that would yield a modest $50 a month.

Discouraged, Wheeler decide to press on to Spokane, Washington. While waiting at the depot for his late-arriving train, Wheeler was approached by two friendly men who claimed that they, too, were waiting for the train out. Wheeler did not drink, but he agreed to wait in the saloon with his two newfound friends, where he met another friendly fellow who kindly offered to engage him in a card game. Wheeler thought a game of "auction pitch" for "a penny a point" would be nice, but the gentleman shook his hand and smiled, "No, let's play poker." By the end of the first hand, Wheeler had lost the $65 he had in his pocket and the remainder of his personal fortune, a $150 bank balance in Montrose, Colorado. Suddenly, the $50 a month offer with Attorney John Sheldon looked attractive. Wheeler returned to Sheldon and accepted the job, securing for himself a tiny foothold on "the richest hill on earth."

In 1906, Butte, Montana, was one of the great mining towns on the planet. A quarter of a century earlier, Marcus Daly and cohorts had sunk a shaft to one hundred feet and turned a young silver camp into a booming city of copper. The city of 45,000 boasted the "longest bar in the world" (long as a city block and manned by fifteen bartenders) and a red-light district with more than 700 girls for hire from all over the world. Trestles, tracks, transmission lines, and other monuments of industrial activity crisscrossed the city as smelters belched fire and arsenic-laden smoke into the sky.

Wheeler quickly adjusted to his new home, leaving Sheldon after a few months and setting up office with a fellow alumnus of the University of Michigan Law School. That arrangement became unsatisfactory as well, however, and Wheeler began practicing alone in a "suite," which also contained the cot on which he slept.

Debt collections and criminal defense appointments composed Wheeler's first case inventory, but soon he was representing Butte's working people in personal injury cases. In his second year of solo practice, Wheeler had saved enough money to make a down payment on a $4,000 four-room house, and his situation was sufficiently stable that he could invite Lulu to their new home.

Wheeler spent the next few years handling a variety of cases, taking every opportunity to appear in the courtroom. Despite his desire to focus on his law practice, Wheeler was unable to avoid the swirling political activity in Butte. He assisted the Democratic Party "boss" in his ward in 1908 and became a delegate to the Silver Bow County Democratic Convention. There, Wheeler was asked to join the ticket of Democratic candidates for the state legislature but declined after receiving advice that the delegation was owned and controlled by the Company. In 1910 Wheeler received the invitation again and accepted, convinced that no one could force him to abandon the dictates of his conscience.

In 1910 Wheeler was assigned to campaign with John K. O'Rourke, Butte's colorful sheriff who was standing for reelection. According to Wheeler, "The prescription for a successful campaign was simplicity itself: you planted a foot on the bar rail and bought 'drinks for the house' in every saloon and casino in Silver Bow County and as often as possible." O'Rourke was said to spend as much as $100 nightly in the saloons, which was a small investment considering that, according to Wheeler, "the job of Sheriff in wide-open Silver Bow County was reputed to be worth $40,000 to $60,000 a year on the side."[7]

In contrast to his campaign partner, Wheeler suffered from chronic Quaker tightfistedness and spent as little in the saloons as possible. Nevertheless, he was elected easily in the heavily Democratic district.

Wheeler had no sooner set foot in the legislature of 1911 than Company confederates began to turn the screws on him. The legislature's most significant task was to fill the United States Senate seat, which had been occupied by conservative Republican stalwart Thomas Carter. The Democrats held a solid majority in the legislature and were confident of their ability to fill the position with one of their own, but the party split between Company loyalists, who supported Great Falls banker W. G. Conrad, and the progressive Democrats, who leaned toward Helena's eminent trial lawyer Thomas J. Walsh.

The entire Silver Bow delegation was expected by the omnipotent Company to fall quietly in line behind Conrad and defeat Walsh, who posed a threat to Company domination. The Silver Bow delegation complied, with few exceptions. One exception was twenty-eight-year-old Burt Wheeler, who broke from the ranks and made his stand for Walsh.

Balloting for the Senate dragged on throughout the session with Democrats split between Walsh and Conrad, Carter holding the Republican minority, and no candidate able to collect a majority. Company strongmen began to threaten Wheeler, but the young man stood firm. He later reported that he was repeatedly offered bribes as high as $9,000 but rejected the grafters' overtures.

Wheeler spoke fervently in Walsh's favor and became recognized as the leader of the Walsh forces. Eventually it became obvious that Walsh could not garner the majority necessary for election, and the Democrats settled on Judge Henry Myers of Hamilton as a compromise candidate. Wheeler's activity gained the attention of both the Company and Walsh. The Amalgamated saw a potential troublemaker and Walsh found a loyal ally.

Wheeler's strong stand for Walsh was not his only distinguishing act in the legislative session of 1911. Wheeler was the primary sponsor and proponent of a bill drafted by the American Federation of Labor to reform the personal injury tort laws. The Wheeler bill abolished the "fellow servant" doctrine, which prevented injured employees from recovering compensation when their injuries were caused by a fellow employee, and it replaced contributory negligence with "comparative negligence," so that recovery could be reduced in proportion to the injured employee's own negligence, but not barred altogether.

Members of the judiciary committee, pressured by Company forces, tagged the measure "altogether too radical and sweeping," and reported out a diluted measure that applied only to the most hazardous jobs. Neither version attracted a majority in the Senate, however, and the matter was tabled to be taken up in a more enlightened era.

Wheeler also voted for the constitutional amendment to enfranchise women. He was perplexed by the alliance between labor leaders and the Company, but was "pleasantly surprised" by his fellow lawyers. "Although lawyers are probably more criticized than any other class of men," Wheeler wrote, "it was a group of young lawyers in the Montana Legislature who courageously fought for liberal legislation, for Walsh's election, and against corporate control." He chided the "Company stooges" in the body, who he said wore "the copper collar," but he took neither battles nor fractional alliances personally. He later explained, "I never carried the bitterness around in my soul because I knew it would not hurt the other fellow, only me."[8]

When Wheeler returned to Butte, word had spread of his stand against the Company. At Butte's city Democratic convention, Wheeler sought the party's nomination for mayor. He enjoyed some support, but former sheriff John Quinn was chosen instead. The final victor in the race was the Socialist candidate, Lewis T. Duncan. Quinn complained that Duncan bought more votes than he got at the polls. Duncan took office in friendly company, as the Socialists elected every candidate for city office and five of nine candidates for alderman.

To the public, young Wheeler was a standard bearer who dared to confront the Company, and the image brought Wheeler a steady flow of personal injury business. In one such case he assisted Thomas Walsh, and Walsh suggested that Wheeler run for state attorney general in 1912. Although only thirty years old, Wheeler agreed and allowed his name to be presented to the Democratic convention for nomination. Wheeler was nominated by Walsh's Helena law partner, Col. C. B. Nolan, but was narrowly defeated by the county attorney from Boulder, Dan Kelly. Kelly won in November, later resigning to become a legal counsel for the Company.

Thomas Walsh had his own place on the general election ballot under new rules that allowed the electorate to "provide advice" on the selection of the United States senator. Walsh overwhelmingly defeated incumbent senator Joe Dixon, who busied himself outside the state by managing the Bull Moose presidential campaign of Teddy Roosevelt. The margin of Walsh's victory before the populace was so substantial that the legislature convening in January had no real political alternative but to confirm the election of Walsh, which they did by acclamation.

. . .

Burton K. Wheeler, circa 1915. The nation's youngest U.S. attorney, Wheeler defied war hysteria, refusing to cooperate in the persecution of German-Americans.

Courtesy of Montana Historical Society, Helena.

When Thomas Walsh went to Washington, he did not forget the courageous young legislator from Butte. Among Walsh's first acts of patronage after Woodrow Wilson moved into the White House was the selection of Wheeler as United States attorney for the district of Montana. Wheeler accepted the appointment and at age thirty-one became the youngest federal district attorney in the country.

Wheeler determined at the outset to present all criminal cases to the grand jury himself and to personally try or participate in the trial of all cases handled by his office. He was paid only $4,000 per year, but was allowed to maintain a private practice, which frequently kept him in his office until late in the night.

During the first five years of his term as district attorney, Wheeler was preoccupied with cases involving counterfeiting, white slavery, postal violations, land fraud cases, and charges involving the sale of liquor to Indians. His approach to the office was distinctive. For example, the commissioner of Indian Affairs for the United States at that time was a fervent

Prohibitionist who directed Indian agents to send part-Indians who appeared to be non-Indian into saloons, where they would "sting" the saloon keepers who were prohibited from selling alcohol to Indians. At one time all of Helena's saloon keepers were under indictment. Wheeler traveled the state, advising tavern owners of the undercover operation and refused to seek further indictments for conduct elicited by the practice.

Wheeler was less generous to Ben Phillips, a prominent Montana Republican charged with land fraud. Phillips had engaged people to move onto public land and claim homestead rights, whereupon he would purchase the land from the settlers. In this manner, Phillips put together an enormous spread of land in eastern Montana. Ultimately, Phillips County, much of which he owned, was named after him. Wheeler achieved a conviction in the case, though the fine imposed by the court was nominal.

Wheeler's most controversial prosecution was aimed at the Northwestern Trustee Company organized ostensibly to build houses and apartment buildings throughout Montana and lend money to farmers. The company sold stock saying the proceeds would go into the company's treasury; a substantial portion of the revenue, however, was used for promotional expenses. Prosecution of the case put Wheeler's political future in jeopardy, as numerous prominent Democratic politicians were charged with or accused of using the mails to defraud. Democratic governor Sam Stewart was pictured on a company brochure as a leading stockholder, although he had never actually purchased any of the company's stock. The case ended in the conviction of two of the ringleaders.

Typically, a district attorney's time is divided between prosecuting criminal cases and defending the United States in civil cases. Occasionally, but rarely, the D.A. may bring a civil action on behalf of the United States. Wheeler brought such a civil action when he sued the Great Northern Railway for damage caused by forest fires in the Flathead and Lewis and Clark National Forests. Wheeler prevailed, and recovered $50,000 in compensation for damage to the national forests.

Wheeler's service as district attorney coincided with mounting tension between labor and Company forces in Butte. On Miner's Union Day in June 1914, the radical wing of the Butte

Miner's Union (BMU) boycotted the annual union parade and then attacked it, beating up labor leaders and ransacking the union hall. The rebels were joined by Wobblies, activists from the Industrial Workers of the World (IWW).

A week or so later, when BMU regulars held a meeting at what was left of the union hall, shooting broke out and two men were killed. Before the night was through, the hall was completely destroyed by an explosion of planted dynamite. Governor Stewart declared martial law and mobilized the national guard to quell the growing anarchy. By September the Anaconda Company announced that it would no longer recognize either union, and an open shop policy went into effect, robbing the union of the power it drew from exclusive representation of all miners. The developments only aggravated tensions between union members and the Company.

Labor and management problems mounted in Butte, and in 1917, when the United States intervened in the Great War, anti-German and anti-Socialist sentiment added to the situation's volatility. Fire in Butte's Spectator Mine that year killed 164 men. Superpatriots blamed German spies; unionists demanded safer working conditions. The possibility of crushing radical unionists by charging sedition was not lost on the Company. It organized over 200 detectives into goon squads to spy on union activities.

Wheeler later wrote that "the most bizarre element of the war hysteria was the spy fever, which made many people completely lose their sense of justice. All labor leaders, miners, and contented farmers were regarded by these superpatriots as pacifists—and ipso facto agents of the Kaiser." Reports of the German Air Force operating out of the Bitterroot Valley spread. Hundreds of cases were brought before Wheeler, inspired by "old grudges, malicious gossip, barroom conversations, etc."[9]

In July 1917, as the flames of war hysteria engulfed the Mining City and the entire state of Montana, IWW agitator Frank Little stepped into the spotlight. Little told a rally in Butte that American soldiers mobilized to work in mines in Colorado were nothing more than "uniformed scabs." He attacked Wilson as being antilabor and proclaimed that if the Germans did not get the "capitalists," the IWW would. Montana patriots were infuriated and less than two weeks later, a team of vigilantes kidnapped Little from his boardinghouse, stripped him to his underwear, and hanged him by the neck from a railroad trestle at the edge of town. Following a pattern established by vigilantes during the Gold Rush days, the new-age vigilantes labeled Little's corpse with a note that read: "L-C-D-C-S-S-W-T. 3-7-77." The numbers were a familiar vigilante insignia, possibly referring to the dimensions of the victim's grave. The initials supposedly stood for troublemakers who faced the same fate. In this case, some speculated that the *W* stood for Wheeler.

Wheeler issued a public statement condemning the lynchers as murderers, and called the mob spirit "unpatriotic, lawless, and inhuman."[10] Three thousand five hundred followers marched in Little's funeral procession as more than 10,000 spectators looked on. Little unquestionably had his followers, but even in these numbers, they amounted to no more than a tiny minority. The hanging of Little created no moral backlash. Rather, it served to fan the fire. Helena's *Independent* said "There was but one comment in Helena, 'Good work: let them continue to hang every IWW in the state.'"[11]

The lynching also fueled ever-growing animosity against Wheeler. He had reviewed Little's inflammatory remarks under the Federal Espionage Act with the chief counsel of the Anaconda Company, but both determined that the elements of an offense did not exist. Nevertheless, Wheeler faced criticism from two sides. Some said Little would not have been lynched had he been properly prosecuted. Others said that Wheeler's failure to prosecute showed that he was, like Little, sympathetic to the enemy.

Tremendous pressure was applied against Wheeler by the Montana Council of Defense, established by Governor Stewart at the request of President Wilson. The ostensible purpose of the council was to promote the sale of war bonds and to stimulate support of the war effort, but the group devolved into little more than a witch-hunting posse, attempting to reveal and prosecute "traitors" and draftdodgers.

By the end of 1917, Wheeler had been wildly chastised by Company newspapers for restraining the activity of federal officials and for seeking search warrants before raiding the homes and possessions of suspected traitors. People began to avoid him on the street and mutter threats that he could overhear.

The heat of public discontent with Wheeler had nearly

reached the boiling point in early 1918, when a Rosebud County stockman named Vess Hall made some casual remarks critical of America's involvement in the war. Hall became the object of public outrage. Wheeler permitted the special prosecutor to obtain an indictment against Hall under the espionage law, but Judge George M. Bourquin of the United States District Court in Butte dismissed the charges as unsupported by evidence. In so ruling, Judge Bourquin explained that "U.S. attorneys throughout the country have been unjustly criticized because they do not prosecute where they cannot."

The Council of Defense was not satisfied. The governor was pressured to call a special legislation session in February 1918, to strengthen the power of the superpatriots against dissenters. Although the session failed to pass a resolution demanding the removal of Wheeler and Bourquin, it impeached State District Judge Charles L. Crum for criticizing the war and testifying on behalf of Vess Hall. The powers of the Montana Council of Defense were expanded, and the Criminal Syndicalism Act was passed in an attempt to outlaw the IWW. The session even passed a gun-control law. Most significantly, the special legislature enacted the Montana Sedition Law, which read in part:

> . . . Any person or persons who shall utter, print, write or publish any disloyal, profane, violent, scurrilous, contemptuous, slurring or abusive language about the form of government of the United States, or the Constitution of the United States, or the soldiers or sailors of the United States, or the flag of the United States, or the uniform of the army or navy . . . or shall utter, print, write or publish any language calculated to incite or inflame resistance to any duly constituted federal or state authority in connection with the prosecution of the war . . . shall be guilty of the crime of sedition.[12]

Tragically, this violent encroachment upon First Amendment guarantees became the model for the federal Sedition Law. The only real blemishes on the political record of Senator Thomas J. Walsh came in 1918 when he succumbed to pressures created by war hysteria. In May, Walsh was responsible for making the Montana Sedition Law the model for federal law. Then, facing reelection in November, Walsh was forced to confront the question of whether to retain the controversial Wheeler as United States attorney. Walsh's political friends warned him that he could not win if Wheeler remained as U. S. attorney.

At first Walsh resisted, but ultimately he succumbed to the political reality and met privately with Wheeler. After the meeting, Wheeler issued a simple statement that he would withdraw from office "in order to satisfy the friend of T. J. Walsh who believed my retention in office would mean his defeat as a candidate to succeed himself in the Senate."[13] Walsh was reelected, although not by the greatest of margins. One historian later wrote, "Wheeler stuck to his principles and lost his job, while Walsh bent with the wind and kept his."[14]

Wheeler returned to private practice, but kept one foot in the political arena, determined to wrest the Democratic Party from the stranglehold of the Anaconda Company. In one case, Wheeler represented a railway shop machinist in Livingston who brought suit against six prominent local residents for "violating his liberty and bringing him shame and disgrace" by forcing him to kneel in the public square and kiss the American flag. The jury came in for the plaintiff, although a token $1 was awarded for damages.

Wheeler's continued law practice denied the Company the result it desired—driving Wheeler from its midst. Meanwhile, Wheeler remained active in politics. The Non-Partisan League (NPL) had been organized in North Dakota in 1915, and by 1919 claimed some 220,000 members, concentrated between Wisconsin and Montana. Fearing the power of the NPL, the Montana legislature attempted to revoke the direct primary election law and return to the old convention system. The attempt was thwarted through NPL's grassroots organization, and the party resolved to nominate sympathetic candidates for governor on both the Democratic and Republican tickets. The leaguers turned to Wheeler in the Democratic Party. B. K. warned Mrs. Wheeler that the race would be difficult and, at times, painful but she agreed to stand with him in the fight. After some deliberation, Wheeler began his battle for the Democratic nomination.

The first campaign stop was in Dillon, where the city council had passed an ordinance to prohibit Wheeler's scheduled rally at the courthouse. When he proposed to speak on a street corner, the chief of police threatened to arrest him. The candidate was relegated to a farm outside town, where he planned to speak from the flatbed of a truck. A band of local businessmen appeared at the field, shouting anti-Wheeler slogans. "It's Wheeler we want," they shouted. "Get a rope!" A local Dillon barber who supported Wheeler pulled out a penknife and stabbed one of the ringleaders.

Wheeler narrowly escaped and spent the night, attended by a rifle-armed supporter, in a boxcar near the railway tracks. When the lynchmen came calling and attempted to board the railroad car, Wheeler's protector cocked his gun and warned, "I'll shoot anyone full of lead who opens that door!" Wheeler was still alive the next morning, after a sleepless night, when the Silver Bow County sheriff arrived to return him safely to Butte. The opposition press began to refer to Wheeler as Boxcar Burt.

The scene was repeated in Choteau when a group of angry Republicans charged Wheeler and demanded his hanging. This time, Wheeler's deliverer was a Great Falls physician and former college boxer. He retorted, "If any one of you touch this man, I'll knock the hell out of you!"[15]

The mainstream of the Democratic Party feared Wheeler because of his positions and affiliations with the Non-Partisan League. Party leaders backed Lt. Gov. W. W. McDowell for the Democratic nomination. The Council of Defense issued a bulletin describing the primary race as "a street fight between the reds and the Americans." The Company-owned *Butte Miner* proclaimed that "no man can sit quietly by and see his state virtually made an annex to Bolshevik Russia."[16]

Boxcar Burt was becoming known as Bolshevik Burt. The sole newspaper supporting Wheeler, the *Butte Daily Bulletin*, quoted Wheeler in its headline: "If elected governor of Montana, I will not put the A.C.M. out of business, but I will put it out of politics." Wheeler ended his primary campaign in Butte, where he spoke to a crowd of 5,000 from the balcony of the Butte Hotel. Wheeler and the other NPL candidates handily captured the Democratic nomination on August 26, 1920.

Wheeler's Republican opponent was former United States congressman and Senator Joe Dixon. The Non-Partisan League could not have been happier, as Dixon was a solid Progressive himself who sought the endorsement of the league. The *Butte Miner* was frustrated, writing, "there is [no] lesser evil offered in this case."[17]

Wheeler was endorsed by Senator Walsh and Democratic presidential and vice-presidential candidates James Cox and Franklin Roosevelt. Other Democrats continued to resist Wheeler, fearing the influence of the Non-Partisan League. But Wheeler's most vicious opponent, of course, was the Company. Company leaders determined "that the time had come not merely to beat this fellow, but to obliterate him, to wipe him out politically, socially, professionally, and every other way." To this end, the Company staged a campaign "scurrilous in the extreme."[18]

Wheeler was labeled a "red socialist." He replied, "I was born in the shadow of Bunker Hill and know no other form of government than the American system—and want to know no other."[19] The Company-owned *Billings Gazette* charged that Wheeler was an advocate of free love on the basis of his affiliation with the NPL and the fact that some books discussing free love had been found in the state libraries of North Dakota. Pointing the finger back at *Gazette* publisher Charles Bair, Wheeler told a crowd, "Now let me ask you something: If there was free love in North Dakota, do you think Charlie Bair would still be in Montana?" The same barb was fired at the editor of the ACM-owned *Anaconda Standard* on election eve in Butte.

Company confederates circulated a story among the Lutherans that Wheeler was Catholic and a story among the Catholics that Wheeler was an anti-Catholic. Wheeler publicly replied, "My mother was a Methodist, my father was a Quaker, I attended the Baptist Sunday school as a child, I am married to a Methodist, and like most of you men, most of my religion is in my wife's name."

Wheeler was crushed in the general election, probably more a victim of the Republican presidential election landslide than the Company's vicious attacks. The *Anaconda Standard* applauded the people's choice under the headline, "Butte Kicks Out the Red and Elects Americans to Office." According to the *Standard*, "Mr. Wheeler, an accident in politics, chewing the cud of bitter reflection today, has found this lesson an expensive one. . . . Butte spat him out of her mouth with all the noisome crew of Reds and Wobblies who followed him."[20]

After the 1920 election, Wheeler was confronted on the streets of Butte and beaten up by a strong-arm thug of the Company. Although the assailant was taken before the police judge for the assault, the judge dismissed the case, advising that, "Any man with red blood in his veins would have done the same thing. . . . "[21]

Figuratively and literally, B. K. Wheeler had been badly beaten. He staggered to his corner, seemingly bereft of political strength. Then began his revival. Economic depression hit shortly after the election, and the Anaconda Company reduced operations 50 percent. Thousands of employees found their wages cut or lost their jobs altogether. Wheeler's gubernatorial defeat began to appear fortunate indeed. As Joe Dixon wallowed in the economic mess and scrambled to contain panic rising up from all corners of the state, Wheeler seemed vindicated.

Speaking at gatherings across the state, Wheeler began telling a story about a young man applying for U.S. citizenship in Montana who was asked by the examining judge to name the governor of the state, to which he replied, "Wheeler." When he was corrected, he said, "All I know is that all the papers, the bankers and the politicians said that if Wheeler was elected all the mines would close, the banks would foreclose the mortgages on the farms, and everybody and everything would go broke. Now, judge, the mines have closed, the farmers are losing their farms and it looks as if everybody's going broke—so I think Wheeler must be governor."[22]

Before the political waters had stopped rippling from the 1920 governor's race, Wheeler challenged incumbent senator Henry L. Myers for the Democratic nomination to the United States Senate. Myers soon announced he would not seek reelection, and several other Democratic hopefuls emerged. Much of Wheeler's rhetoric remained the same. In his formal announcement he denounced "exploitation by unscrupulous financiers," and pledged to "give to labor its just proportion of the products of its toil and grant its just demands concerning its right to organize, hours of labor, and working conditions."[23] Still, B. K. was wiser from his experience in 1920. He told the leaders of the Non-Partisan League that he would mount this candidacy only if they promised not to endorse him. The league agreed. After an exhaustive speaking tour, Wheeler easily garnered enough votes to capture the nomination. The Republicans nominated Congressman Carl W. Riddick after his primary battle with United States District Attorney J. Wellington Rankin.

Many events worked in Wheeler's favor in 1922. Conditions following the election of 1920 had shown the need for much of Wheeler's platform and discredited the scare tactics of his opponents. Because the Democrats had been badly beaten after a divisive election season, they were naturally inclined toward a unified ticket in 1922. Company closures responding to economic depression exacerbated public animosity toward the Company.

At the Democratic convention, Wheeler's old intraparty enemy, ex-governor Sam Stewart, introduced Wheeler as "the hero of the lost battle of 1920."[24] Senator Walsh told the convention that Wheeler "has never had the patronage of the wealthy and powerful corporate interests that have so largely influenced public affairs. On the contrary, he has encountered their stubborn and . . . their vindictive opposition. Nevertheless, he has prospered. . . . "[25]

Company henchmen pledged to maintain a low profile. The Company was probably skeptical about Wheeler's chances of victory given his defeat in 1920. Wheeler fostered this notion of his poor chances and a good deal less money was spent by the Company to defeat him. While the Company gave some financial support to Wheeler's opponent and brought speakers into the state in support of the Republican candidate, gone were the slanderous tactics of 1920 and the tremendous expenditures aimed at saturating the media with anti-Wheeler propaganda. The Company also sensed that Wheeler would do them less harm in Washington, D.C., than in Montana.

When the votes were counted in November 1922, Wheeler won with 56 percent. He proclaimed that the victory represented "a repudiation of the reactionary policies of the Harding administration. Montana people are progressive," he said, "and want to join with progressives of other states in waging the battle for some constructive legislation in the interests of the average citizen."[26] The political career of Burton K. Wheeler, "accident in politics," was just beginning.

. . .

By the time Senator Wheeler arrived in Washington, Montana's other senator, Thomas J. Walsh, had undertaken his investigation of the handling of naval oil reserves by Harding administration officials. Wheeler, a natural fighter, doubtless found the investigation intriguing and the national attention surrounding it politically appealing. After less than a year in the Senate, Wheeler introduced a resolution to create a select committee to investigate Attorney General Harry M. Daugherty. Daugherty was one of the "Ohio Gang" who came with Warren Harding to Washington in 1920. Not long before Wheeler became prosecutor for the committee, Jess Smith, a Justice Department operative, shot himself and "died with his bullet-punctured head in the Attorney General's metal wastebasket."

Smelling a connection between the suicide and suspected graft, Wheeler obtained a subpoena and traveled to Ohio himself to serve it upon Roxy Stinson, the ex-wife of the deceased Smith. When he returned to Washington he brought Stinson with him. She revealed stories of startling corruption among the members of the Ohio Gang. Her testimony was later corroborated by direct evidence. One of the nation's infamous bootlegging kings had paid more than $250,000 to Smith to ensure immunity from prosecution. Fight promoters had paid tens of thousands to escape prosecution for illegal interstate transportation of boxing films. Japanese backers of a New York aircraft firm had paid $100,000 in $1,000 bills so that the Justice Department would not file an action for $6 million in government overpayments to the company.

The Ohio Gang conducted many of its activities at the "little green house on K Street." One witness happened into a bedroom where he saw stacks of Liberty Bonds piled upon the bed as members of the gang sorted the loot. Roxy Stinson herself testified that she saw her husband on one occasion with seventy-five $1,000 bills in a belt around his waist.

The revelations, especially when combined with Walsh's deliberate, if unsensational, investigation of the oil leases, brought the Republican administration to its knees and elevated Wheeler to national prominence. Years later, a screenplay writer developed a script for a movie based upon Wheeler's success in exposing the graft. The movie, tentatively titled *The Man From Montana*, eventually appeared as the now-American classic, *Mr. Smith Goes to Washington*.[27]

Unlike actor Jimmy Stewart's character Jeff Smith, Wheeler's investigation did not fade out with a happily-ever-after ending. After a month of the investigation, President Calvin Coolidge demanded Daugherty's resignation. The attorney general's friends in the Justice Department remained, though, and sent agents to Montana to find any information that could be used against Wheeler. As the investigators dug, Wheeler became involved in national presidential politics. In 1924 Senator Walsh presided over a divisive Democratic National Convention. Rival factions promoted New York governor Al Smith and former treasury secretary William McAdoo. The battle was left versus right, Catholic versus anti-Catholic, and after more than one hundred ballots, the convention settled on compromise candidate John W. Davis, an eminent Wall Street lawyer. Wheeler opposed the nomination furiously, convinced that "the more respectful the figurehead, the more villainous the operations carried out by the underlings."[28]

Meanwhile, in Cleveland, the newly formed Independent Progressive Party nominated Indiana senator Robert M. LaFollette for president. A longtime Progressive, LaFollette had become especially controversial for his isolationist positions during the war years. A few days after the Progressive convention adjourned, LaFollette visited Wheeler at his home and asked him to run as his vice presidential candidate. Wheeler resisted initially, but then decided to join the ticket.

A couple of LaFollette-Wheeler campaign songs exemplified the values espoused by the Progressives. To the tune of "Jingle Bells," supporters sang,

Profits big, profits big,
Profits all the day,
Oh, what fun it is to stop
the profiteers at play.

Profiteers, oh profiteers,
we've got you on the thigh,
We'll chase you out of the marketplace
and then, we'll wring you dry[29]

To the tune of "John Brown's Body," the Progressives sang:

The people have awakened and are rising in their might,
From North and South and East and West, they come to join the fight,

To rid the state of evil, and to put their foes to flight.
The people now march on.

Victory, victory for the people (repeat)
They now come marching on.

Their champions are ready and have answered to the call,
They come from Senate chamber and from legislative hall
Theirs is the might of David, and Goliath's sure to fall,
As the people now march on.

Victory, victory for the people (repeat)
Their day at last has dawned.

The farmers and workers, they have joined the gallant band,
Their slogan is "no privilege," on this they take their stand.
For "justice to all classes," they will pledge both heart and hand,
They now are marching on.

Glory, glory to the people (repeat)
Their hosts are marching on.[30]

Daugherty's boys in the Justice Department had, by that time, obtained an indictment against Wheeler for illegally practicing law before the Department of the Interior after he had become a senator. Wheeler's trial, to be held in Montana, was delayed until the opening day of his vice presidential campaign. Counsel for the defense was none other than Senator Walsh, who had distinguished himself before and after entering the Senate as a great lawyer. Although the Justice Department brought every tactic to bear against Wheeler, the jury deliberated only ten minutes before returning a verdict of not guilty. The Justice Department then sought to reprosecute Wheeler under the same charges in the District of Columbia, but the case was properly dismissed there in the federal court.

Bastards!

The Progressive Party's hopes of an election being thrown into the House of Representatives went unfulfilled, although the Progressives ran strongly as a third party. In Montana, the Progressive ticket received 39 percent of the vote to Coolidge's 42.5 percent. Nationally, Coolidge won handily and the Republicans, in spite of the Ohio Gang, retained the White House. After the election, Wheeler realigned himself with the Democratic Party and considered his third-party candidacy a protest against "reactionary control of the Democratic Party."[31]

In the years that followed, Wheeler stood strongly in favor of legislation to benefit labor and agriculture, the constituencies most responsible for his election in 1922. In 1927 and 1928, Wheeler supported the McNary-Haugen Bill aimed at providing agricultural aid during the worst agrarian crisis since the 1890s. The measures were passed by Congress but vetoed by President Coolidge. For labor, the 1920s were described as the lean years. Major legislation favorable to workers would not come about until the election of Roosevelt in 1932.

In 1928 Wheeler felt no need to bolt the Democratic Party for ideological reasons when the convention, again presided over by Montana's own Senator Walsh, nominated Al Smith for president. Although Wheeler agreed philosophically with the New York governor, he knew that the Democratic candidate's provincial eastern views would prove unacceptable to Montanans and so did not become actively involved in the presidential race. Instead, Wheeler concentrated on his own senatorial campaign and was easily reelected. The vanquished Republican in the race was Joseph Dixon, whose victory over Wheeler in 1920 for the governor's chair ensured his own political demise. Dixon never recovered from his association with the economic collapse of the early 1920s and Wheeler was given the opportunity to forge onward with his rising senatorial career.

The election of 1928 behind him, Wheeler began to search for a Democratic candidate who could end the Republicans' long tenure in the White House and promote the Progressive principles that Wheeler held dear. Wheeler's attention fastened upon Franklin D. Roosevelt, the vibrant governor of New York. Roosevelt, like Smith, hailed from an eastern tradition and carried the baggage of the Empire State. Unlike Smith, though, Roosevelt had spoken directly to the problems concerning westerners. Moreover, while Roosevelt was dependably Progressive, he maintained an air of political acceptability that made his election a realistic possibility.

Early in 1930, Wheeler spoke nationally on the NBC radio network on behalf of Roosevelt, becoming the first politician of national stature to endorse the FDR candidacy. For the next two and a half years, Wheeler worked tirelessly to build a national political base for Roosevelt. He campaigned throughout the West during the presidential primary season and brought together such unlikely bedfellows as Joseph P. Kennedy and Huey Long under the banner of FDR's New Deal.[32]

The election of Franklin Roosevelt in November 1932, promised great possibilities for the national political career of Burton K. Wheeler. Wheeler had been in at the ground level, and had played an instrumental part in assembling the Roosevelt coalition that led to his election. Even more significant, perhaps, was Roosevelt's selection of Thomas Walsh to serve as attorney general of the United States. Walsh had been at once Wheeler's idol and staunch political supporter. Wheeler respected Walsh's tremendous talents and integrity, and each had advocated and protected the other over the years. But Walsh died two days before Roosevelt's inauguration, and Roosevelt, acting quickly, named Connecticut Democrat Homer Cummings to the post. Cummings was a close friend of J. Bruce Kremer, who was chairman of the Montana Democratic Party and one of Wheeler's mortal political foes.[33]

Many of Daugherty's cronies remained in the Justice Department and now the captain of that team was intimate with one of Wheeler's greatest detractors. Perhaps the move was calculated by Roosevelt to strangle any challenge from Wheeler before it began. If so, Roosevelt made a political mistake. Perhaps the affront to Wheeler was unintentional. In any case, the powerful Montana senator's view of the new president suddenly shifted from rosy and hopeful to dour and suspicious.

The Roosevelt administration came into power preoccupied with the enormous domestic economic collapse that had crippled the Hoover administration. The acute symptoms of the Depression were present on every street corner in America. The breadth of the problems demanding attention was staggering. Roosevelt responded forcefully and increasingly demanded extraordinary executive power. Wheeler's support for the early New Deal measures was inconsistent. Independently, he espoused remonetization on the silver standard to increase money supply and thereby combat severe deflation with inflation. With Wheeler's support the Thomas Amendment was passed, giving the president power to expand the money supply, a policy that later became the orthodox macroeconomic approach.

Wheeler took early issue with Roosevelt, however, by opposing the Industrial Recovery Act of 1933, which to him "went beyond curbing economic power and sought to put behind the natural economic power of business combination and concentration the coercive power of government."[34]

As chairman of the powerful Interstate Commerce Committee, Wheeler supported the Public Utility Company Holding Act of 1935, which was designed in part to eliminate monopolistic control of the electric power industry. According to Wheeler, "The only difference between Jesse James and some of these utility men is that Jesse James had a horse."[35] Wheeler's strong public position infuriated the politically powerful Montana Power Company, and newspapers owned by the ACM, a frequent ally of the power company, gloomily predicted the demise of the electric power industry.

The bulk of the New Deal legislation contained goals philosophically attractive to Wheeler. However, the legislation concentrated unusual power in the hands of the chief executive. Roosevelt was granted power to dictate wage reductions, to control the railroads, and to fix the gold content of the dollar. Wheeler's instinctive suspicion of "bigness" led him to proclaim that the concentration of power in the chief executive was "going a long way toward destroying our form of representative government and coming mighty close to setting up a dictatorship in the White House."[36]

In spite of these rifts, Wheeler ran again in 1934 as a Roosevelt ally. Wheeler's Republican opponent was Judge George M. Bourquin, who helped Wheeler protect the justice system against public hysteria during World War I. Bourquin's liberalism, though, apparently did not extend beyond the Bill of Rights. As a Republican politician, he attacked the New Deal and denounced the Fort Peck Dam project as a useless duck pond. Wheeler carried every county in the state and defeated the judge by a margin of better that two to one.

Wheeler's campaign successfully relied upon his early support of Roosevelt, his advocacy of free silver, the public works project bringing dollars and jobs to Montana, favorable loan programs for farmers, generous compensation for war veterans, and a copper tariff to protect Butte miners from cheap foreign labor. Wheeler could also point to his support for

collective bargaining, unemployment insurance, old-age pensions, reasonable wages, and improved working conditions, all
issues dear to the workers of Montana and the nation. When
Wheeler addressed the Democratic State Convention in Helena in September 1934, he proclaimed:

> We have no fears. We shall win and win easily. Let the To-
> ries rail! Let the reactionaries howl! Let grasping and
> greedy exploiters think and act as they please! We have
> started the great task of returning this country to the peo-
> ple and we shall continue until the job is completed.[37]

In 1935, after Wheeler was returned to the Senate, *Collier's*
magazine wrote, "The man from Montana, it may be explained, is a progressive whose progressivism takes in a whole
lot of territory, and anyone following his lead is quite likely to
find himself far from friends and the old familiar faces."[38] The
magazine spoke of Wheeler's vigorous advocacy of "economic
democracy," saying:

> [I]t irks him no little that some 200 great corporations,
> "controlled by a handful of men," should dominate the
> business of the United States. Taxation is his method of
> decentralization; taxes so heavy that only a corporation
> demonstrably efficient will be able to avoid breaking up
> into smaller units.

> He hates war as much as he dislikes swollen fortunes; he
> believes with all his heart that it is an obligation of society
> to provide work for the strong and willing, and to guard
> old age against poverty and despair.[39]

Tensions between Wheeler and the Roosevelt administration
mounted until early 1937, when Bolshevik Burt locked horns
with the eminently popular Roosevelt in the greatest fight of
Wheeler's pugnacious career. The repeated invalidation of
New Deal legislation by the United States Supreme Court in-
censed Roosevelt, whose power seemed otherwise unchecked.
On February 5, 1937, Roosevelt submitted to Congress a plan
for "reorganizing" the federal judiciary. Paramount among the
act's provisions was expansion of the United States Supreme
Court from nine members to a maximum of fifteen if judges

reaching the age of seventy declined to retire. The act also added fifty judges to all levels of the federal judiciary.

Wheeler's support for the measure was solicited, but instead he rose up against the proposal and became the leader of an intense lobbying effort to defeat it. Wheeler opposed the reorganization plan as a liberal, defending the independence of the judiciary, which he believed to be the sole bulwark against radical swings of public opinion during times of national hysteria. Wheeler's position could be traced to his World War I days as a U.S. district attorney when "the Bill of Rights remained in force only because of an independent judiciary."[40]

On March 4, Roosevelt addressed the Democratic victory dinner in Washington, decrying the "personal economic predilections" of the Supreme Court's majority. In a fireside chat a few days later, the president declared that the courts had "cast doubts on the ability of the elected Congress to protect us against catastrophe by meeting squarely our modern social and economic conditions."[41]

Wheeler responded to Roosevelt's appeal in his own radio address:

> Create now a political court to echo the ideas of the Executive and you have created a weapon; a weapon which in the hands of another president could well be the instrument of destruction; a weapon that can cut down those guarantees of liberty written into your great doctrine by the blood of your forefathers and that can extinguish your right of liberty of speech, or thought, or action, or of religion; a weapon whose use is only dictated by the conscience of the wielder.[42]

In the end, Wheeler prevailed, with the assistance of various outside circumstances. Chief Justice Charles Evan Hughes provided a letter that Wheeler presented to Congress, refuting Roosevelt's suggestion that the Supreme Court was buckling under a burdensome workload. Hughes advised that the Court was fully abreast of its work and needed no new justices. Further, in the coming months, the Supreme Court delivered a series of decisions sustaining important New Deal legislation, including a minimum wage law, the Social Security Act, and the Wagner Labor Relations Act. On July 22 the Senate reassigned the original Judicial Reorganization Bill to the Judiciary

Committee, where it died. Congress then passed, and Roosevelt signed, the Judicial Procedure Reform Act, a modified measure that reformed the procedures of the lower courts, but made no provision for the appointment of additional judges and justices.

Back home in Montana, Wheeler's traditional constituents failed to see the "liberalism" in Wheeler's position. The sanctity of the Constitution was less important to them than the fact that Wheeler had apparently sided with a court that denied them the economic relief promised by Roosevelt and delivered by Congress during the 1930s.

In the span of a mere few months, Wheeler suddenly found himself the darling of conservative Democrats and even a good number of Republicans. Wheeler was assailed by Senator James Murray and the outspoken young Montana congressman Jerry O'Connell, who reported that Roosevelt had encouraged him to wage a fight to defeat Wheeler's political machine and purge him from the Senate. O'Connell pledged that indeed he would challenge Wheeler for the Senate nomination in 1940. Meanwhile, representatives of the American Federation of Labor and the Congress of Industrial Organizations, the Farmer's Union, and ranks of unemployed workers coalesced in 1938 to create the Montana Council of Progressive Political Action, paralleling similar farm-labor coalitions in Minnesota and North Dakota.

Every great and otherwise courageous political leader seems to have a darkest moment when the instinct of personal political survival conquers and consumes ideological values. For Senator Wheeler the moment came during the divisive Western District congressional election of 1938. Jerry O'Connell, son of a Butte miner who died of silicosis, was elected to the Western District seat in 1934 at the age of twenty-five. He was an aggressive and ambitious opponent of the Anaconda Company and the Montana Power Company, which he denounced as the Montana Twins. His rhetoric recalled images of the young B. K. Wheeler, but O'Connell distinguished himself from the senior senator and attacked him for his position on the Court-packing legislation.

By 1938 O'Connell had patently threatened Wheeler's leadership in the Democratic Party in Montana, and Wheeler's political lieutenants undertook the formidable task of defeating O'Connell in the primary. Democratic and Labor newspapers began to black out O'Connell's speeches, fearing the consequences of a fissure in the Democratic Party. O'Connell received the same treatment from the Company press, for obvious reasons. Wheeler remained in the shadows, but personally visited political operatives across the Western District urging O'Connell's defeat. O'Connell survived the primary with half his usual margin of votes, as the candidate pushed by Wheeler allies ran a strong second.

O'Connell's Republican opponent was Dr. Jacob Thorkelson, a physician and naval reserve officer who was given little chance of unseating the young firebrand representative. The Wheeler machine, masters of political organization, quietly went to work for Thorkelson. At the state Democratic convention, Wheeler's efficient organization pushed O'Connell's crew aside and controlled the proceeding. As the convention adjourned, the *Lewistown Democrat News* wrote: "Through some peculiar oversight, none of O'Connell's adherents were named on any of the committees, they had but a weak and futile voice in the work of the convention and they finally abandoned the idea even of offering a candidate for the chairmanship."[43]

While Wheeler publicly maintained no opposition to O'Connell, the furious efforts of Wheeler supporters made the senator's position painfully obvious to O'Connell, who decried Wheeler as a "Benedict Arnold to his Party and a traitor to his President."[44] In one of the most shocking political upsets in the history of Montana, Thorkelson defeated O'Connell on election day by a convincing margin. One writer later explained, "O'Connell had climbed too fast and had challenged the wrong man; the Wheeler of the 1930s was the most powerful politician Montana had ever seen."[45]

Having defrocked the only Democrat who posed a threat to him in Montana, Wheeler returned his attentions to America's role in the increasingly explosive international arena. The 1936 German "elections" had given Adolf Hitler 99 percent of the vote, and the Fascist leader had joined with Mussolini to proclaim the Rome-Berlin Axis. Spain was engaged in a civil war. In 1937, across the Pacific, Japan had adopted an aggres-

Senator Wheeler. In his later years, Senator Wheeler clashed with President Franklin D. Roosevelt. Wheeler led the opposition to Roosevelt's "court-packing" plan and opposed American involvement of World War II, until the Pearl Harbor attack. Wheeler was a favorite for the Democratic presidential nomination in 1940, until Roosevelt announced his intention to run for a third term.
Courtesy of Montana Historical Society, Helena.

sive war policy and was rolling over northern China. Later that year, Japan sank the U.S. gunboat *Panay* in Chinese waters. President Roosevelt immediately urged the construction of a billion-dollar navy.

True to the isolationist policies he supported during World War I, Wheeler opposed the president's naval buildup, seeing "no necessity for spending millions and millions of dollars for armaments and battleships when one-third of our people are ill-housed, ill-fed, and ill-clothed." Meanwhile, Jacob Thorkelson had dubiously distinguished himself as a raging anti-Semite and pro-Fascist. While Wheeler had shown the political sense not to align himself with Thorkelson officially, the development allowed Wheeler's opponents to question the motives underlying his aggressively isolationist position.

In 1939 Wheeler returned to his birthplace, Hudson, Massachusetts, where he addressed the building pressures for America to enter the European conflict. Republican senator Henry Cabot Lodge, Jr., introduced Wheeler to the Yankee crowd, saying, "He hates monopoly and dictatorship if it wears the garb of big business, but he detests it just as strongly if the desire for power comes from those in public office. He hates a tyrant, whether he is in business or whether he occupies a judicial bench. To him the economic royalist and political royalist are on the same footing."[46]

Lodge's remark was clearly a swipe at Roosevelt's attempt to pack the court, but it underscored the philosophy firmly and consistently held by Wheeler—that bigness is bad, that power corrupts. The same notion was responsible for Wheeler's opposition to American involvement in World War II, an involvement he believed to be spawned and powered by Wall Street and industrial giants. An article written a few years later reasoned, "Wheeler is not a subtle man. He regards the world, after the fashion of Andrew Jackson, as being populated by two classes—honest men and scoundrels; and the more prominent interventionists he regarded as belonging almost exclusively to the latter class."[47]

In his own speech to the Bay Staters, Wheeler declared:

> If man must hate, let us not hate each other; let us hate poverty. If man must make war, let us not fight each other; let us make war on poverty. . . .
>
> War profits will destroy true neutrality. They lure and corrupt. . . .
>
> We are neither Germans, Poles, Britains, Frenchmen, Italians, nor Russians. We are Americans, and in this hour of world strife our country is a haven for peace. We must so maintain it. Cries of Nazism, Fascism, or Communism that we presently hear neither frighten nor interest me. Working democracy can withstand their attacks. The only 'ism' in which I am interested is Americanism. We should build up our national defense so that no nation will dare attack us; we must build up our trade in the Americas where our natural markets lie.
>
> As a member of the United States Senate, I will never vote to send a single American boy across the water to fight on foreign soil. Neither will I, by my vote, approve a single step that in my judgment may lead this country down the road to war.[48]

Wheeler's speech came on the heels of escalating European conflict. Only a month earlier, Germany had invaded Poland while Britain and France had declared war on Germany. American popular opinion had not yet unified, however, behind a policy of American intervention. As the election of 1940 approached, Wheeler's stand on peace would be put to the popular test.

Franklin Roosevelt was slow in revealing his intention to seek a third term, but he advised that the Democrats could only win in 1940 if they nominated a liberal. As prospective candidates emerged to succeed FDR, a Wheeler candidacy for the White House slowly gathered broad support. In December 1939, the *Washington Evening Star* reported, "If Senator Burton K. Wheeler of Montana enters presidential preferential primaries in a number of the states which have such elections—it is entirely probable that he will win—he will be a tough adversary."[49]

With Roosevelt undecided, Wheeler won the support of the Senate's dependable band of progressives, including Edwin C. Johnson of Colorado, George W. Norris of Nebraska, Robert M. LaFollette, Jr., of Wisconsin, D. Worth Clark of Idaho, and Hiram Johnson of California. The ire raised by Wheeler's confrontation with Roosevelt did not prevent labor from returning to his ranks as the presidential primaries approached in 1940. The AFL remained friendly, and the CIO's controversial John L. Lewis campaigned openly and vigorously for Wheeler.

A Pennsylvania newspaper endorsed the Wheeler candidacy, saying, "This paper gave its blessing to Burton K. Wheeler years ago, and we never changed our minds about him. We never wiped him off our list because we didn't see eye to eye with him, on every issue. We recognized Burton K. Wheeler as a man of brains, as a man of courage and as a man who cherished intense convictions. No one had a halter on Wheeler. He was a free soul. That's why we liked him."[50]

A Kentucky newspaper echoed the praise: "During the booming 20s, Senator Wheeler was an outspoken liberal at a time when it was dangerous to be one, and when liberalism was at the peak of its political popularity in 1936–37, he did not fear to encounter criticism by raising his voice in a note of caution."[51]

Early in 1940, another syndicated columnist noted: "The

way Senator Wheeler of Montana is rising up as the Democratic candidate for President beats about anything I've seen in American politics along this line. Three or four weeks ago he was 'mentioned' as having a bare chance. Now he is taken seriously by most of those who feel an interest, and a good many of the wise ones are saying he's the Party's best bet—IF—Roosevelt does not run."[52]

Of course, Roosevelt did run for a third term, and by the time the Democratic convention of 1940 rolled around, Wheeler's campaign headquarters was empty. Roosevelt was easily renominated without serious opposition from Wheeler, but the Montana senator was able to preserve his place in the American political forum by winning reelection to his senate seat in Montana. The Montana Council for Progressive Political Action set out to defeat Wheeler and Democratic governor Roy Ayres, but Wheeler was still invincible. While Ayres fell to Republican gubernatorial candidate Sam C. Ford, Wheeler assembled a number of loyal liberals, a broad base of conservative Democrats, and thousands of Republican votes to win a landslide reelection for his fourth Senate term.

The great foreign policy debate concerning American intervention in the war continued during 1940 and 1941, but Wheeler found increasingly few adherents to his staunch antiwar position. In 1940 Germany invaded Norway, Denmark, Holland, Belgium, Luxembourg, and France. Heavy air raids crippled London; Japan, Germany, and Italy signed a military and economic pact. In 1941 Roosevelt signed the Lend-Lease Act to support Britain.

Finally, the great debate was closed when the Japanese bombed Pearl Harbor on December 7. Within days, the United States and Britain declared war on Japan, and the Axis Powers and the United States and Britain declared war on each other. After Pearl Harbor, Wheeler voted in favor of the declaration of war. But he continued to echo isolationist themes and maintained that American participation in the war was responsible for the survival of the Soviet Union, its domination over Eastern Europe, and its threat to Western Europe and other regions of the world. Because of such rhetoric, Wheeler's credibility as a national leader quickly declined as Americans zealously unified behind the country's war effort.

Wheeler's remaining years in the Senate were anticlimactic even though on March 4, 1943, his congressional career became the longest of any Montanan. He was, at that time, still Chairman of the Interstate Commerce Committee, ranking member of the Agriculture and Indian Affairs Committees, a "freshman" member of the Judiciary Committee, a member of the Senate Steering Committee and an ex officio member of the Appropriations Committee. No Montanan—and few Americans—had ever held such an array of powerful committee assignments.

As 1944 approached, Wheeler vehemently opposed a fourth term for Roosevelt, or for any president. "While I should prefer to support the Democratic Party," Wheeler explained, "I am prepared to support any man who is a realist at heart and who is interested in the welfare of the people of the United States and our institutions."[53]

Wheeler continued to criticize Roosevelt's foreign policy, but his protests were barely noticed by the distracted nation that now concentrated on the unified, worldwide American effort to save society from the clutches of Hitler and the empire of Japan. Trying to look past the conflict, Wheeler advised, "We must be prepared to find work for our boys coming back from war and for the men and women who will be thrown out of work when the war industries fold up."[54]

The New York press was reporting, in early 1943, that Montanans had come to regard Wheeler as a Democrat "in name only." The reins of the state party machinery had been taken by a new political team captained by Montana's junior senator, James Murray.

By 1946 Wheeler's stubborn isolationism and apparent disloyalty to the Democratic Party had dissolved the political foundations upon which his great senatorial career had been built. In the primary election of that year, Wheeler drew opposition from Leif Erickson, spokesman for the proposed Missouri Valley Authority, a public works project that Wheeler opposed in the Senate. As an isolationist, Wheeler found himself abandoned by a unified, patriotic electorate. As a perennial critic and antagonist of Roosevelt, he had alienated the farmer-labor groups, which perceived that his truculent disposition toward the president marked an ideological shift to the right.

Despite the decay of Wheeler's political base, he was expected to win as he always had. But with considerable assistance from the Murray machine, Erickson accomplished a stunning upset only to fall to Republican Zales Eckton in the general election.

Wheeler's four-term Senate career and his career as an elected official closed when he was sixty-four years old. He would remain in the public eye for the remaining twenty-eight years of his life. Dividing his time between his primary residence in Washington where he practiced law with his son and his Montana home on Lake McDonald, Wheeler participated in campaigns and issued public statements on salient issues of the day.

During the 1950s Wheeler insisted that America's policies and alliances during the Second World War were mistaken and led to the rise of Russia and China as Communist threats to world security. "After the war, if anyone intimated that Russia wasn't peaceloving," said the ex-senator, "he would be called a fascist or reactionary. But today, we are urging Germany and Japan to re-arm and helping them financially—in order to protect us from our former 'peaceloving' allies, Russia and China."[55]

Before Dwight D. Eisenhower issued his famous caveat against the dangers of the military-industrial complex, Wheeler told the Montana press, "All the time I was in the Senate, a lot of propaganda was given out when appropriation bills were pending that some foreign country was very strong and we might be involved in war overnight. This was done to get a huge appropriation from the Congress. The same technique is being used today.[56]

In 1962, before the rapid escalation of American presence in Vietnam, Wheeler declared, "I oppose the give-away policy in which some $100 billion has been expended on the theory it is necessary to keep some foreign countries from going communist. It has been demonstrated we cannot buy friends, as individuals or countries."[57] Ten years later, when the Vietnam War had become an albatross upon the American conscience, Wheeler maintained his position that the war in Southeast Asia had been a mistake. Nonetheless, he chastised the tactics of antiwar demonstrators of the 1960s. Distinguishing his own opposition to American involvement in foreign wars, Wheeler explained, "We were progressives who wanted to correct abuses by corporations and others. Now it would seem that some ultra-liberals want to tear down the government and that would lead to dictators—it happened in Italy, Germany and Russia."[58]

In spite of the shift of Wheeler's traditional support against him at the end of his Senate career, he remained in his later years gracious toward Montanans. In 1971 he told a Livingston journalist, "Say hello to Montanans and say thank you for me. I owe a lot to Montana and hope I have made some small contribution to the Treasure State."[59] In 1975 Burton K. Wheeler died at the age of ninety-two.

B. K. Wheeler had been, by most accounts, the most powerful politician in Montana's turbulent political history. During his long career, he assembled a bipartisan political force that exercised domination in Montana politics equaled only by the Anaconda Company earlier in the century. Until his final defeat, he won repeatedly by lopsided majorities, although at every turn, he battled those whose influence threatened the diffusion of authority, which he deemed indispensable to democratic government. He attacked despots without apology, whether they donned the garb of business monopoly or political autocracy.

Through it all, Wheeler possessed a peculiar capacity to fight vigorously in the professional arena without jeopardizing personal friendships. Years after his last political defeat, Wheeler would reflect, "In Montana and the West, you have friends. In Washington you have acquaintances." Indeed, B. K. Wheeler had more friends than he ever knew, and when the storm clouds cleared, his career remained standing as a model of courage, vigor, and independence.

Suggested Readings on Burton K. Wheeler

The most comprehensive work on Wheeler's life is his autobiography: Burton K. Wheeler and Paul F. Healy, *Yankee from the West* (Garden City, New York, 1962). Much of the factual background in the foregoing chapter is drawn from Wheeler's book. The volume contains many recollections of Wheeler not documented elsewhere. Wheeler's life and career are also examined in the biography of his wife, Lulu White Wheeler, by their daughter Elizabeth Wheeler Cronin, *Mrs. Wheeler Goes to Washington* (Helena, 1989).

A collection of letters and photographs is maintained at the Montana State University Library's Special Collections Archives in Bozeman. The Montana Historical Society's Burton K. Wheeler vertical files contain copies of many newspaper and magazine articles that covered Senator Wheeler during his career.

Wheeler is frequently discussed throughout M. P. Malone, R. B. Roeder and W. L. Lang, *Montana: A History of Two Centuries* (Seattle/London, 1991). Malone et al., address Wheeler's protection of civil liberties as U.S. attorney during World War I, the 1920 gubernatorial campaign against Joseph Dixon, the investigation of Attorney General Harry Daugherty, the "Court-packing" battle with Roosevelt, the opposition to World War II, and Wheeler's defeat in the Democratic primary of 1946.

Richard T. Ruetten has written several authoritative pieces on Wheeler, including "Burton K. Wheeler and the Montana Connection," *Montana: The Magazine of Western History* (Summer 1977), which provides a sound biographical overview of Wheeler. The election results for each of Wheeler's statewide races are compiled in Ellis Waldron and Paul B. Wilson, *Atlas of Montana Elections* (Missoula, 1978).

VII

James E. Murray,
Stalwart of the New Liberalism

I would rather die a martyr to a righteous cause than to enjoy the luxury and happiness of a thousand years on a sun-blessed fairy isle . . . if it meant that I would be a turncoat to the sacred philosophy of the New Deal.

With the New Deal, the domestic policy debate turned to jobs, health care, economic security, rural development, civil rights, education—in short, the protection of human dignity and the cultivation of human potential. Among the engines pulling this revolutionary movement was a wealthy, tenacious Irish-Catholic Democrat who one day would be called "the greatest senator Montana ever sent to the nation's capitol."[1]

James Edward Murray agitated for creative social reform and saw government as the only agent capable of confronting unrestrained business while protecting and advancing fundamental rights. For twenty-six years, longer than any other Montanan, Murray labored in the Senate. At the end of his career, most of his greatest dreams remained unfulfilled. Some were accomplished in part, some materialized after his death, others retain prominence in modern political dialog. On the occasion of Murray's retirement, young Senator William Proxmire of Wisconsin joined the multitude praising Murray and observed, "the greatest senators who ever served in this body have been primarily known for what they strove to do. In most cases their work was unfulfilled when they left."[2]

So it was with Jim Murray of Montana. Facing relentless and monstrously powerful opposition, Murray held true to the

Opposite: *Senator James E. Murray. Murray was a staunch supporter of President Franklin D. Roosevelt's New Deal and helped engineer passage of many New Deal reforms.*

Courtesy of Montana Historical Society, Helena.

course of the new liberalism. His immediate successes were understandably limited, but he planted the seeds of conscience and left glowing upon the American firmament a legacy of vision, hope, and compassion.

Like most of his predecessors, Senator Murray was not a native Montanan. He was born on a farm near St. Thomas, Ontario, May 3, 1876. He was the son of Andrew Murray, who with his parents and thousands of other Irish refugees, escaped their homeland during the Great Famine of the mid-1840s. Andrew had married Mary Cooley, and James Edward was the third of their four children. When Jim was still a young boy, the family moved from their rural farm into the town of St. Thomas, where Jim entered Catholic school. He studied hard and performed well as a young student. When he was eleven, his father died and he became closer to his Uncle James, who took responsibility for Andrew's widow and children.

In contrast to his brother, who struggled to provide a subsistence to his family, James A. Murray had made it rich in the West. At the age of eighteen, he had set out from St. Thomas and migrated to Butte, Montana, where he climbed from among the throngs of hopeful prospectors to the top of financial society. James A. Murray became one of the copper kings. From that high station on the American frontier, Murray provided money and guidance to his young namesake and the rest of his brother's family. In spite of his virtually unlimited means, Murray counseled the importance of hard work and helped young Jim secure a job on the Michigan Central Railroad when he was only thirteen. In 1893 Jim entered St. Jerome College, where he distinguished himself as a student and athlete.

Over the years, Uncle James planted grand visions of the western frontier in the mind of his nephew. He spoke of the "great opportunities" in the West for men of industrious spirit. So when Jim graduated from St. Jerome, he and his mother and sister packed their belongings and went to join their kin on the Richest Hill on Earth.

Jim began his career in the West with a pick and shovel. His uncle knew this experience would serve Jim well in his intended life as an attorney and public leader. Jim worked for several months in Murray's Ticon Mine, where he witnessed firsthand the harshest realities of the human condition. He saw the struggle of organized labor to protect the dignity of the working man, and he watched his coworkers and fellow Butte citizens suffer the most crippling health maladies of the day.

In the fall of 1898 Jim left the mines for New York University Law School. He earned his bachelor of laws degree after two years and his master's degree a year later. It was in New York that Jim cut his teeth in politics. Irish-Catholics had long been indivisible with the Democratic Party, and New York's Tammany Hall was perhaps the strongest Democratic political machine in the country. Jim worked alongside Robert Wagner and Al Smith, whom he would later join in the highest echelons of national leadership.

Jim returned to Butte in 1901 after becoming a naturalized American citizen. He opened his law practice in a city that was rapidly changing. For years, workers had enjoyed high wages and an organized labor presence that allowed at least a voicing of grievances. The early copper kings, most notably Marcus Daly, adopted relatively beneficent management styles as they competed for the loyalty of the area's productive workforce. Workers won the eight-hour day, the right to strike, and the power of collective bargaining in these early years. The honeymoon, such as it was, ended when Daly sold much of his interest in Butte to William G. Rockefeller and other eastern business magnates from the Standard Oil Company and New York's National City Bank.

From its inception in 1899, the Amalgamated Copper Mining Company began systematically to eliminate its competitors and employed hardball tactics, including mass layoffs, to crush the influence of the trade unions. It purchased much of the Treasure State's resource base, a number of public utilities, and all but one of the state's important daily newspapers. Opposition was not tolerated. When dissenters spoke out, the Anaconda would tighten its grip, crushing its antagonists and sometimes strangling the community. The company made itself the enemy of the people and engendered a public hatred that defined the face of Montana politics for decades.

Most of Jim Murray's time as a young lawyer was occupied by the affairs of his uncle's multifarious holdings in Butte and around the western United States. In 1905 Jim was married to Viola Edna Hogan, the daughter of a Butte merchant. A short time later he tested Butte's turbulent political waters. Murray won the Democratic nomination for county attorney in 1906 and was easily elected in the increasingly one-party town.

Murray quickly, if infamously, distinguished himself as a vigorous prosecutor. He cracked down on illegal gambling and the sale of liquor to minors. Powerful interests of the city were held to the same tough standards. Labor laws were vigilantly enforced and the likes of F. Augustus Heinze and William A. Clark were the object of proceedings to compel full payment of taxes. The young prosecutor showed no timidity. In one colorful episode, Murray called a presiding judge a fool and was held in contempt of court. When the bailiff came forward to apprehend the offending lawyer, Murray flipped him onto his back. The ensuing skirmish left the courtroom in shambles before Murray was escorted to jail for the evening.

At the end of his two-year term, Murray did not seek reelection. Instead, he withdrew to private practice where he again concentrated on the affairs of his uncle's business. He remained a player in Democratic politics, however, and financially supported the efforts of union leaders in their repeated futile attempts to reorganize mine workers.

The First World War drew new attention to the ongoing struggles of Irish citizens for independence from England. Murray was among the many Irish-Americans in Butte who sympathized with the demands of his native brethren for sovereignty and self-determination. Accordingly, he joined the delegates to the 1919 Irish Race Convention in Philadelphia to pass resolutions endorsing Irish independence for President Woodrow Wilson's consideration. That same year, Murray led fund-raising drives for the Irish freedom fighters throughout Montana and hosted the president of the Irish Republic before a cheering crowd of 10,000 in Butte.

In 1920 Murray was urged to run for a local judicial position, but declined in order to continue his efforts on behalf of the Irish. As a delegate to the Democratic National Convention that year, Murray fought single-mindedly but unsuccessfully for a platform plank calling for diplomatic recognition of the Irish Republic. In 1922 the American Association for Recognition of the Irish Republic elected Murray its president, introducing him to national politics.

James A. Murray died on May 11, 1921, leaving a $10 to $15 million fortune to Jim as the primary beneficiary. Murray continued to manage the small empire throughout the 1920s without great success. His most significant setback, though, came in 1929 when the stock market crash devastated the value of many of his holdings. Murray was certain that the crash was the product of Wall Street interests that had manipulated the market to their own advantage. Convinced that the abuses could be rectified most effectively in the political arena, Murray rekindled his activity in the Democratic Party.

After working to elect a Democratic slate in 1930, Murray remained Silver Bow County Democratic chairman for two years and helped to build a coalition for Franklin Roosevelt in Montana. Again, he served as a delegate to his party's national convention and was instrumental in the Montana campaign of 1932, which swept Democrats into the governorship, both congressional seats, and majority leadership of the state legislature. Shortly after taking office, Roosevelt appointed Murray to Montana's advisory board for the new Public Works Administration (PWA). Murray chaired the board and led its efforts to address the catastrophic consequences in Montana of the economic collapse.

Political events in the state unfolded quickly after the 1932 election. Sen. Thomas Walsh, who had been appointed attorney general of the United States by President Roosevelt, died on the eve of Roosevelt's inauguration. Gov. John Erickson was vested with the responsibility of choosing a successor to Walsh's Senate seat. A crowd of ambitious Democratic hopefuls clamored for the job, but Erickson, encouraged by Sen. Burton K. Wheeler, decided to appoint himself.

On March 13, 1933, days after Walsh's death, Erickson resigned and turned over his office to Lt. Gov. Frank H. Cooney. Cooney, in turn, appointed Erickson to fill Walsh's seat in the Senate, igniting a public outrage. Cooney labored to build a meaningful gubernatorial administration in the face of public scorn until he died of heart failure in 1935. Erickson faced the same opposition and was eminently vulnerable as the Senate election of 1934 approached. Butte Democrats looked to Jim Murray to challenge Erickson and fill the shoes of the late Senator Walsh. Despite such backing, Murray was considered a dark horse when he became a candidate in the six-person Democratic primary.

Erickson squandered the advantage of incumbency by absenting himself from the campaign. Meanwhile, Murray had his own advantages as an Irish-Catholic Democrat from the powerful political base of Butte. He also had money, which hindered as much as it helped his electability. The family fortune was a potent political resource, but it divided the candidate from the average elector. Murray was not far down the campaign trail when his advisers convinced him to trade in his Cadillac limousine for a Ford.

Day after day, Murray battled Senator Erickson and the Wheeler machine, powerful Livingston Democrat James F. O'Connor, and other challengers. When the primary votes were totaled, Murray nosed out O'Connor, surprising pundits. In the general election, he faced the state's ten-year Eastern District congressman Scott Leavitt, a veteran of the Spanish-American War. The election was a referendum on Roosevelt. Leavitt chastised "the subtle changing of our form of free government through the amazing growth of controlling bureaus set up in the name of an oddly continuing emergency," while Murray pledged "100 percent" support for President Roosevelt and the New Deal.

The general election handed Roosevelt a landslide mandate, and Murray was swept into the United States Senate. While Murray won by nearly 40,000 votes and carried all but eight counties, senior Senator Wheeler carried every county and won by over twice as much. Murray pledged unwavering allegiance to the policies of FDR, but he went to Washington in a position clearly subordinate to the popular, powerful, independent, and unpredictable Wheeler.

Murray was constrained in his first year in the Senate by that body's entrenched seniority system that unofficially forbade meaningful activity by freshman members. Nevertheless, Murray captured appointments to the Senate's important and prestigious Foreign Relations and Education and Labor Committees. In March 1935 the Education and Labor Committee began hearings on Sen. Robert Wagner's National Labor Relations Bill. The bill proposed to create the National Labor Relations Board to settle disputes between unions and management and to list conduct by employers considered to be unfair labor practices.

Murray built a close personal relationship with Senator Wagner, whom he had known since his law school days in New York, and worked tirelessly to help secure congressional approval of the Wagner Act. Murray thus began to distinguish himself as a stalwart of organized labor. During the same Seventy-fourth Congress, Murray supported bills calling for a thirty-hour workweek and payment of prevailing wage scales on all public works projects.

Murray was immediately involved in agricultural issues as well. The Montana farm economy continued to hobble through an economic crisis born not just of the Depression but of the drought-stricken farm regions of eastern Montana. Murray supported Roosevelt's farm programs and helped increase the number of Works Progress Administration (WPA) positions available to struggling Montana farm families. By the end of 1936, Murray had played an instrumental role in obtaining nearly $12 million in federal grants and loans for water projects in the state as well.

For the first few years, Murray maintained generally friendly relations with Senator Wheeler, although the two occasionally clashed over patronage. Many of Wheeler's appointments were objectionable to organized labor, for example, and Murray was largely powerless to see to the appointment of his supporters and the friends of labor.

When the election of 1936 approached, labor was disgruntled and Murray faced a challenge from the left. Western District congressman Joseph Monaghan was a fellow Butte Irishman. He had gained recognition in the House as Montana's leading spokesman for the old-age pension plan of California's Francis Townsend. Monaghan rode this proposal hard through the primary. It was a single-issue campaign that drew enormous popular support in a state staggering through the depths of the Depression. Murray nosed Monaghan out by barely over 2,000 votes.

In the general election, Murray faced Republican Thomas Larson, a cattle rancher and state senator from Choteau, who found himself in the unfortunate position of opposing the popular policies and programs of President Roosevelt. In a Labor Day speech in Billings, Senator Murray reacted to the attack on government relief and revealed the essence of his own political philosophy:

The purpose of government is not merely to protect the life and property of citizens, nor is its main object merely to aid and encourage the development of vast industrial and business enterprises. . . . To be enlightened, progressive government, it must give consideration to the moral, social and human problems that directly affect the lives, the happiness and the security of its people.[3]

Murray faced not only Larson in the general election but also Congressman Monaghan, who continued to wage his candidacy as an independent. Murray campaigned hard to make people aware of the economic benefits derived from the New Deal programs and to defend the administration's free trade policies against the protectionist proposals espoused by Larson. Murray's campaign was a success. Roosevelt scored a smashing victory in Montana and around the nation; the governor's seat was won by Democrat Roy Ayres; Democrats took control of the legislature and won every elective administrative office. The congressional seats both went to Democrats as well, Jerry J. O'Connell in the west, and James F. O'Connor in the east, and Murray marched into his first full six-year term.

If the 1936 election was a hallmark of Democratic Party unity, the cohesion did not last. The votes barely were counted when the Democratic Party began to divide into vehemently opposing factions. At the national level, the party began to separate into liberal and conservative, pro-Roosevelt and anti-Roosevelt factions. Party lines crumbled. Perhaps the greatest wedge driven into this fissure was Sen. Burton K. Wheeler's vigorous opposition to Roosevelt's court reform plans in 1937. Wheeler became one of the first liberals in the Senate to declare his opposition to Roosevelt's proposal, which sought to expand the federal judiciary with judges of the president's choosing. Wheeler portrayed the fight as the only means of blocking a presidential power play that threatened to destroy the independence of the American judiciary.

Murray was also concerned about Roosevelt's plan. "If [Roosevelt] had asked me about it," he wrote, "I would have told him not to do it."[4] Simultaneously, however, Murray was as frustrated as Roosevelt that the conservative court consistently struck down New Deal legislation. Fearing the battle would fracture the New Deal coalition, Murray pled for conciliation. In the spring of 1937, the Supreme Court voted to uphold the Wagner Act, and a month later a conservative justice retired. Murray argued that the Supreme Court no longer threatened to obstruct the economic reforms of the New Deal and that the court bill was no longer necessary.

In spite of his reluctance to back the court-packing measure, Murray resented Wheeler's vocal opposition to the president and viewed it as an attempt to undermine the administration generally. What began in private rooms with confidants soon grew public. Montana's two Democratic senators became overtly contentious toward one another. Meanwhile, the president's coalition had been fragmented, and Roosevelt, the man, appeared fallible.

In the Senate, Murray's stature continued to grow. He received national attention for his pro-labor comments during the sit-down strikes in the automobile industry in 1937. In the final conference-committee sessions on the Fair Labor Standards Act, Murray fought for strong provisions prohibiting sweatshop practices and oppressive child-labor conditions.

He continued to fight for public water and reclamation measures for Montana, most notably the Buffalo Rapids project, which proposed to irrigate some 80,000 acres in southeastern Montana. After Roosevelt had notified Wheeler that the project would be dropped as economically infeasible, Murray persisted and arranged for WPA workers to participate in the construction, which made the proposal financially possible. The project was approved and Murray's success broadened his base of support back home.[5]

The federal programs pushed by Murray and others unquestionably brought relief, but by 1938 inflation and a growing deficit began to concern the administration. Roosevelt ordered cuts in the WPA rolls and a tightening of the money supply. Unemployment rose 5 percent in response. Senator Murray had already called for a presidential commission to study the problem of unemployment and federal relief, a resolution that died before obtaining bicameral approval. But in 1938, the Senate created its own special committee to study the problem.

Murray was appointed to the investigatory panel and became a central figure in the hearings. He challenged financial and industrial leaders who opposed further federal relief and

forced them to concede that relief measures already imple-
mented substantially had improved the economic climate and
fostered an upturn in business performance. Murray charged
that the monopolistic schemes of eastern capitalists caused inflation. He argued passionately for the Work Relief Bill of 1938,
and in June of that year congress passed the bill, infusing billions of dollars into the national economy.

At the conclusion of its investigation, the Unemployment
and Relief Committee of the Senate recommended increased
federal funds for unemployment compensation, public assistance for the aged and dependent children, and more public
work projects where needed. The measure might have passed,
but for the election results of 1938, which reacted to the recession and repudiated Roosevelt by sending eighty new Republicans to the House and eight to the Senate.

The complexion of the Congress thus changed, Murray's
beloved New Deal agenda faced new hurdles. As he and others
committed to further relief struggled forward, Murray wrote to
a constituent, "I would rather die a martyr to a righteous cause
than to enjoy the luxury and happiness of a thousand years on
a sun-blessed fairy isle . . . if it meant that I would be a turncoat to the sacred philosophy of the New Deal."[6] Meanwhile,
Roosevelt's attention was turning away from domestic policy
and toward the escalating conflict among nations. As a member of the Senate's Foreign Relations Committee, Murray was
bound to confront the pressing question of America's role in a
chaotic world.

Murray was chosen for the Foreign Relations Committee
shortly after he assumed office in 1935, at least partly because
of his declared allegiance to the programs of Franklin Roosevelt. Although the thunderheads of World War II had not yet
gathered, Murray's commitment to the president suggested to
the Democratic majority leader that Murray would remain a
dependable ally of the administration in times of international
crisis. This assumption was ill-founded. Roosevelt was decid-
edly an internationalist, while Murray immediately aligned
himself with the isolationist wing of the Senate. Murray had
barely taken his seat on the committee when he defied the administration by voting against the World Court, thus helping to
defeat the measure.

That same year, North Dakota senator Gerald P. Nye chaired hearings to investigate the international arms trade. The hearings exposed corruption and avarice in large financial concerns and suggested that they were responsible for America's involvement in the First World War. Responsive legislation placed an embargo on the sale of American arms and ammunitions abroad. Murray supported and helped to pass the embargo bill. Throughout 1936, Murray voted against appropriations for the War Department and the navy. In 1937 he voted again for a neutrality act and, while he acknowledged a role for American presence in the Pacific during the Sino-Japanese conflict, he backed a constitutional amendment in 1938 requiring a popular referendum to declare war.

The outlook of Murray and others was upended in September 1939, when Adolf Hitler's Germany invaded Poland. Murray shared the opposition of the great majority of U.S. citizens to American involvement in another European war, but his instinctive isolationism was challenged by Hitler's aggression and a transformation of perspective began. Murray supported Roosevelt's plea to repeal the arms embargo, so America could provide assistance to Britain and France whose security was now threatened by Nazi expansionism.

In May 1940, Hitler rolled into France and the threat to England and the Atlantic intensified. The prospect of American combat involvement became real, and the urgency of American financial support undeniable. Murray remained opposed to participation by American soldiers and so voted against the president's peacetime conscription bill, but he publicly backed the administration on the lend/lease measure, making American ships, aircraft, and other tools of war available to England.

Although the majority of American citizens favored providing some aid to England, the lend/lease measure came under attack from those charging that it would irreversibly lead America into the war. Murray's Irish friends in Montana opposed any aid to England, and Murray increasingly found himself at odds with his own constituents. In 1941 Murray supported White House–sponsored legislation, against the will of his constituents, to allow the president to arm American merchant vessels.

The rift between Murray and Wheeler was perhaps never greater than at this time. As Murray had converted from a non-internationalist to an internationalist, Wheeler had grown more staunchly isolationist and was active with the America First Committee. Further, while Murray had pledged to support Wheeler's presidential candidacy in 1940 if Roosevelt chose not to run, Roosevelt remained in the race and enjoyed Murray's support at the Democratic convention. Taking this stand of loyalty to the president, Murray found himself isolated from his own state's delegation to the convention, which was pledged to Wheeler.

When the Japanese bombed Pearl Harbor on December 7, 1941, even Wheeler and the other isolationists save Jeannette Rankin whose war opposition sprang from a different source, joined the American call to arms. Still, the stage was set for a political battle between Wheeler and Murray as the 1942 election approached. Wheeler quieted rumors that he would resign his Senate seat to run against Murray, but his opposition was no less felt. The full force of the Wheeler machine was brought to bear against Jim Murray as he sought reelection.

Wheeler unsuccessfully recruited candidates to challenge Murray in the primary. A nominal fight was waged by Murray's longtime rival Joseph Monaghan, but the opposition did not become formidable until the general election. Wheeler campaigned hard against Murray, and his machine openly supported the Republican candidacy of Wellington Rankin, brother of the first congresswoman. Rankin had distinguished himself as a top trial lawyer, state attorney general, and United States district attorney. Each candidate carried twenty-eight counties and Murray's margin of victory was only 1,200 votes. Murray even lost his hometown Butte, a Democratic stronghold. Notwithstanding the narrow margin, Murray's success ratified the positions he had taken with respect to the war and extinguished the bipartisan Wheeler political machine's last embers of hegemony.

As events in Europe and the Pacific waged onward, Senator Murray did not forget his responsibilities to domestic economic concerns. Murray always had distrusted the giants of American industry and blamed many domestic and world problems, including World War I and the Great Depression, on the monopolistic practices of greedy financiers. Such sympathies motivated Murray in 1940 to press the Senate to investigate the mortality of American small business in a climate characterized by increasing concentrations of economic power and wealth. The proposal enjoyed bipartisan support and the Senate Small Business Committee was created with Murray as its chairman.

Murray's commitment to small business and opposition to monopoly was consistent with the populist heritage of the Montana Progressives. "If we permit small business to be destroyed," Murray cautioned, "we shall destroy the American way of life."[7] In 1942 Murray sponsored a bill directing Roosevelt's War Production Board (WPB) to use the productive capacity of small enterprise and establishing the Smaller War Plants Corporation within the WPB. The Murray-Patman Act passed both houses unanimously and resulted in billions of dollars of general contracts and subcontracts being awarded to small businesses during the war.

Still, by 1943 Murray was dissatisfied with the attention given to small business in the war effort and believed that Roosevelt unfairly permitted war production to be controlled by large business interests. He continued to warn citizens of the steady march toward concentration of business and industry in the hands of a few gigantic monopolistic corporations. Murray's fears about concentrating economic power proved prophetic. Within two years after the bombing of Pearl Harbor, the percentage of goods manufactured by the nation's one hundred largest corporations rocketed from 30 percent to nearly 70 percent.

In 1943 Murray also won the chairmanship of a subcommittee of the Senate Committee on Military Affairs, which dealt with war contracts. Although the war raged on, many public leaders recalled the difficulties following World War I presented by reconversion of war production businesses to peacetime economy. As chairman of the War Contracts Subcommittee, Murray undertook efforts to lay the groundwork for a smooth reconversion to peacetime production for small businesses. Arguing for his own reconversion bill, Murray warned, "We cannot afford at the end of the war to let our servicemen and our war workers fear that Hoovervilles are just around the corner."[8]

The final War Mobilization and Re-Conversion Act, which was passed by both houses, was stripped of most of the labor-oriented provisions backed by Murray, including the Federal

Employment Service, retraining and transportation of war workers to new jobs, federal housing and public works programs, and the expressed commitment to full employment. So disappointed was Murray at the final legislation that he voted against it. Although a central agency was created to coordinate reconversion, Murray's counsel to protect labor and small business went largely unheeded.

Murray's warnings again proved prophetic. By 1946 as America wound up its war efforts, a study by the Smaller War Plants Corporation concluded that the most significant economic development during the war was the disproportionate growth in size and influence of large corporations. The report predicted that the financial strength and technological know-how gained by these corporations during the war put them in a position to dominate the postwar economy. In Congress, Murray lamented, "We have just waged a terrible war and sacrificed the lives of our youth in order to prevent collectivism from being imposed from without. Are we now willing to let it develop from within?"[9]

The Small Business Committee fell into Republican hands and the focus of its efforts were shifted away from protecting small business against big business. Murray, however, continued his fight for a permanent Small Business Corporation, ultimately leading to the creation of the Small Business Administration in 1953, ensuring that the interests of small business would continue to be tended and nurtured by concerned members of Congress.

During the war years, Murray remained very much involved in world affairs. After the Allied victory, he demanded that harsh punishment be dealt to German industrialists. Murray suspected that big business, concerned only about its own financial gain, had sponsored Hitler's adventurism and perpetuated the war. Murray also developed an odd affection for the Soviet Union. Although the Soviet invasion of Finland in 1940 had been one of the factors that converted Murray to his internationalist position, by 1942 Murray was praising the Soviet Union as a "young, vigorous and mighty republic." Few would ever argue with the accuracy of this description, but many would later charge that Murray went too far in articles he wrote between 1943 and 1945 for the magazine *Soviet Russia Today*, praising Nikolai Lenin, the Soviet government, and the

Senator Murray with John L. Lewis, leader of the United Mine Workers.
Senator Murray tirelessly defended organized labor and maintained a
close friendship with Lewis.
              Courtesy of Montana Historical Society, Helena.

Red Army.[10] Murray's pro-Soviet positions at the time drew few criticisms as the Soviet Union was deemed America's chief ally in the battle against Nazi conquest. In the postwar era, opponents of Soviet communism would not be so forgiving.

Closely tied to Murray's commitment to small enterprise during and after the war was his struggle to ensure full employment in the postwar period. Many of the government-sponsored work projects utilized in the 1930s to put the unemployed masses to work were based upon the pump-priming economic philosophy of John Maynard Keynes. The recession of the late 1930s, which preceded America's entry into the war, convinced Murray and other liberals that the role of government in stimulating the American economy to ensure full employment should be permanent. In 1944 Murray and his staff worked to develop a postwar full-employment bill.

Introduced in December of that year, the Murray Full Employment Bill declared for every American, "the right to useful, remunerative, regular and full-time employment." The legislation was to "provide such volume of federal investment and expenditure as may be needed to assure continuing full employment" when the private sector proved inadequate to this task.[11] The bill vested in the president the responsibility to encourage private sector investment necessary to maintain full employment and, failing that, the duty to present Congress with a program of federal investment sufficient to ensure full employment. Critics charged that the proposal would lead to a planned economy. Murray responded that it simply created a supplement to the private sector that would enable the free market to perform more effectively.

Murray argued that "jobs for all is the best safeguard of freedom and security for the American people."[12] He reminded America that the soldiers of World War I who pounded the Germans came home to find themselves pounding the pavement or selling apples on street corners to support their families. Murray warned that civilian workers in war production would be dislocated, that demand for farm products would shrink, that the country's population had grown during the war, and that 15 to 20 million people would be unemployed if production returned to the 1939 level. Murray explained the philosophy behind the bill:

> We have witnessed the vast extent of our productive capacity when management, labor, farmers, and the government were mobilized for a single purpose—the successful prosecution of the war. I have a deep conviction that in peace Americans can put aside greed and selfishness and work together in preventing a recurrence of the tragic waste and demoralization of mass unemployment—that we can marshall our large productive capacities and resources for a high and expanding level of national well-being.[13]

Coalitions of powerful political interests lined up on either side of the Murray Full Employment Bill. Supporting the measure were the American Federation of Labor (AFL), the Congress of Industrial Organizations (CIO) and other trade unions, the National Farmers Union, the Anti-Nazi "Union for Democratic Action," the National Catholic Welfare Conference, the National Association for the Advancement of Colored People (NAACP), and other liberal organizations. Opposing the bill was an alliance that included the National Association of Manufacturers, the United States Chamber of Commerce, and the American Farm Bureau Federation. Antagonists labeled the measure "state socialism" and the "Fool Employment Bill."[14]

Layoffs in late 1945 and projections of 8 million unemployed workers spurred President Harry Truman to designate Murray's bill a matter of the highest priority on the domestic-legislation agenda. Hearings held before Senator Wagner's Banking and Currency Committee presented mainly supportive testimony, but the bill was ultimately diluted by a series of conservative amendments. The bill passed the Senate in amended form but took on more compromising amendments in the House. In the meantime, the postwar economy began to grow with a new demand for civilian products. By early 1946, the country had achieved nearly full employment.

Truman's strong support for the Murray Full Employment Bill notwithstanding, the measure was stripped of even its most essential elements in the conference-committee process. The committee purged from the legislation all references to federal investment and spending to maintain full employment. The resulting product, a toothless skeleton of its former self, was passed easily and signed into law.

Full employment was only part of Senator Murray's dream of social security for all Americans. With equal vigor Murray fought the first great battle for national health insurance. Great Britain had enacted a national health plan in 1911, stirring interest in such a program in other free industrialized countries. The call for national health care grew in America, too, but with the vehement and vitriolic opposition of the medical profession.

In 1939 Murray chaired the Education and Labor Subcommittee that heard testimony on Senator Wagner's national health insurance proposal. Murray brought to the chair a background of personal exposure to some of the most debilitating diseases and injuries and the compounding tragedy of those afflicted who were financially unable to obtain basic medical treatment. In the mines as a young man, Murray had seen miners develop silicosis as their lungs filled with particles of silicate dust. He saw tuberculosis and innumerable industrial injuries. The testimony heard by his subcommittee confirmed these experiences for Murray and drew the health care crisis into focus. At the completion of the hearings, Murray's sub-committee reported and endorsed the Wagner Bill to the full committee. Murray argued that the measure would provide financial and technical aid to the states and would ensure the availability of insurance. At the same time, he rebutted cries that the proposal would lead to "socialized medicine." Despite Murray's effort, Wagner's bill languished in the congressional labyrinth.

In 1941 40 percent of the million men called up for the draft were found to be physically unfit for service. At the same time, national polling showed that nearly three-fourths of the American people favored national health insurance. In 1943 Murray and Wagner united with Congressman John Dingle of Michigan to prepare a comprehensive social security package including a national health care plan. The health program would be financed by contributions from employers and employees.

The medical establishment erupted again against the proposal. The American Medical Association helped form the National Physicians' Committee for the Extension of Medical Services, which boasted that it printed 15 million pamphlets and issued 18,000 press releases attacking the Murray-Wagner-Dingle Bill. The bill moved slowly against this current of propaganda. Murray publicly charged the National Physicians' Committee with spreading "dishonest and vicious literature" designed to deceive the public.

In 1945 Murray, Wagner, and Congressman Dingle revised their bill to expand coverage to include independent farmers, professionals, and businessmen. The new bill added dental and nursing care benefits and broadly expanded coverage for hospitalization. The sponsors employed every legislative tactic to advance the health care plan, but the medical lobby struck back at each turn.

By 1946 the Truman administration delivered to Congress a comprehensive health care plan of its own. It provided for more doctors for needy areas, development of public health services and maternal and child care, federal support for medical research, protection against wage loss from illness or disability, and prepaid national health insurance. The AMA branded Truman's proposal "the first step in a plan for general socialization not only of the medical profession but of all professions, industry, business and labor."

Nevertheless, Murray's crusade for public health was forcing the AMA to confront the reality of certain public needs. The AMA backed voluntary prepaid insurance plans and endorsed various provisions of the Murray-Wagner-Dingle Bill, including hospital construction, federal funds for maternal and child health services, and sickness compensation for workers. At the end of 1945, Congress passed the Hill-Burton Hospital Survey and Construction Bill providing some $375 million to the states for construction of nonprofit hospitals.

Murray observed that controversial programs such as national health insurance, which offered dramatic solutions to critical problems, typically went through three stages. First, the plan is attacked as communist or radical. Second, opponents express agreement with its objectives while proposing alternative methods. Finally, opponents are swayed to jump on the bandwagon. Murray's determined approach was generating acceptance for the health programs' objectives and a universal recognition of the need for better public health care.

In April of 1945 Murray's Education and Labor Committee commenced hearings on the merits of national health insurance. During Murray's opening remarks, Republican senator Robert Taft interrupted the chairman, charging that the proposed national health care plan was "the most socialistic measure that this Congress has ever had before it." Murray fired back and the argument escalated until the chairman exclaimed, "Shut up right now or I'll call the officers here and have you removed from the room." Taft branded the hearings "a propaganda machine" and marched out of the room vowing never to return.[15]

By 1948 national health insurance had gained little ground, although Murray still hammered at opponents in his campaign literature. The Democratic victories of 1948 gave sponsors reason for optimism that the time for national health insurance had finally come. But the AMA rose again to hold back the tide, building a war chest of $3.5 million and mounting an unprecedented national public relations campaign.

The comprehensive health care plan offered by Senator Murray and his colleagues never attained passage. Murray fought tenaciously through the Eisenhower years to the end of his own career for a comprehensive national health plan. He decried the inadequacies of the voluntary prepayment plans and championed the cause of elderly Americans, whose life savings could be wiped out by a single illness. National health insurance remains a vital and divisive topic of debate in modern political discussion, but the profile of American public health has changed, from Hill-Burton to Medicaid, much to the credit of Sen. James E. Murray.

By 1944 the Tennessee Valley Authority or TVA was known around the world as a successful public works project that addressed the problems of uncontrolled floods, soil erosion, and lack of resource development in the Tennessee Valley. Murray had long believed that a TVA-style program would be appropriate for the Missouri Valley. Problems in the Missouri River valley, from Montana to Missouri, had long been dealt with on a piecemeal basis with little success. During the war years alone, uncontrolled floods in the Missouri River valley took lives and caused property damage in excess of $150 million. By 1945, a million people had left the valley in a five-year period and the productive capacity of 40,000 acres had been destroyed by erosion. In a ten-year period, 80,000 families gave up farming in the valley.

The idea of a central, coordinating agency for the Missouri Valley was first advanced by Sen. George Norris of Nebraska in the 1930s. The objective still had not been accomplished by August of 1944, when Murray introduced his bill to establish a Missouri Valley Authority. Murray's bill created a regional corporate agency empowered to construct, operate, and carry out projects to control and prevent floods, to safeguard navigable waters, to reclaim the public lands, to encourage irrigation, to promote family farming, to foster navigation, and to generate electric power. The proposed agency was further charged with the duty of reconciling the conflicting demands of reclamation, flood control, navigation, and power.

Like the legislation to provide national health insurance to Americans, Murray's MVA drew opposition from powerful lobbies. Sen. Burton K. Wheeler and Montana governor Sam Ford denounced the MVA as a communistic threat to state sovereignty. The Montana Power Company was among more than 150 private utilities from across the nation that formed the National Association of Electric Companies to battle the MVA. Power company lobbyists swarmed Capitol Hill. State and lo-

Senator Murray with President Harry S Truman and Missouri senator Thomas C. Hennings, inspecting a Missouri River flood area, 1948. Senator Murray fought unsuccessfully for years to create a Missouri Valley Authority comparable to the Tennessee Valley Authority.

Courtesy of Montana Historical Society, Helena.

cal officials opposed the MVA as an encroachment on state rights. The United States Chamber of Commerce attacked the MVA measure, too, and local reclamation and land and water development associations warned of totalitarianism and bureaucracy. In June of 1946, Murray introduced a Senate resolution calling for an investigation of the "strongly financed and unscrupulous lobby maintained by the private power interests of the country."[16]

Murray had his own supportive constituency for the MVA, but none substantial enough to overpower the coalition united against the measure. The bill struggled through congressional committees, making little progress.

When Senator Murray reintroduced his bill in 1947, the climate had grown worse. Zales Ecton had become Montana's first popularly elected Republican senator and quickly distinguished himself as a spokesman for the private utility industry. On the Democratic side President Truman provided little encouragement or support. Murray spent most of the Eightieth Congress cultivating grassroots support for the MVA. From the Senate floor, he confronted his colleagues with the dire statistics showing economic decline in the Missouri River valley and comparing the Missouri Valley to the Tennessee River valley, which had prospered after implementation of the TVA.

Murray charged that "the great problem of the United States is the huge concentration of industry in certain favored sections, which in many instances has produced serious economic and social problems. We need a more nearly balanced economy in the sparsely settled states of the west."[17] He explained that the Missouri Valley was responsible for nearly half of the foodstuffs of the nation, with a tremendous untapped production capacity.

Murray described the Missouri River valley as "the greatest river basin of the United States with unsurpassed scenic wonders, rare natural beauty, and undeveloped recreational features."[18] He noted vast hydroelectric potential as well as timber and mineral deposits, but lamented that the flood waters of the Missouri and its tributaries in this undeveloped area destroyed annually thousands of acres of rich lands and irreplaceable resources.

Though the Missouri Valley Authority would never become reality, Murray succeeded in forcing recognition of the need for regional oversight of the federal agencies regulating various activities in the Missouri River valley. In 1952 President Truman finally created a commission to study the problem, which recommended a five-member board to supervise the activities of existing federal agencies, but legislation to effect this board died in committee.

Murray also succeeded, in the course of the MVA campaign, in obtaining important public works programs for Montana, including the Hungry Horse dam on which construction began in 1948. Even the fight for local public power development was a bitter battle for Murray. Murray fought doggedly against what Rep. Al Gore called "this monstrous thing that is being done to the people of the West, the shameless surrender to the power lobby and its determination to destroy, by subterfuge, the established policy of public power development."[19] During a battle over a public power project at Canyon Ferry, Murray scolded Sen. Zales Ecton, charging that the only reason Montana was not getting western power projects, "is that the power interests do not want them. That is the truth of the matter, and everyone who knows the situation understands that."[20]

In the 1948 Democratic primary, Murray swamped his lone Democratic opponent five to one, polling more votes than any other partisan candidate for any office. In the general election, Murray faced Republican Butte attorney Tom J. Davis. Davis was a favorite of business and industrial interests that were furious with Murray for his aggressive promotion of populist causes. The daily press organs owned by the Anaconda Company either ignored Murray's crusades or branded them communistic.

Montana's premier journalist-historian of the day, Joseph Kinsey Howard, called Murray "an outstanding figure in the dwindling band of indomitable liberals," and explained that "few men in public life today have so steadfastly pursued 'the truth of the matter' and few have done so at greater cost. Personal abuse is an old story to Murray."[21] Howard wrote during the 1948 campaign:

> . . . throughout his career, undismayed by the later divagations of the New Deal, the defection of Truman, or the temporary triumph of reaction, he has clung stubbornly to the liberal position. Call him naive or call him courageous; he stands today right where he stood in 1934 when everybody was a liberal and the power tryst was on the run. That is why liberals everywhere will tune in anxiously for the Montana election returns.[22]

Liberals were indeed anxious about how Murray would fare in the general election in 1948. Although Murray enjoyed the support of prominent Republican Wellington Rankin who had been defeated by Davis in the Republican primary, Murray faced vigorous opposition from the powerful interests he had confronted over the past six years. Pundits widely predicted Murray's defeat. The *United Press* and *The New York Times* both predicted victory for Davis. Nationally powerful political leaders from both parties came to Montana to campaign for their respective candidate. On the eve of the election, the Anaconda Company–owned newspapers ran huge ads headlined, "Do You Want a Hero of the American Communists as a Senator from Montana?"

Despite such accusations, Murray never compromised his liberal positions. He stood by his ideology and record. The 1948 election results were stunning. Truman unexpectedly defeated Dewey, and Murray won by more than 30,000 votes. Murray's fidelity to principle was rewarded and vindicated by the result.

During the 1940s and 1950s, Murray distinguished himself as one of the Senate's most steadfast advocates of the interest of organized labor. A vocal supporter of Wagner's Labor Relations Act, Murray became chairman of the Senate Committee on Education and Labor in 1945. From the chair, Murray fought the efforts of large corporations to curb union activity. When General Motors threatened to close down during a massive strike by the United Automobile Workers, Murray presented Congress with evidence of large increases in profits and net worth of the nation's largest corporations during the war, arguing that wage increases could be made without price increases.

In 1946 Republicans in Congress pushed through legislation demanding greater use of injunctions during strikes, a cooling-off period before strikes could be called, and a labor-management mediation board with binding authority. Murray used his committee to strip the bill of all but a nonbinding federal labor mediation board. Many of the provisions offensive to labor were added on the Senate floor over a Murray filibuster, but President Truman vetoed the bill, and Murray helped stave off congressional override. When President Truman asked Congress to grant him the authority to declare a state of emergency whenever strikes threatened vital industries, Murray stopped the bill in the Senate, although the House had easily passed the legislation.

As chairman of the Education and Labor Committee, Murray was also active in educational policy. He introduced comprehensive legislation to provide for school construction, college scholarships, public libraries, special education, and vocational education. Murray's chairmanship of the committee was short-lived though. The Republicans won a majority in 1946 and assumed the chairmanships of all the committees.

The Congressional Reorganization Act, which went into effect in 1947, further cost Murray top party seniority status in the Education and Labor Committee. Nevertheless, he continued to fight for the interests of labor, opposing the Taft-Hartley Bill, which promised to outlaw mass picketing and industry-wide collective bargaining. The bill was passed overwhelmingly by the House and Senate as a reaction against the perceived power amassed by the unions. Again, Truman vetoed the bill, but Murray, stripped of his own official power, was this time unable to prevent a bicameral override. In late 1947, Murray told a convention of lawyers in California, "We have not merely turned the clock back in the field of collective bargaining, we have stopped it dead."[23] Murray and his colleagues responded by introducing a measure designed to restore the provisions of the Wagner Act.

Murray's crusade to protect trade union activity and advance the causes vital to labor never waned. He presided over a special committee in 1950 that investigated industries where labor's influence had been eroded. Along the way, he took every opportunity to spotlight the failings of the Taft-Hartley Act. When the Eighty-second Congress convened in 1951, Murray resumed chairmanship of the Senate's Labor and Public Works Committee. Revision of Taft-Hartley was impractical in the face of strong Republican opposition so Murray and sympathetic colleagues pushed smaller initiatives to advance the interest of labor.

In 1951 the Congress of Industrial Organizations awarded Murray its highest tribute, the Philip Murray Award, for his tireless advocacy of the interests of working Americans. Despite few legislative victories on major bills affecting labor, Murray had steered the debate over labor-management relations in a manner that kept the plight of workers and the cause of social justice constantly before the public. "Through democratic processes," he said to the members of the CIO, "we have forged a liberal philosophy, and under that philosophy we have strengthened political freedom and brought into being an economic freedom never before known anywhere on this earth."[24]

By the late 1940s, scattered allegations that New Deal policies were socialistic or communistic converged into a witch hunt for Communist sympathizers. Liberals, opponents of big business, and advocates of organized labor became targets for smear campaigns. Murray's outspoken liberal politics and apparent affection for the Soviet Union at the end of the war exposed the Montana senator to charges of un-American activity.

Murray accused the Republican leadership and big business of attempting to distract the public from corporate misconduct by "conjuring up an enormous communist menace," calling the campaign "part of the basic strategy of monopoly in this country."[25] "There is a very important distinction," Murray said in a speech to a convention of Catholics in California, "between minimum wage legislation and totalitarianism, between the Employment Act of 1946 and socialism, between public low-cost housing and the so-called servile state."[26]

The "red scare" was used on a small scale against Murray in the 1948 election. After that, the frenzy of "red baiting" assumed center stage in American politics. Joseph McCarthy's inquisitions in the un-American activities committee set out to purge Communist collaborators from government and private industry alike. Murray's enemies collected every shell of ammunition available as the 1954 election approached.

With no serious opposition in the 1954 Democratic primary, Murray advanced to the general election against the popular Eastern District conservative congressman Wesley Abner D'Ewart. D'Ewart and his cronies lashed out early at Murray with accusations that Murray had associated with the "communist front" on no less than two dozen occasions. Following the lead of those who had defeated Claude Pepper in Florida with the same propaganda offensive, D'Ewart supporters prepared and circulated a twenty-three-page booklet titled *Senator Murray and the Red Web over Congress*.

The *Red Web* publication charged that six of the nine congressional staff members questioned about affiliations with the Communist Party had been employed on committees of which Murray was a chairman or ranking Democratic member. One Labor and Public Welfare Committee staff member was called a confessed Communist spy-ring member. The booklet further alleged that Murray and Sen. Claude Pepper "appeared as sponsors of various activities promoted by Communist front organizations." It cited "13 Communist front organizations" with which Murray was "identified by membership, sponsorship or association."

The *Red Web* pounded Murray with a multipage collage of newspaper clippings highlighting the senator's sympathy toward the Soviet Union and speeches Murray had made to organizations identified by Attorney General Tom Clark as "subversive and Communist." The paper charged that Murray was "the only Senator who regularly receives a Communist newspaper from overseas," and called him "an author for Communist magazines," printing excerpts from Murray's articles in *Soviet Russia Today*. Finally, the publication concluded, "God help America or any other country if the Communist Party ever gets strong enough to control labor and politics. God help us all!"[27] D'Ewart's campaign published and distributed more than 50,000 copies of the *Red Web* throughout Montana.

In the 1954 election, Murray faced not only D'Ewart's Communist smear effort, but a nationwide recession and a terrible year for agriculture. National party leaders lined up on either side of the battle. President Eisenhower appearing for D'Ewart and Lyndon Johnson and Adlai Stevenson were among those who campaigned in Montana for Murray. Murray survived, with a plurality giving him a margin of less than 2,000 votes. At seventy-eight years of age, James E. Murray began his final term in the United States Senate.

When he returned to the Senate, Murray elected to chair the Senate Interior and Insular Affairs Committee rather than the Labor Committee. While he remained active in legislation addressing full employment, labor reform, and health care, his primary focus shifted to federal power projects, irrigation, land use, mining, conservation, and Native Americans.

A public power advocate, Murray clashed with private utilities constantly. To Murray, public power meant bigger sources of electricity for the people and jobs for thousands. In 1952 he pushed for construction of a multiple purpose dam in Idaho's Hells Canyon and went toe to toe with the Idaho Power Company. Power company lobbyists cried socialism, while Murray and his colleagues denounced the monopolistic practices of the "power trust." In 1957 the Senate finally passed legislation authorizing construction of the Hells Canyon Dam.

Murray also fought for a major dam project in the Bighorn River Canyon in Montana but was opposed there by the Crow Indian Nation, as well as the Montana Power Company. Murray worked out an agreeable compensation plan for the Crow Nation, but President Eisenhower's acquiescence was not obtained until 1960. Construction on Yellowtail Dam, named for the Crow Tribal Council chairman, finally began after Murray's retirement. Throughout the 1950s, Murray also advocated the Libby Dam project on the Kootenai River. Eisenhower opposed this project, too, and construction did not begin until after both Murray and Eisenhower had passed from the scene.

Despite his aggressive campaigns for large publicly financed dams, Murray was considered a conservationist in an era that predated the rise of politically effective environmental coalitions. Murray blocked certain public projects when the scenic values of a proposed site appeared in danger. "Vigilance is ever the watch word," he warned, "for those who would preserve and develop the public domain."[28]

Murray became an early supporter of Senator Hubert Humphrey's proposed wilderness bill in 1956. In 1957 Murray opened hearings on the bill and again found himself in the throes of a heated battle. This time, conservationists and outdoor enthusiasts were pitted against the chambers of commerce, mining interests, and wood products concerns. When flaws were revealed in Humphrey's bill, Murray introduced his own wilderness proposal in 1960. He attacked opponents saying, they "will object to any preservation of wilderness they think might interfere, even at some uncertain future time, with their own interests in exploiting such preserves for profit."[29]

While Murray's wilderness bill was never enacted, it became the model for the Wilderness Act of 1964. During the 1950s, Murray sponsored bills to control air and water pollution. As early as 1951, he condemned the environmental insensitivities in turn-of-the-century Butte where, he said, "smelter smoke stacks spewed forth eternal dark clouds laden with poisonous fumes that hid the sun and drifted downward to spread injurious chemicals over the earth."[30] In 1959 Murray introduced legislation to create ten new national parks.

Murray's most celebrated achievement as Interior Affairs Committee chair was his successful sponsorship of statehood bills for Alaska and Hawaii. The campaign for Alaskan and Hawaiian statehood was under way at the end of the World War II. By the 1950s, the African-American communities' battle for equal rights was escalating, and southern states adamantly opposed the admission of two territories whose votes would enhance the chances of civil rights legislation. In

1953 and again in 1958, Murray introduced separate bills for Hawaii and Alaska. Notwithstanding opposition from elements of both parties, Murray guided the bills to successful passage. In 1958 Alaska gained statehood and in 1959, over the opposition of the solid southern block, Hawaii was admitted, too.

Murray devoted another substantial portion of his last term to education issues. Public teachers in the 1950s earned subsistence wages and classes became overcrowded with the wave of postwar children. In 1957 Murray and Congressman Lee Metcalf, assisted by the National Education Association, introduced a comprehensive proposal to provide federal aid to the nation's public schools. The bill promised more classrooms and higher teachers' salaries. Critics charged that Murray sought socialistic control over curricula.

The Eisenhower administration was opposed to federal aid, but relented after America's presumption of technological superiority was burst by the Soviet Union's Sputnik satellite in 1957. The following year, Congress passed Eisenhower's National Defense Education Act to provide student loans and strengthen science, math, and vocational training.

Metcalf and Murray introduced a revised version of their education bill in 1959. It came before the Senate unexpectedly in 1960 when a floor amendment bearing the same provisions was appended to a smaller school construction bill. Vice President Richard M. Nixon cast the tie-breaking vote to defeat the measure. Although the Murray-Metcalf Bill did not ultimately pass, it aroused public consciousness and created pressure that led to other federal school assistance including Eisenhower's Defense Education Act and the Elementary and Secondary Education Act finally signed by President Johnson in 1965.

Murray was eighty-four years old at the end of his fourth full term. While he entertained the idea of seeking one more term, his friends and family convinced him that in twenty-six years he had satisfied his obligation to the people of Montana and the nation. Murray had served his state in the Senate longer than any other Montanan before him. He figured prominently in the New Deal and became at once a champion and lightning rod for controversial causes. From trade unions to the environment, from full employment to national health care, from public works to education, Jim Murray's career did much to define the modern liberal agenda.

Murray's legacy would not be abandoned by his retirement. Montana's junior senator, Mike Mansfield, was elected majority leader of the Senate in 1961 and Lee Metcalf, who earned his spurs in the House backing legislation dear to Murray, stepped forward to fill the senator's vacancy. Murray turned over his office in January 1961. On March 23, he died quietly at the home of his son, United States District Judge William D. Murray.

For Jim Murray, the battle for social justice was not a cause for compromise. In a most remarkable way, he resisted intimidation by powerful monied interests and survived for more than a quarter century as an advocate for the common man. At times he moved swiftly, at other times slowly, but always he moved, never losing hope that the ideals of the new liberalism would finally prevail.

Suggested Readings on James E. Murray

The details of James E. Murray's life and public career have been effectively and painstakingly collected from the Murray family's private papers and Murray's senatorial papers by Donald E. Spritzer. Much of the background information about Murray's life set forth in this chapter has been drawn from Spritzer's book, *Senator James E. Murray and the Limits of Liberalism* (New York/London, 1985). Enough cannot be said about the thoroughness of Spritzer's work. Spritzer also prepared the pamphlet titled "James E. Murray Collection," for the University of Montana's Maureen and Mike Mansfield Library. The pamphlet provides a brief biography of Murray and identifies the categories of Murray's papers, which are deposited at the University of Montana Archives.

The Montana Historical Society's James E. Murray vertical files contain copies of a wide assortment of articles, speeches, and campaign materials—including the scurrilous *Red Web over Congress*, which the Wesley D'Ewart campaign used to smear Murray in the 1954 Senate race. Specific election results are compiled in Ellis Waldron and Paul B. Wilson, *Atlas of Montana Elections* (Missoula, 1978).

VIII

Mike Mansfield,
Giant on the Hill

Too many bewildered men and women and children are being burned, bloodied and broken by this war. Too much is in ruins. Too many lie dead. Vietnam is not a game.

It is just another morning at the Oxford Bar and Cafe in Missoula, Montana. At the end of the lunch counter sits a rangy, blue-eyed, sixtyish-looking fellow with pale skin and a dark cap of receding hair. He is reading the morning paper, a pipe clenched in his teeth. "Mornin' Mike. What'll you have?" says the cook. "Brains and eggs and a cup of coffee will be fine, Joe," the man replies.

It is not obvious that the plain-spoken customer dines weekly with the president of the United States, or that others recently advanced his name for president. Nor would a stranger guess that this seemingly ordinary Irish-American just engineered passage of the most far-reaching, controversial civil rights legislation in the nation's history or that he has rattled the military-industrial complex by persistently denouncing American involvement in Vietnam. He speaks easily with the other customers. They know he is considered powerful, perhaps among the most powerful men in the world, but it does not frighten them because they know Mike Mansfield, and he is a friend.

Mansfield. The name alone invokes legend and inspires awe. In his long and colorful career, he was known as Professor Mansfield, Congressman Mansfield, Senator Mansfield, Majority Leader Mansfield, and Ambassador Mansfield—lofty

Opposite: *Mike Mansfield of Montana, shown here with his trademark pipe. Mansfield was elected to Jeannette Rankin's congressional seat in 1940 and ascended to the United States Senate in 1952. Shortly after the 1960 elections, he commenced the longest career as majority leader in Senate history.*
Courtesy of Montana Historical Society, Helena.

titles conferred upon the Montanan who fled his home and school in search of adventure before he had begun ninth grade. Mostly, Montanans knew him as Mike. From sailor to soldier to marine to miner to student to teacher, his path to power was far from conventional. Mike Mansfield never sought leadership so much as it sought him. His humble origins, early independence, and gradual education produced a unique kind of man: a man of principle who respected the opposing principles of others; a man of integrity who accorded every other man and woman a rebuttable presumption of honor; a patriot who did not question the patriotism of others; a stubborn fighter who often prevailed through peacemaking; an erudite scholar at home in the halls of academia, but equally comfortable in a coffee shop with a table of Montana mill workers.

The model of an up-by-the-boot-straps Montana man, Mike Mansfield stoically strolled to the forefront of national policy-making and left his profile permanently etched in the chronicles of his state, his nation, and the world. Others share recognition as Montana's greatest senator, but none has more profoundly influenced the complexion of society and been so universally revered by his colleagues. The Democrats in the United States Senate made him the longest serving majority leader in that body's history, while Republican minority leader Everett Dirkson called Mansfield "the most disarming man in the world," and archconservative senator Barry Goldwater, described him as "one of the finest people I have every known."[1]

Mike Mansfield was born to Irish immigrant parents the day before St. Patrick's day, March 16, 1903. His home was a small apartment on Perry Street in Greenwich Village, New York City, years before that place became chic. Mike's dad, Patrick Mansfield, was a hotel porter who came to the United States from County Kilkenny, in the south of Ireland. Mike's mother was Josephine O'Brien of the western Irish counties of Galway and Limerick, who married Patrick in Ireland and traveled with him to a new life in America in 1896.

Mike was the eldest of three children born to Patrick and Josephine. His first sister Catherine came along in 1905, followed by Helen in 1907. Tragically, Josephine died of pneumonia in 1910 and Patrick was left alone with three small children. Patrick called upon his uncle and aunt in Great Falls, Montana, to look after the children until he was able to do so himself. That summer, Mike and his sisters bade farewell to their father and boarded a train for Montana.

Richard and Margaret Mansfield were proprietors of the Mansfield Grocery, a small business in a small but growing western town. By 1910 15,000 people called Great Falls home. The town was crosshatched with dirt streets; cars were scarce but streetcars rattled along rails through the town. Since it was founded in 1885 by Paris Gibson, Great Falls had developed an ore-processing industry and an ethnically diverse population. Mike was raised a church-going Catholic and imbued with the Christian ethics. Mike served as an altar boy at St. Ann's Cathedral and reluctantly practiced the violin. On Saturdays and sometimes after school he helped his uncle deliver groceries. His customers included a colorful cowboy named Charlie Russell, by then a famous western artist, but a familiar local figure who had not become too big for his friends at the Mint Bar.

Mike's relationship with his Aunt Margaret was more often stormy than peaceful. She took Mike out of public elementary school after fourth grade and placed him in the parochial St. Mary's School. A year later Mike ran away from home for the first time. He was only eleven years old in 1914 when he hopped an outbound freight train and was apprehended by sheriff's deputies in Ulm, nine miles away. He spent the night in jail before he was returned home. Unwilling to permit Mike's recalcitrance, Margaret placed him in the state orphans' home at Twin Bridges, 190 miles to the south, until the next summer when he returned to his home and friends in Great Falls.

By the time Mike reached eighth grade, American involvement in the wars abroad had become a pressing national issue. Mike's dreams began to carry him far away from Great Falls. In April 1917, the United States entered the war. The *Great Falls Tribune* hailed the courage of local boys serving in the forces. Captivated by visions of exotic places, impressed by the public acclaim for local servicemen, and swept up in the nation's patriotic fervor, fourteen-year-old Mike Mansfield returned to the railyard and jumped another freight train in search of adventure. This time he was not to be stopped.

. . .

Mike worked his way around the Pacific Northwest doing odd jobs in the logging camps of Washington and Oregon until October 1917, when he climbed into a boxcar bound for New York City. Weeks later Mike arrived in New York and found his way to the Perry Street apartment in Greenwich Village where his father still lived. Mike and his father quickly and easily rekindled their familial bond.

Despite his months on the rails, Mike was not travel-weary. He told Patrick his dream of joining the navy and seeing the world, but he could not convince him to lie about Mike's age to the neighborhood navy recruiter. Finally, determined to join the service, the fourteen-year-old adventurer forged his father's signature, certifying that he was eighteen years old, and began his military career.

Twelve weeks later, Mike completed basic training—all five feet eight inches and 140 pounds of him. He set sail on the *U.S.S. Minneapolis*, a Spanish-American War cruiser, for combat duty in the Atlantic Ocean.

By the time the armistice was signed, Mansfield had made several peaceful Atlantic crossings. He enlisted for the "duration of the war" and expected to be released after the armistice. When he was not, he wrote to Sen. Thomas Walsh of Montana and asked if it would not be too much trouble for Senator Walsh to have a word with the secretary of the navy about this fifteen-year-old's discharge. Mike sought to return to Great Falls to complete his schooling. Despite Senator Walsh's personal efforts, the request was denied, and Mike unhappily remained in the navy eight months more until his discharge in August 1919.

After his navy discharge, Mike returned to Montana for several months, doing odd jobs in Great Falls and Butte, before enlisting in the army. He hoped to win an assignment with the occupation forces in Germany, but was stationed instead as an orderly at the Military Hospital Base in San Francisco Bay. When he was mustered out a year later (1920), Mike "walked around the corner" into the Marine Corps recruiting office and enlisted for another two-year hitch. It was during this service in the Marine Corps that Mansfield had his first contact with the Far East. Assigned to the Philippines, Mike thought he had finally hit the jackpot.[2]

While Mike was stationed in the Philippines, rival warlords

in northern China clashed, threatening American interests in Peking and elsewhere. Mansfield was sent on an American ship to put down the conflict. Aboard the *U.S.S. Huron*, Mike and his fellow marines, escorted by five navy destroyers, chugged up the Pei-Ho estuary to the port city of Tientsin. By the time Mike's ship dropped anchor, the ten days of fighting were over and 20,000 Chinese lay dead. The marines patrolled the outskirts of Tientsin for several days but stayed out of combat until the crisis was over. Mike never found himself on the battlefield, but the strangeness of this place and the hundreds of Chinese bodies floating face down in the brown river were forever burned in his memory.

After completing his marine corps obligation, Mike returned to Great Falls. At eighteen, he was a veteran of three branches of the military, but without a high school education. Mike landed in Butte where a hardworking miner could make $4.25 a day working in the copper mines. Butte, Montana, in 1923 was a tough town. Only a few years earlier, leftist union organizer Frank Little had been lynched, murders were not uncommon, and ethnic conflict was a way of life. Scores of speakeasies defied Prohibition, and Butte's Chinese pushed illegal opium. Immigrants comprised nearly two-thirds of Butte's population, then numbering more than 40,000. The foreign contingent included people from all parts of Europe and Asia. The largest of all ethnic communities was the Irish, which represented over 20 percent of the foreign-born white population of the city.

Young Mike Mansfield joined the ranks of the Butte Irish as a mucker in William Clark's Colorado Mine on East Park Street. Mike and the other muckers kept the tunnels clean and maintained the timbers and the mine shafts. Some 6,000 miners worked the deep shafts and tunnels of the mineral labyrinth. Mike moved freely from job to job, working at many of the mines in town. Along the way, he watched friends and acquaintances succumb to silicosis and other respiratory illnesses and witnessed many others who died of physical injuries in falls and mine disasters.

Steering away from such misery, the young mucker set his sights on a career as a mining engineer and enrolled at the Montana School of Mines in Butte. Despite his work demands,

Mike found time to box, play football, and join his friends for an occasional game of poker, but his grades suffered. One professor later recalled, "Mike was a D student. The only reason I kept interested in him was because he was so dead in earnest."[3]

On the campus of the School of Mines in 1928 Mike met Maureen Hayes, a copper-haired young woman who had just returned to Butte to teach English at Butte High School after four years of college in Indiana. Maureen's father, Frank, owned and operated the Western Fuel Company, a successful coal-delivery firm in Butte. The tall, handsome Irishman was well known in Butte political circles and had run unsuccessfully for mayor in 1923.

Maureen became what Mansfield later described as "perhaps the only genuinely close friend in my life."[4] It was not long, though, before the disparity of their educations began to bother Mike. Years later, he confessed, "the fact that she had a college education while I'd never gotten beyond the eighth grade troubled me." Maureen was devoted to Mike, but not passive. "If it bothers you," she told him, "do something about it."[5]

During the summer of 1928, with Maureen's help, Mike applied for admission to the University of Notre Dame and to Montana State University in Missoula. Montana admitted him as a "special student," but required a completion of high school equivalency courses, which he undertook by correspondence. Meanwhile, the Anaconda Company had promoted him to assistant mining engineer, and Mansfield began drawing a small salary. Throughout the winter of 1928–29, Mansfield read extensively in history and civics, while debating the political issues of the day with the other residents of Mary Flemming's boardinghouse in Butte. There, Mansfield met the energetic, young Irishman Jimmy Sullivan, who would become his closest early political adviser. And there, in the upstairs rooms of Aunt Mary's boardinghouse, he and Sullivan would later hold the strategy sessions for Mansfield's first congressional campaigns.

With Maureen's support, Mansfield journeyed to Missoula for the summer academic quarter of 1929. Not long after his return to Butte that fall, however, the stock market crashed and the Depression shook Butte hill. The mines began to lay off workers. Mansfield later recounted, "I was scared; mining was the only work I knew."[6] Then, in 1930 Mansfield heard from two friends who were working in Chile, where the mining companies offered experienced miners the security of three-year contracts.

Mansfield raised the option of going to South America with Maureen, but she insisted that he remain true to his goal of obtaining a college degree. Mike continued his correspondence courses and his work in the mine until the end of 1931. At a *Crux* time when people were crying for jobs, Mansfield then left his position as assistant mining engineer and moved to the timber town of Missoula to become a full-time college student.

By January Mike was carrying a full load of classes, simultaneously completing his high school requirements and pursuing his bachelor's degree. Mike's schoolwork reflects his early political leanings. Mansfield had supported Wisconsin senator Robert LaFollette and Montana senator Burton K. Wheeler on the Progressive Party presidential ticket in 1924. One of his written exams, some six years later, praised the Progressive team for taking a position "against the capitalists and for more legislation for the working man."[7] In another exam, Mansfield lamented, "Although we live in a land of plenty, we see many good deserving people in dire straits."[8] By the end of summer quarter in 1932, Mansfield had been away from Maureen for eight months. She had waited for him, on and off, for three years. "The separation was becoming too painful," Mansfield recalled, "so one day that autumn Maureen gave up her job and drove down to Missoula, where we were married."[9]

In the spring of 1933, Mansfield completed his final high school equivalency credits and was granted status as a "regular" student in the senior class. Despite several years of mediocre grades, Mansfield finished his last quarter with high marks and in June, the thirty-year-old ex-mine mucker proudly got his bachelor's degree and teacher's certificate from the University of Montana.

Mansfield's applications for teaching jobs in small western Montana towns were rejected, and he was left without solid job prospects. Then the chairman of the history and political science department approached Mansfield about pursuing his master's degree and teaching a few history courses at the university. This was the break that Mansfield had been searching for. Thirty years later, he still recalled the "joy and excitement I felt at that moment." "Tonight, Mrs. Mansfield," Mike said with a stern voice when he returned home, "we are going out for a steak dinner." Perhaps partly because Maureen at one point had cashed in an insurance policy to keep Mike in school, Mansfield called this his "first payment on a long overdue bill."[10]

Mansfield's master's thesis focused on diplomatic relations with Korea. Supporting his analysis with detailed data, Mike concluded that the United States had "no business" in Korea, signaling his early opposition to direct involvement of American troops in Asia, a conviction he retained in later years, throughout his congressional career. Commenting on America's departure from Korea in 1910, Mansfield commended the decision to avoid "what might have been an entangling venture," and condemned those American officers who had "imperialistic ideas as to America's destiny in the Pacific."[11]

Mike and Maureen won their master's degrees together in June 1934. For the next two years, Mike worked in Main Hall as assistant registrar in charge of admissions and graduation for the university. In 1936 Mansfield took his place on the regular history faculty. Mike and Maureen spent the summer of 1937 in the Ph.D. program at the University of California, Los Angeles, studying the Far East and Latin America and, in the fall of 1937, Mansfield became the University of Montana's first instructor of Asian history. "Professor Mike" quickly became a popular teacher and distinguished himself as a colorful and knowledgeable speaker. As his popularity grew, Mansfield's attention turned to politics.

With Maureen's encouragement, Mansfield considered running for office as early as 1936. In 1937 Mansfield became active in the University Teacher's Union and became well acquainted with political leaders across the state. His years in Butte drew Mansfield to the causes of the Democratic Party and organized labor. After his summer session at U.C.L.A. in 1937, Mansfield ventured to Washington, D.C., to visit Senators Wheeler and Murray and Western District congressman Jerry O'Connell.

In 1939 Mansfield's public appearances increased, and he spoke frequently to labor groups, women's clubs, service organizations, and veterans. He emphasized the need for "a more equitable distribution of our wealth," and, after Germany invaded Poland in September 1939, he echoed isolationist themes, advocating protection of America's democratic form of government from the ravages of World War.[12] Helena's liberal weekly newspaper, the *People's Voice*, called Mansfield a "militant progressive."[13] Meanwhile, Mike courted the support of Senators Murray and Wheeler and received at least private encouragement from Murray.

In 1940 Mansfield officially entered the race for Montana's Western District congressional seat. Mansfield was not apologetic about his congressional ambition. "While nobody asked me to," he later told a reporter, "I decided to run for Congress."[14] His best-known opponent in the Democratic primary was the bombastic Butte Irishman Jerry O'Connell, who had been ousted two years earlier from the seat by a coalition of Republicans and Wheeler forces. Before June, two other candidates climbed into the ring, and Mansfield finished third in the field of four. O'Connell captured the nomination but lost in the general election to Jeannette Rankin, who was making a comeback some twenty-four years after her historic first term in Congress.

Mansfield was not discouraged. Immediately after the election, he toured the state thanking supporters and building his foundation for 1942. The professor's expertise in history and world affairs placed his speeches in demand as America leaned closer to the growing world war. The University Teacher's Union came out for Mike, and Maureen organized a letter-writing campaign for him. Mike used the network of his former students across the state, as well, and Jimmy Sullivan rounded up support in Butte and elsewhere.

The day after the bombing of Pearl Harbor, the United States Congress voted to declare war against Japan. The sole dissenting vote came from Jeannette Rankin, who also had voted against entry into World War I as Montana's and the nation's first congresswoman. This antiwar vote evoked even more public outrage than the first one. Rankin did not even bother to seek reelection in 1942. Five candidates filed in the Democratic primary but Mansfield's careful preparation since 1940 prevailed, and he easily took the nomination. In November he won all seventeen counties in the Western District, soundly defeating his Republican opponent, former newspaper man H. K. Hazelbaker. The year 1942 was drawing to a close, America was engulfed in the century's second World War, and an ex-Butte miner who nearly missed out on a formal education was on his way to Washington to take his seat in the United States Congress.

Mansfield's star rose swiftly on Capitol Hill. Because of his teaching background and military experience, he secured a precious seat on the House Foreign Affairs Committee and was soon touted—perhaps overtouted—as a preeminent expert on Far Eastern affairs. Some articles reported that Mansfield had spent as much as four years in China, and a Washington columnist erringly called Mansfield "one of the few Americans who knows the Chinese language."[15] Other sources said that Mansfield had carefully studied the Far East for some twenty years. As China staggered between the competing forces of Japanese imperialism and Marxist insurrection, Mansfield pled for increased aid for the government of Chiang Kai-shek in Peking. Arguing in favor of a lend-lease bill to China, Mansfield warned that "the Chinese are being starved and worn out because of our inability to get materials to them."[16]

The frequency and authority with which Mansfield spoke on the Asian situation—one of the most pressing international issues of the day—launched him into the national spotlight. At the request of the National Broadcasting Company (NBC), he delivered a nationally broadcast radio address on the Pacific war less than three months after joining the Foreign Relations Committee. Explaining patterns of Japanese history, he warned of that nation's fanaticism and the danger of relegating the Pacific war to a "side show."[17] He advised the U.S. government to deal candidly with the American people, saying "it would be good policy in this war to keep our eye on the ball and not on the grandstand. We seek not plaudits and acclaim but victory, absolute and complete, for our United States."[18] The speech was met with almost universal public praise and Mansfield followed it with a steady stream of public statements, including two more national radio addresses, urging increased aid to China and addressing other Pacific issues.

In June 1944, just a year and a half after his election to Congress, Mansfield was invited to the White House and asked by

Congressman Mansfield meeting with Montana GIs in Burma, 1944.
K. Ross Toole Archives, Mansfield Library. The University of Montana.

President Franklin Roosevelt to undertake a confidential fact-finding mission to China. Later, the president allowed Mansfield to make the fact of the trip public, which Mansfield did just weeks before the 1944 congressional election. While Mansfield missed the state Democratic convention in Montana and stirred criticism among Democratic Party regulars for his aloofness, he returned to Montana from Washington late in the campaign, stumping hard for President Roosevelt and the state Democratic ticket, including himself. Mansfield easily surpassed his Republican opponent, M. S. Galasso, on election day, more than doubling the Republican vote and again sweeping all seventeen Western District counties.

Two weeks later, Mansfield was in India beginning his assignment as the president's emissary to Asia. Wearing combat boots and GI fatigues, Mansfield traveled by Jeep over the treacherous Burma Road and into China. Mansfield met with American military personnel and took detailed notes as he moved north through southwest China to Kunming and on to Chongqing, a teeming metropolis on the banks of the Yangtze River. On his return, Mansfield briefed the Congress publicly and the president privately.

His report sounded a prudent tone that later characterized his opposition to American involvement in Vietnam. "From a combat point of view," he said, "we have no interests in Burma, Malaya, Thailand, or French Indochina."[19] Mansfield warned against a commitment of American forces that would involve the United States in "political squabbles" in that region: "We have no direct interest in that area and we will have enough to do to concentrate our energies on the main job of defeating Japan through aid to China."[20] A soldier himself, Mansfield was acutely conscious of the heavy toll exacted from the Americans already deployed in Asia, and his report personalized the conflict by explaining the difficult conditions under which American personnel were then laboring in that part of the world.

Mansfield's China trip fueled his growing reputation as a candid, independent Far Eastern expert. He was pictured together with Chiang Kai-shek in *Time* magazine and enjoyed speaking engagements about the trip in Montana and Washington. He continued to emphasize the importance of aid to China without expanded involvement of American troops. Mansfield recognized the evils of Chiang Kai-shek's Kuomintang regime and acknowledged certain relatively democratic procedures of the Communist revolutionaries, but concluded that American allegiance must remain with the established government of China.

In the summer of 1945, Japan surrendered, and Mansfield took a strong public stand against a continued American military presence in China. American generals in that country asked to remain, but Mansfield advised President Harry S Truman that "the quarrel in China is a problem for China to solve and not the United States or any other foreign power."[21]

Mansfield displayed a keen awareness of the inception of a new international community when he wrote home to Montanans about the humbling task that faced the United States in the postwar period. "Since I last was with you, the war has been brought to a close and victory is ours," said Montana's junior senator. "But in achieving victory, what have we won; what are we going to do with it; what has it brought us?" He continued:

> . . . Unless we are careful—very careful—we face a future
> which, because of man's ingenuity, may lead us into far

more dangerous situations than the war from which we
have just emerged. . . . Are we going to use the bomb to
make war more horrible, or are we going to try to use
atomic energy for peaceful purposes and human security? Are we, as nations of the world, going to continue
old-fashioned policies of imperialism, subjugation, and
distrust, in light of the release of atomic energy? Never in
all history has man faced a greater challenge.[22]

Mansfield worked closely with President Truman after Roosevelt's death. After Truman scored his historic upset of
Thomas Dewey in 1948, he offered Mansfield the position of
assistant secretary of state. Mansfield declined the chance to
pursue a diplomatic career, choosing instead to remain Montana's Western District congressman. The public statement released to his constituents graciously thanked the president for
the honor of the offered position but reiterated Mansfield's
commitment to "the development of our state's resources and
the betterment of our people."[23]

In 1951 Truman appointed Mansfield to serve as a delegate
to the sixth session of the United Nations, it would meet in
Paris. Mike distinguished himself there in a vigorous debate
with the foreign minister of the Soviet Union over an incident
in which American planes had been forced down in Hungary.
When he returned to the States, his attention turned toward
the Senate seat occupied by Zales Ecton.

The powerful Burton K. Wheeler had been defeated in the
Democratic primary in 1946 and the Democratic Party's nominee fell to Ecton in the November general election. Ecton was
then the only Republican ever popularly elected to the Senate
from Montana. His first four years there were unimpressive
and he was generally viewed to be vulnerable. Still, Mansfield's conciliatory stand toward China at that end of the war
had earned him a niche on the most-wanted list of the vicious
McCarthyites.

McCarthy and his "red-baiting" cronies set out to smear
Mansfield in much the same fashion that they would attack
Senator James Murray two years later. With McCarthy's back-
ing, Zales Ecton accused Mansfield of promoting "Communist-
coddling practices." One of McCarthy's aides, Harvey
Matusow, traveled to Montana under the bogus banner of

Montana Citizens for Americanism. Matusow toured the state speaking to service organizations, veterans groups, and schools claiming to have documented proof that Mansfield had written articles for Communist publications.

In fact, the Communist Party's *Daily Worker* magazine had merely reprinted certain of Mansfield's remarks from the *Congressional Record*, but that was sufficient fodder for the McCarthy invective. Matusow called Mansfield "either stupid or a dupe," and then attacked the entire Democratic Party leadership in the state of Montana, claiming to have copies of their signatures on a Communist petition, which was actually a petition calling for equal civil rights. Mansfield fought back, perhaps too hard, but understandably so. He warned Montanans that the Communists "want to make all of us their slaves" and pledged that if he could, he would "outlaw the communist party."[24] Mansfield squeaked into the Senate with a 5,800 vote margin out of more than 260,000 votes cast. Matusow later confessed in his memoirs: "As hard as I tried, Congressman Mansfield was elected to the Senate. But the harm I had done with the distortion and lies will probably never be completely erased."[25] When Mansfield took his seat in the Senate in January 1953, Joseph McCarthy congenially approached him on the Senate floor, slapping Mansfield on the back, and asked, "How are things in Montana these days, Mike?" Mansfield, despite his dependably kind manner, flatly replied, "Much better since you left."[26]

Joining Mansfield in the freshman class of 1953 was young John Kennedy of Massachusetts. Thanks to Majority Leader Lyndon Johnson's policy of giving at least one plum committee to each freshman, Kennedy and Mansfield both won assignments to the Senate's prestigious Foreign Relations Committee. At the same time, Dwight Eisenhower was moving into the White House to commence an eight-year presidency that set the tone for a decade of relative national complacency and quietude.

For the next few years, Mansfield continued to polish his skills and to refine his reputation as an expert on the Far East. In particular, he continued to warn against imprudent American entanglement in the internal affairs of Asian countries. By 1954 the Vietnamese of Indochina finally succeeded, after eight years of bloodletting, in their effort to oust the French colonists who had long occupied the country. In July of that year, Mansfield rose to criticize the role of Secretary of State John Foster Dulles in a Geneva conference, which was designed to settle affairs in Southeast Asia but, in Mansfield's view, destabilized the situation and allowed the Communist-bloc countries to gain an upper hand in the region. Mansfield supported substantial financial assistance to the anti-Communist government of Ngo Dinh Diem, but he warned that "the defense of freedom in Asia must rest in the first instance on the will and determination of the free peoples of that region."[27] Mansfield argued further that "the United Nations should serve as the only world wide marshaling center for resistance, in the event of aggression or threat of aggression in Asia."[28]

Even then, some ten years before the major escalation of American activity in Vietnam, Mansfield warned of the dangers of American intervention. "I think it would be suicidal," he predicted. "I believe the worst thing that could happen to the United States would be to have our forces intervene in Indochina and then bog down in the jungles there. . . . "[29]

Partly because of Mansfield's profile on issues of international concern and partly because he was acceptable to Southern "Boll Weevil Democrats," eastern liberals, and western conservatives alike, Johnson tapped Mansfield to serve as majority whip after the 1956 election. The position would be largely powerless under Johnson, because of the tight grip he personally kept on the members and the fact that his chief staff assistant, Bobby Baker, took most of the more critical arm-twisting assignments himself. Mansfield was reluctant to take the job in the first place, preferring to devote his time to foreign affairs and matters of local interest to Montana. "I don't like it, I don't want it, and I won't take it," Mansfield initially replied.[30] But Johnson was insistent and, after he enlisted the aid of several influential senators, Mansfield finally acceded.

For the next four years, Mansfield worked as Johnson's deputy at the helm of the Senate's Democratic membership. Johnson had already distinguished himself as the most powerful majority leader in the Senate's history. He won votes for the Democratic agenda by strong-arming members through political leverage and making compliance with his program the safest and most desirable course for each member. That was not Mansfield's style. He followed Johnson quietly and served him loyally, but did not participate in the coaxing and cajoling of his colleagues.

By 1958 when Mansfield sought election to his second term, his national prominence had become a powerful political asset. He won reelection with a whopping 76.2 percent of the vote, sweeping all fifty-six counties. His margin of victory was bigger than that of any other senator outside the South.

As Mansfield's profile grew, so did American aid to the Saigon government of South Vietnam. Mansfield's earlier statements about the dangers of American entanglement in Asia appeared prophetic and his continued warnings grew more urgent. Mansfield condemned the inflexible, militant opposition to Communist nations in every corner of the globe and called for a spirit of peaceful coexistence characterized by civility as well as vigilance. Despite Mike's caveats, the commitment of the United States grew. The American "advisers" to South Vietnam suffered their first fatalities. Mansfield warned that "the time to study, to doubt, to review and revise is now."[31]

When John F. Kennedy was elected to the White House in 1960, he brought with him Lyndon Johnson as vice president. The Senate needed a new majority leader, and Mansfield was at the top of Kennedy's list. Kennedy called Mansfield, asking him to take the post and to become the chief engineer of the Kennedy legislative agenda in Congress. Mansfield again overcame initial reluctance and agreed to seek the position. His main rival, Senator Hubert Humphrey lacked the necessary support among southern Democrats, who feared and despised his strident tone on civil rights issues. Taking Humphrey as his whip, Mansfield was easily elected and began what would be the longest term as majority leader of the United States Senate in the history of the Union.

Initially, Johnson maintained such a dominant presence in the Senate that critics raised questions about violation of the separation of powers. Johnson continued to occupy the majority leader's luxurious office suite and actually attempted to continue running the Senate's Democratic caucus, traditionally part of the majority leader's job. Mansfield deferentially permitted the usurpation until members voiced their objections. Eventually, Johnson bowed to his critics and retreated grudgingly into his nebulous position as vice president, while Mansfield ascended to the full powers of majority leader.

Mansfield brought a new style to the Senate's top leadership post. "They are sent here to do their own thinking," he said of his fellow senators, "and I hope by logic and understanding they'll do the right thing. I don't believe in arm twisting and high pressuring. The leader should not lay down by command or ukase what the senator should do. Collectively, they are the ones who decide. There is no difference between senators—all are on the same level. I am one among my peers."[32]

Mansfield's laissez-faire approach to party leadership was so unlike Johnson's that more than a few eyebrows were raised among Senate onlookers during Mike's first few months in office. While Mansfield was very different from Johnson, however, he had his own source of authority and his adversaries underestimated him. Lyndon Johnson assessed Mansfield as "one man who does not have an enemy in the true meaning of the word," and explained that Mansfield was one "who can be as aggressive as a tiger and as mild and meek as a mother."[33] The *Christian Science Monitor* wrote: "Under Lyndon B. Johnson the United States Senate was a three ring circus with Senator Johnson in every ring; under Mike Mansfield it is a quieter place with collective leadership in which every senator seems to have grown an inch taller."[34] But the *Monitor* also noted that "there is a sort of subconscious feeling among friends who call him the best loved man in the Senate, that he would be a tough customer to tangle with if anyone departed from his own high code of fair dealing and self respect."[35]

Mansfield quietly built an effective coalition of Democrats from the North and West and liberal Republicans as he laid the groundwork for Kennedy's ambitious legislative program. He operated under a self-imposed system of simple courtesy and respect. Where Johnson would often hold the Senate well into the night until the fatigued body capitulated to his demands, Mansfield adopted a friendlier approach, virtually abolishing night sessions and allowing senators, as he put it, to go home and enjoy dinners with their families.[36] "It isn't that Mike doesn't enjoy a good fight," one writer noted, "that would belie his Irish ancestry. But Mike is an orderly sort of chap who would like to go down in history as a leader whose administration was noted for smooth, business-like operation."[37]

One episode is particularly illustrative of Mansfield's leadership technique. When astronaut Alan Shepard returned from space, he was honored at a White House reception, but Republican Senator Norris Cotton, a senator from Shepard's native state of New Hampshire, was not invited. Mansfield knew Cotton had a potentially difficult reelection campaign and, when Shepard reached the Capitol for a second reception, Mike seated Cotton in the front row where he was photographed with Shepard. Later that day, the grateful Senator Cotton crossed party lines and voted with Mansfield to confirm a controversial ambassadorial nomination.

It was said that Mansfield generously distributed quids without demanding quos. He explained in his simple, forthright manner, "On the basis of personal friendship and trust I might in a close situation get five or maybe ten senators to give me the benefit of the doubt," and that was the way Mike Mansfield built the foundation for senatorial leadership. The effectiveness of Mansfield's light touch was undeniable, but a truth hard for some traditionalists to grasp.

Part of Mansfield's reluctance to become majority leader stemmed from his own hard-minded independence as a senator. During his first year in office, a Northwest newspaper wrote: "His philosophy is that he is a Democrat, yes, but first he is a United States Senator. He sometimes is a liberal, sometimes a conservative. But always upper most in his mind is the thought: What is best for the people? . . . Mike Mansfield is an individualist. But he will work with anyone and everyone when he feels the net result will produce something beneficial to the nation."[38] Mansfield's independence was evidenced in the first instance in his selection of Humphrey as majority whip. Part of the reason for Kennedy's draft of Mansfield was the political notion that Humphrey would alienate conservative southern Democrats.

Mansfield also showed his independence in June of 1961 when he suggested that Berlin be made a free, neutral city under international guarantees and protection. He proposed that access to the city be guarded by international peace teams with freedom guaranteed by the North Atlantic Treaty Organization (NATO) and Warsaw Pact countries. Because of Mansfield's renowned stature as a leader in American foreign policy, world leaders wondered whether he spoke for the Kennedy administration. West Germany was particularly upset and Kennedy disavowed the proposal. Critics claimed Mansfield's public pronouncement was impulsive, but it clearly demonstrated that Mansfield placed the highest priority on his role as a individual senator and his independent leadership in foreign policy debates.

Part of the reason for Mansfield's apparently effortless influence was the authority he delegated to his colleagues. Where Johnson grabbed for power, Mansfield disfused it. Instead of manipulating committee assignments as Johnson had, Mansfield would assign struggles over appointments and promotions to the Senate Steering Committee to settle by secret ballot.[39] Likewise, Mansfield frequently permitted committee chairs to manage floor debate on bills that were recommended by their committees.

In the meantime, Mansfield diligently kept his own desk in order. He was often quoted as saying "If I forget Montanans, then they'll forget me." Mansfield's fifteen-hour days began at 6:30 A.M., before the Senate office buildings officially opened. On most days, by the time staff members arrived at 8:00 A.M., Mansfield had already read and sorted the mail and was joining his colleague, Republican senator George Aiken of Vermont, for breakfast in the Senate cafeteria. Mansfield and Aiken shared breakfast nearly every morning for most of their Senate careers, and their friendship was a well-known institution on the Hill.

During the 1,000 days of the Kennedy administration, Mansfield helped enact legislation fortifying education, providing aid to impoverished areas, protecting reciprocal trade, raising the minimum wage, improving infrastructure and public housing, combating water pollution, creating the Peace Corps, and advancing the goal of equal pay for women. Arguably the greatest legislative accomplishment of the Kennedy administration was the ratification of the nuclear test-ban treaty. Atmospheric testing of nuclear weapons during the cold war of the 1950s was contaminating ecosystems and finding its way into the world's human food supply. Leaders of the military-industrial complex vigorously opposed an atmospheric test ban, and the Senate was hotly divided over the issue.

Mansfield's address to his colleagues called upon them to give the president the benefit of "those vague and residual hesitancies" that accompany difficult foreign policy decisions. Mansfield showed characteristic respect for the treaty's opponents but urged the course of common reason. He explained that "neither this nation nor the Soviet Union seeks the dubious distinction of being the foremost contaminator of the earth's physical environment with radioactive substances." At the conclusion of his well-reasoned appeal, Mansfield told his colleagues:

> This nation, the Soviet Union and the world are destined to live for a long time with feet dangling over the grave that beckons to the human civilization that is our common heritage. Against that immense void of darkness, this treaty is a feeble candle. It is a flicker of light where there has been no light.
>
> The Senator from Montana will vote for this light, and he will hope for its strengthening by subsequent acts of reason on all sides. He will vote for approval of this treaty because it is, on clear balance, in the interests of the people of his state and the United States. He will vote for it because it is a testament to the universal vitality of reason. He will vote for it because it is an affirmation of human life itself.[40]

Mansfield's speech on the nuclear test-ban treaty exemplifies two leadership tactics that gave Mansfield his seemingly stringless authority. By avoiding overstatement about the significance of a legislative initiative, Mansfield defused potentially explosive political situations. Further, by summoning the "universal vitality of reason" and the interests of the people of the United States, Mansfield brought down walls that divided ideological foes.

During the Kennedy years, Mansfield also maintained his opposition to American involvement in Vietnam. Mansfield had made several investigatory trips to Southeast Asia in the 1950s. After France abdicated its colonial presence in South Vietnam, Ngo Dinh Diem rose to power, claiming to be the defender of democracy. When his administration weakened, though, he imposed martial law and was soon assassinated in a military coup.

A few days later, concerned about American overreaction to this internal Vietnamese struggle, Mansfield again warned the nation against intervention.

Mansfield called upon the president to reduce the commitment of U.S. forces in Southeast Asia and to improve relations with Vietnam, Cambodia, and Laos. Mansfield cautioned that the coup d'etat and death of Diem should not be viewed as a victory or defeat for the United States and recalled the statement issued by himself and other senators after returning from Saigon a year earlier. They had concluded that "there is no interest of the United States in Vietnam which would justify, in present circumstances, the conversion of the war in that country primarily into an American war, to be fought primarily with American lives."[41]

Significantly, Mansfield had met with Kennedy the day after Christmas 1962 to discuss his written report about withdrawal from Vietnam. One of Kennedy's chief aides, Kenneth O'Donnell, later wrote in his memoirs that Mansfield had persuaded Kennedy in that meeting and in the months following that the United States should pull out of Vietnam. Fearing an anti-Communist backlash, Kennedy planned to delay the withdrawal until after the 1964 presidential election, but according to O'Donnell, pledged to leave Vietnam after his reelection.

On November 25, 1963, President John F. Kennedy lay in state in the rotunda of the United States Capitol, felled by assassination bullets. Mike Mansfield stood before the assembled dignitaries with the humbling task of eulogizing the leader of the free world at the moment of a historic national tragedy. Moved by Jacqueline Kennedy's placement of her ring in the president's coffin at the funeral, Mansfield began:

> There was a sound of laughter; in a moment, it was no more. And so she took a ring from her finger and placed it in his hands. . . .
>
> A piece of each of us died at that moment. Yet in death he gave of himself to us. He gave us of a good heart from which the laughter came. He gave us of a profound wit, from which a great leadership emerged. He gave us of a kindness and a strength fused into a human courage to seek peace without fear.

> He gave us of his love that we too, in turn, might give. He
> gave that we might give of ourselves, that we might give to
> one another until there would be no room, no room at all,
> for the bigotry, the hatred, the prejudice, and the arro-
> gance which converged in that moment to strike him
> down.

> In leaving us these gifts, John Fitzgerald Kennedy, Presi-
> dent of the United States, leaves with us. Will we take
> them, Mr. President? Will we have, now, the sense and the
> responsibility and the courage to take them?

> I pray to God that we shall, and under God we will.[42]

Perhaps the Kennedy administration's most ambitious legislative undertaking was the introduction of the omnibus civil
rights bill. The bill promised to end structuralized segregation,
and the issue cut across party lines as it opened a chasm in the
Democratic majority. Mansfield's task was to harmonize the
warring factions that clung to the same diametrically opposed
ideologies that sparked the Civil War one hundred years before. The bill, HR7152, undertook, in fifty-five pages, to settle
the nation's oldest and deepest value conflict, and to define,
perhaps for the first time, a single national character. The bill
had successfully passed through the hazards of committee-
level political maneuvering, but a protracted floor debate most
certainly lay ahead.

With a sober understanding of the gravity of this challenge,
Mike Mansfield rose in the well of the Senate chamber and began to speak. His words were measured, but infused with un-
mistakable feeling. "There is," he said, "an ebb and flow in
human affairs which at rare moments brings the complex of
human events into a delicate balance. At those moments, the
acts of government may indeed influence, for better or for
worse, the course of history. This is such a moment in the life
of the nation. This is the moment for the Senate."[43]

Mansfield could have collected the votes to pass the civil
rights act immediately, but for the power of filibuster. Led by
Georgia's Richard B. Russell, southern Democrats organized
three six-man talk teams, each assigned to a twenty-four-hour
shift. Mansfield's challenge was to gather sufficient votes to in-
voke "cloture" under Senate rule XXII. Two-thirds of the sena-

tors present were required for cloture, which meant that Mansfield had to commandeer a coalition of sixty-seven Democrats and Republicans to overpower the stalling strategy of the southern bloc, composed largely of Democratic senators. *Time* magazine declared that "never in his time as majority leader has Mansfield had to cope with so important and controversial a measure."[44]

Smaller civil rights bills had passed the Senate in 1957 and 1960 addressing voting rights and school segregation, but both wound up largely toothless. The new omnibus bill would bar discrimination in voting rights, public accommodation, schools, jobs, and government-aided welfare programs, while giving the United States attorney general substantial enforcement powers.

Democratic segregationists assailed the bill as "an instrument of unparalleled tyranny and persecution," that would "commence the processes of socialism" and lead to the "mongrelization of our people."[45]

Mansfield fought to defeat the southern bloc's delay strategy, but defended the right to filibuster as a protection against domination by a tyrannical majority. Later, Mansfield successfully would convince the Senate to lower the cloture threshold to three-fifths, but Mansfield recognized and respected the shield represented by the filibuster. He came under some criticism from the liberal corners for not ordering round-the-clock sessions, as Lyndon Johnson had, but Mansfield thought such tactics were inconsistent with sound strategy.

"We debated a civil rights measure twenty-four hours a day for many days on end," he told his colleagues, recalling the 1960 bill:

> We debated it shaven and unshaven. We debated it without ties, with hair awry and even in bedroom slippers. In the end, we wound up with compromise legislation. And it was not the fresh and well rested opponents of the civil rights measure who were compelled to the compromise. It was, rather, the exhausted, sleep-starved, quorum-confounded proponents who were only too happy to take it.[46]

The filibuster droned on for three months. Twenty or so of the sixty-seven Democrats were counted as southern segregationists. It was the same group that often strayed from the party line to stake a more conservative position on other issues. Mansfield would need the same number of Republicans to garner the necessary two-thirds majority for cloture. For three months Mansfield steadily persuaded moderate Republicans. Compromises were made and the dogmatic minority was given full opportunity to vent its views. Nevertheless, after three months, the guts and spirit of the civil rights bill remained intact, and Mansfield met with Senator Russell to tell him he had collected the necessary votes for cloture. Eleven prior attempts had been made to end Senate filibusters of the civil rights bill, but this was the first to succeed. After cloture, the bill easily passed the Senate seventy-three to twenty-seven. Soon thereafter, President Johnson signed the Civil Rights Act of 1964.

Throughout 1964 the United States was without a vice president, and Lyndon Johnson was considered a shoe-in to succeed himself as president. Whomever Johnson chose for the second spot of his ticket, therefore, was almost certain to become vice president of the United States. Mansfield was at the top of Johnson's short list. William S. White, columnist for the *Washington Evening Star,* was regarded as the newsman closest to President Johnson. He wrote that Mansfield was being considered by Johnson as a vice presidential running mate "in the most meaningful of ways."[47] White explained that Mansfield was a personal favorite of Johnson.

Mansfield responded swiftly. When asked about his interest in the vice presidency by a reporter, the majority leader said, "count me out." The reporter continued: "You mean you would turn down the nomination if it were offered to you?" "Yes, I would," Mansfield replied. "My interest is being a senator from Montana. I achieved my life's ambition when I came to Congress. I have gotten more out of life than I deserve and I am happy where I am." Mansfield added, "There are many men being mentioned who are far better qualified than I am."[48]

Mansfield's genuine reluctance to advance himself beyond the halls of the Senate won him credibility and authority in the nation's most difficult policy debates. As Hubert Humphrey once said, "Keep in mind, the things he says, no matter how critical, do not spring from personal ambition but rather as a reflection of his own mind and conscience."[49]

Mansfield used this credibility in 1965 to engineer the passage of the Voting Rights Act, which augmented the Civil Rights Act by forbidding literacy tests and voting qualifications designed to deny or abridge the right to vote on account of race or color. By far the greatest object of Mansfield's concentration during the Johnson years, however, was the ongoing conflict in Vietnam.

By the summer of 1964, plans were under way to bolster American support of South Vietnam and commence air raids in North Vietnam. Mansfield repeatedly warned Johnson against the escalation and cautioned that if it must be done, the American people must be more convincingly marshaled behind the effort. The Tonkin Gulf Resolution was passed in response to charges that American war ships had been attacked in the gulf. The resolution affirmed the president's power to "take all necessary measures to repel any armed attack against the forces of the United States and to prevent further aggression."[50]

After the Tonkin Gulf incident, the pressure on President Johnson to expand America's presence in Vietnam increased. In December 1964, Mansfield wrote to Johnson: "We remain on a course in Vietnam which takes us further and further out on the sagging limb."[51] But Mansfield's was a lonely voice. Defense Secretary Robert McNamara, Secretary of State Dean Rusk, and National Security Advisor McGeorge Bundy all advised the president that vast expansion of American commitment in Vietnam was both necessary and inevitable. Within a few months, the first U.S. combat troops landed in Vietnam.

As late as May 1965, the U.S. force in Vietnam was limited to a relatively small contingent of 34,000. Word of a massive infusion of troops reached the Senate, and Mansfield vigorously denounced the plan. "We are in, not for a summer of pain and difficulty," he said on the Senate floor, "but for an ordeal of infinite duration and increasing sacrifice which will persist until the problem can be resolved at the conference table."[52] Mansfield persisted by pronouncing his opposition in a memo to the president. "Even if you win totally, you still do not come out well. What have you achieved? It is by no means a vital area of U.S. concern. . . . We are too deeply enmeshed in a place where we ought not to be. . . . The situation is rapidly growing out of control. . . . Every effort should be made to extricate ourselves."[53]

Over Mansfield's vehement dissent, the administration flooded Vietnam with American soldiers. By December 1965, when Mansfield and several colleagues made a fact-finding trip to Vietnam, nearly 170,000 young Americans had been funneled into the country. Mansfield decried the policy not only because he viewed American entanglement in Southeast Asia as imprudent and unnecessary, but also because he believed the White House was usurping congressional authority by immersing the country in a military conflict without a congressional declaration of war.

Nevertheless, Mansfield remained charitable and sympathetic toward Johnson personally. When Johnson announced his decision to send American combat troops to Vietnam, Mansfield watched him on television and said, "I feel so sorry for him. I can imagine what he is going through."[54] On the Senate floor in January 1966, Mansfield told his colleagues, "So far as the Senator from Montana is concerned, he will do his very best to give the President of the United States as much in the way of support as he possibly can."[55]

By April 1966, American forces in Vietnam and the contiguous waters exceeded 300,000. Senator Mansfield explained to his constituents: "The dominant concern in the Congress at this time is the same as in the nation. It is Vietnam. All other matters take second place. No other single issue in recent years has prompted so much searching of the national conscience, so much probing for an acceptable course of national action."[56] Mansfield warned, "If present trends continue, there is no assurance as to what ultimate increase in American military commitment will be required before the conflict is terminated."[57]

The war dragged on and the carnage mounted. By March 1968, more than 18,000 Americans had lost their lives and the wounded totaled over 110,000. In the first five weeks of 1968 alone, 1,674 Americans were killed. Majority Leader Mansfield addressed the Indiana University convocation of February 23, 1968, and his pain was evident:

> The struggle in Vietnam has turned grim, pitiless and devastating. The casualty figures are staggering. The physical damage is enormous. Men, women, children, soldiers, guerrillas, weapons, machines, cities, towns, and

villages—all are thrown together in an inferno of destruction. . . . I have no desire, therefore, to indulge, today, in
what has been a kind of parlor game called "who's winning in Vietnam?" It is offensive to me, as I know it must
be to you, to hear this deadly conflict treated as some sort
of athletic contest. The lives of too many young Americans are on the line in Vietnam. Too many bewildered
men and women and children are being burned, bloodied
and broken by this war. Too much is in ruins. Too many lie
dead. Vietnam is not a game. There can be no winners;
there are only losers and the longer the war persists the
greater are the losses for all concerned.[58]

Mansfield sadly explained that in spite of the immense effort of the United States, the Vietcong remained entrenched
along the Mekong Delta of South Vietnam and controlled
approximately the same percentage of the South Vietnamese
population as they had when American troops were first deployed in 1965. Mansfield chastised American policy for al-
tering "the character of what was once a struggle among
Vietnamese."[59] "To strip the Vietnamese struggle of its Vietnamese character," he pled, "to convert it into a war to be won
or lost by this nation, is to detract from its relevance both to the
people of Vietnam and to the people of the United States."[60]

Not long after this speech, President Johnson removed himself from the presidential campaign of 1968. During the
months that followed, the country seemed to come apart at
the seams in a year that has become known as the "crack in
time." Civil rights leader Martin Luther King, Jr., was gunned
down in Memphis, Tennessee, and a few weeks later presidential candidate Robert Kennedy was assassinated by a gunman
in California. Mandatory conscription had begun, and young
people cried out in fierce opposition to a war that made no
sense to them. While the mainstream of America denounced
the rebellious youth as treasonous, Mansfield heard their call
and stood up for their cause by advocating a constitutional
amendment to lower the voting age from twenty-one to eighteen years of age.

In a move that embroiled him in wild controversy back
home, Mansfield became a sponsor of S3634, the National Gun
Crime Prevention Act, calling for registration and licensing of

firearms. Montanans were furious about Mansfield's sponsorship of a gun-control bill and flooded his office with letters. Mansfield wrote back explaining that the people in America's inner cities did not use firearms properly and responsibly as Montanans had for many years. Instead, he explained, countless acts of gun violence are committed daily. Mansfield pointed out that in Washington, D.C., Thad Lesnick, a young marine from Fishtail, Montana, was shot to death while eating at a restaurant counter. Also in Washington, D.C., Mansfield reported, Harry Gelsin, a medical researcher from Helena, was dragged into an alley and shot point-blank by a group of thugs.

These tragedies, and not the shocking assassinations of President Kennedy, Dr. King, and Senator Kennedy, spurred Mansfield to back the comprehensive 1968 gun-control bill. At one point, Mansfield boldly announced, "As far as hand guns are concerned, it is my belief that they should not only be outlawed, as they are in the bill passed by the Senate, but that the most serious consideration should be given to restricting their use to law enforcement authorities or other persons qualified to use them in the line of duty."[61]

Mansfield argued that the act's registrations and licensing requirements would allow guns used in crimes to be quickly traced to their owner and should "weed out persons who, by reason of criminal record, drug addiction, alcoholism, mental incompetence, or age would not be intrusted with a gun in the first place."[62]

Mansfield's stand on gun control was bound to jeopardize his political security, and he knew it. "I know, as much as anyone else in this chamber, what voting on this bill means," Mansfield told his colleagues, "but I believe that those of us who come from the rural West have an obligation to the rest of the country; that all of us, regardless of where we come from, have an obligation to cut down on crime." With Mansfield's staunch and courageous support, S3634 was passed by the Senate and soon became law. The next year, Mansfield sponsored his own bill that required mandatory prison sentences for anyone who used a gun in the commission of a crime.

Richard Nixon assumed the presidency in 1969 after a campaign of promises to reduce the number of American troops in Vietnam. Initially, Mansfield urged support for Nixon's purported policy of troop reduction. Soon, however, Nixon claimed that the Vietnam War was supported by America's silent majority. Mansfield rejected that notion and lost faith in Nixon's sincerity.

In the spring of 1970 the war in Vietnam spilled over into Laos and then Cambodia. Since 1969 the United States had supported movements of Laotian government troops against Communist insurgents in northern Laos. In March 1970 Mansfield warned Nixon from the Senate floor against American involvement in Cambodia and Laos. "If the military see-saw goes down in Vietnam only to rise in Laos, our situation will not have improved; it will have worsened."[63] Mansfield's remarks were prescient, for less than two months later, American and South Vietnamese troops invaded neutral Cambodia.

An angry Congress responded to Nixon's Cambodian adventure with the Cooper-Church Amendment in June 1970, which effectively repealed the Tonkin Gulf Resolution. Mansfield helped to steer the amendment to a successful passage, decrying White House failures to exercise discretion prudently under the Tonkin Gulf Resolution. Mansfield backed a Senate resolution urging withdrawal of American troops from Indochina and relentlessly pressed his arguments against the waste of money and lives in that nonvital region.

On the subject of the expense of war, Mansfield testified before a Senate subcommittee that resources had been allocated toward "military white elephants with a billion dollar price tag," at the expense of "the essential ingredients of a healthy and secure society—good education and health, decent living conditions for all, a safe and clean environment and the absence of poverty."[64]

As a candidate for reelection in 1970, Mansfield sounded similar themes, explaining that "well over one hundred billion U.S. dollars have disappeared in the flames of that conflict. The cost is currently running at over twenty-five billion dollars a year. No economy can take that kind of drain indefinitely without severe strains and damage."[65] Mansfield also emphasized that 50,000 young Americans had lost their lives in the "barbaric war" and 400,000 Americans remained in South Vietnam at that time. Mansfield firmly advocated American withdrawal. For financial reasons, Mansfield also advocated more than halving the American military personnel stationed in Europe.

Mansfield easily won reelection in 1970, despite his forceful and controversial opposition to American involvement in Vietnam, his sympathy toward student opponents of the war, and his sponsorship of the 1968 Gun Control Act.

By 1971 the bill for Vietnam had risen to $130 billion, and Mansfield called the conflict "a root cause of the nation's present economic difficulties."[66] He declared that ending the war was "the most compelling business of this nation," and mourned that "Vietnam is a human tragedy which tears at the fibers of the nation's cohesion."[67]

Between the 1970 military coup d'etat in Cambodia and the final months of 1971, the numbers of American solders there had increased more than tenfold. Mansfield continued to castigate the Cambodian facet of the Indochina conflict in particular, charging that "hundreds of millions of dollars already spent in a year and a half have done hardly anything for the defense of this nation except, perhaps, to weaken it by wastage. Nor have these expenditures helped the Cambodian people who have now been reduced the common denominator of the irrelevant devastation which has been suffered in Laos and Vietnam."[68]

By 1972 with his reelection campaign approaching, President Nixon announced that negotiations with the North Vietnamese were under way. Mansfield then reiterated his consistent position that America had no business in Vietnam, an area not vital to the security of the nation, and called the war "the greatest tragedy which has ever befallen this republic."[69] Mansfield declared unmistakably that the only satisfactory conclusion to the conflict was complete withdrawal, "lock stock and barrel."

In January 1972, he told the Senate Democratic Conference, in his courteous but candid way: "May I say, with all due respect, that it is not enough to wind down the war in Vietnam. The residual obligation is to wind this nation completely out of the war in Indochina and to extricate our forces from the entire Southeast Asian mainland."[70] A month before his reelection, Nixon announced that "peace is at hand," although Americans remained in Vietnam. Mansfield replied, "It is long since past time to start worrying about saving face, and concentrate on saving lives and our sense of decency and humanity."[71]

Nixon removed most of the American troops from Vietnam in 1972 but enlarged the theater of the conflict in Cambodia and Laos. Mansfield chastised Nixon for digging America "deeper into another tragic military involvement, inflicting one more vast compass of devastation on one more hapless land in support of one more irrelevant government, in one more obscure region of Indochina."[72]

Eventually, the opponents of America's presence in Vietnam became a clear, vocal majority, and the last American soldiers were evacuated from Vietnam by order of President Gerald Ford on April 29, 1975. Mansfield deserves much of the credit for shifting American public opinion to the point that final withdrawal became politically feasible, if not necessary. In the beginning, only a handful of senators dared to speak out against the war in Vietnam, and among them only Mansfield had the unassailable credibility slowly to change people's minds. He had foreseen the conflict and warned against it early in the Eisenhower years. After American involvement escalated in spite of his warnings, he doggedly reiterated his condemnation of the whole affair, pleading for the withdrawal of young Americans.

Year after year, the bodies piled up—bodies of boys plucked out of American high schools. Year after year, the financial cost drained strength from the American economy. Mansfield's firm reasoning became unanswerable, and the tide of public opinion finally turned his way. It took a long time for that to happen, and Mansfield considered his slow success in this area to be his greatest disappointment as majority leader. But Mansfield was probably as responsible as any public leader for the fact that public opinion ultimately did demand withdrawal from Southeast Asia. As one commentator noted:

> It was largely because of Mansfield, however, that antiwar sentiment became acceptable not only for those with fashionably long hair and fashionably strident speech, but for middle Americans as well. . . . Mike Mansfield made it difficult to engage in name calling or questioning of motives or patriotism, a tactic each succeeding administration has tried. His reputation, integrity and patriotism are beyond question.[73]

As one national crisis drew to a close, another began. On January 16, 1973, Mansfield dispatched letters to the leading figures in the Nixon reelection campaign, informing them that the Senate intended to investigate the events surrounding the break-in at the Democratic National Committee headquarters in the Watergate building. Mansfield instructed the recipients to retain and preserve all records and documents pertaining to the campaign.[74]

In April Nixon demanded and received the resignation of numerous White House staff members, including presidential assistants Robert Haldeman and John Ehrlichman and presidential counsel John Dean. Hearings in the Senate Select Committee on Presidential Campaign Activities, chaired by Sen. Sam Ervin, were well under way by April 30 when Nixon announced the purging to the American people. Mansfield was careful not to raise accusations against anyone prematurely but firmly stated that the investigation would uncover every stone before it was through.

By the end of October 1973, lurid details about dirty campaign tricks and big money payoffs began to emerge in the testimony of witnesses before the committee. Then, Attorney General Elliott Richardson and Deputy Attorney General William Ruckelshaus resigned after refusing to fire special prosecutor Archibald Cox at Nixon's request. Cox was then fired by Solicitor General Robert Bourke. Nixon's cronies contended that the investigation was compromising national security by damaging ongoing U.S. negotiations in the Middle East. They demanded that the inquiry stop, but Mansfield stood firm, resolutely asking the Senate to extend the authority of the Select Committee.

Dismissing the administration's scare tactics, Mansfield advised: "We would do well . . . to avoid in the name of foreign policy a pretense of national well being when the people are profoundly disturbed by what they see and hear in Washington."[75] Mansfield commended the Senate for proceeding in "an orderly and impartial fashion and without any suggestion whatsoever of partisan politics. They moved deliberately but relentlessly," he said, "to bring about the facts of illegality. They uncovered these facts in great numbers and in sordid detail. They laid them bare for the nation to see and for the Congress to act upon in order that what transpired in the name of a free election does not happen again."[76]

Senator Ervin's committee marched on. By April 1974, there were rustlings of impeachment or resignation. As he pru-

dently and resolutely oversaw the exhaustive Ervin committee investigation, Mansfield cautioned against vigilantism. He
warned his colleagues that they must always ask, "Are we
shunting aside the basic principals of law which presume the
innocence of the accused until found guilty? . . . Are we exer-
cising restraint and patience?"[77] As the evidence of Nixon's
wrongdoing mounted, impeachment by the House and conviction by the Senate seemed inevitable. So, on August 9, 1974,
Richard Nixon resigned the presidency of the United States.

On March 4, 1976, Mansfield announced the end of his own career in Washington. After thirty-four years in the United States
Congress, he told his colleagues and the public on that day that
he would not seek reelection. In his farewell speech, he noted
that his years in Congress encompassed one-sixth of the nation's history since independence and the administrations of
seven presidents. He briefly expressed his gratitude to the nation, the Senate and the people of Montana for "the great public trust" that had been reposed in him. "There is a time to stay
and a time to go," he said. "Thirty-four years is not a long time,
but it is time enough."[78]

The spontaneous tributes from colleagues who happened to
be on the floor lasted nearly an hour. Republicans and Democrats alike hailed Mansfield for his integrity, intellect, fairness
and compassion. On September 16, 1976, Mansfield's final day
in the Senate, the final hours of the Ninety-fourth Congress
were taken up with tributes that occupied twenty-five printed
pages in the *Congressional Record*.

Mansfield, too, extended his remarks and reinforced his
faith in the U.S. Senate as a tool and bulwark of the people. "So
long as the Senate persists," he assured his colleagues, "I am
confident that the liberties of the American people will be
maintained and the government of the republic will remain
receptive to their needs and aspirations. . . . I do not leave this
place in sadness. I leave as one who has lived as a part of it and
loved it deeply."[79]

When Mike Mansfield walked off the Senate floor that day, he
and Maureen intended to retire, but freshly elected President
Jimmy Carter had other ideas. He wanted Mansfield to join the
foreign-policy team in the new administration. He offered

Mansfield the position of ambassador to Mexico, but Mike respectfully declined. Next, he asked Mansfield to be the ambassador to Japan. After discussing the option with Maureen and considering his lifelong interest in Far Eastern affairs, the seventy-three-year-old Mansfield embarked on yet another career.

Soon, Mike and Maureen had settled into their new home in Tokyo, and Mansfield stood before his first Japanese press conference. "Ladies and gentlemen," he announced, "I am the new boy on the block. Shoot."[80] On that note, the Land of the Rising Sun was introduced to the Gary Cooper of American politics, marking the advent of a long relationship of profound mutual respect.

After serving the longest term as majority leader in the history of the United States Senate, Mansfield began what would become the longest tenure as his country's ambassador to Japan. He served as America's chief liaison in a country where the United States dropped two atomic bombs and where, barely thirty years later, the native people had built an economy so powerful and vibrant that many Americans feared the consequences of free trade. Simultaneously, the other major cities of the Pacific basin of Asia were asserting themselves as international financial powers. The potential for transpacific conflict required the most delicate diplomatic treatment. As usual, Mansfield handled the competing forces adroitly.

Consistent with his thirty-four-year congressional career, Mansfield built his service in Japan on a foundation of candor and sensitivity. Some Americans felt that he was too sensitive to Japan, at the expense of American interest, but Mansfield emphasized that "our interdependence is a fact that we deny at our own peril."[81] Mansfield opposed protectionism and encouraged Americans to develop a new relationship among management, labor, and government consistent with the framework that had been so successful on the Pacific Rim.

When Jimmy Carter was defeated by Ronald Reagan in 1980, Mansfield's position was in jeopardy. The ambassador clearly served at the pleasure of the president, and Reagan was unlikely to retain Carter appointees. Mike contacted former president Gerald Ford to speak with Reagan about keeping Mansfield on. Ford, who was grateful to Mansfield for advocating his appointment as vice president to Richard Nixon, did just that. Reagan granted Ford's request, and Mansfield became the only Carter ambassador reappointed by the Reagan administration.

Meanwhile, Mansfield's stature continued to grow in Japan. He was respected for his personal humility and advancing age, as well as his careful attention to the feelings of the Japanese. Mansfield biographer Charles Hood explains that Mansfield "has not done the usual things that an envoy would do to ingratiate himself. He hasn't learned the language. He doesn't particularly like the food—he is a meat and potatoes guy. Yet, he is sensitive to the most important requirements for understanding a culture."[82]

An often repeated anecdote illustrates the manner that endeared Mansfield to the Japanese people. In 1981 a U.S. nuclear submarine inadvertently collided with and sank a Japanese freighter ship. The U.S. sub fled the scene, leaving Japanese sailors floating in the sea, waving for help. For several days, the navy denied the event, but Mansfield visited the Japanese foreign ministry, apologized formally, and bowed deeply to the Japanese officials, as reports and photographs captured the diplomatic event for the Japanese public.[83]

In 1988 Mansfield was sidelined for several months after a triple-bypass heart operation and prostate surgery. Many observers speculated that Mansfield would retire. When he returned to his normal 7:00 A.M. to 4:00 P.M. routine, he was asked about the speculation by a *New York Times* reporter. "Never thought of it," he said, closing the discussion.[84] Mansfield continued to work for a comprehensive trade agreement between Japan and the United States, "based on reciprocity and equal opportunity." He repeatedly advised American officials that "the next century, indubitably, will be the century of the Pacific."[85]

By January 1989, Mansfield was ready to call it quits. He announced, once and for all, his retirement from public life. The quality of his service may be judged partly by the reaction he inspired from the leaders of the two countries he worked so hard to bring together. In 1983 Japanese Prime Minister Yasuhiro Nakasone wrote to Mansfield: "Your valuable contribution to enhancing mutual understanding and friendship between our two great nations deserves highest esteem."[86]

On the occasion of his retirement, on January 19, 1989,

President Reagan invited Mansfield to the White House to receive the Medal of Freedom, the nation's highest civilian award. As he presented the medal, the outgoing Republican president declared, "Mike Mansfield has set his indelible mark upon American foreign policy and distinguished himself as a dedicated public servant and loyal American."[87]

At eighty-six years of age, Mansfield determined that his useful years were not over. He returned to Washington, D.C., where he accepted a position with the international investment firm of Goldman-Sacks. Now over ninety, he continues a regular daily work schedule in which he advises American businesses and helps pave the way for their successful operation in and with the Asian Pacific basin.

Mansfield's life must rank among the most interesting and significant of American public careers. He rose from modest circumstances to become one of the most powerful and widely respected public leaders in the world. His Senate colleagues and his constituents held him in the highest esteem because of his personal qualities. This esteem was never diminished by the firm and sometimes stubborn positions Mansfield staked out on controversial principles that he believed in.

Jack Valenti, a former aide to President Johnson, explained that Mansfield "didn't hide his strongly held views. . . . people mistake courtesy and civility for deference. That is a misreading of a man's demeanor. Mansfield was one of the most dignified people I have every known, but Mansfield bent his knee to man's opinion."[88] As ambassador to Japan, Mansfield said "I try to put myself in the shoes of the Japanese, but I have never forgotten that the shoes I wear are American and that my country's interests come first."[89]

His wisdom was born of careful study and dispassionate consideration. His respect was won with courage and empathy. The nation is different and better because he lived, and Mike Mansfield's career continues to shine as an example of excellence in public leadership.

Suggested Readings on Mike Mansfield

The story of Mansfield's early life is colorfully told and carefully documented in Charles Hood's doctoral dissertation at

Washington State University: "'China Mike' Mansfield, the Making of a Congressional Authority on the Far East" (Pullman, Washington, 1980). Hood's dissertation is the most detailed account of this period of Mansfield's life. Background information in the foregoing chapter—about Mansfield's youth, education, and early career—is drawn largely from this work.

A well-written general biography of Mansfield is Jim Ludwick's *Mansfield, the Senator from Montana* (Missoula, 1988), a series of articles published in the *Missoulian* and reprinted in booklet form. Although Ludwick's work contains no footnotes, it is an excellent source of background information about Mansfield's life and career. A useful compilation of Mansfield's most significant Senate speeches appears in Louis Baldwin, *Hon. Politician, Mike Mansfield of Montana* (Missoula, 1979). Baldwin's book begins with a thirty-page biography of Mansfield. For a broad discussion of Mansfield's thinking on the Vietnam issue, see Gregory A. Olson, *Mansfield and Vietnam: A Study in Rhetorical Adaptation* (East Lansing, Michigan, 1995).

The Mansfield Papers, which are voluminous, are kept in the University of Montana Archives, Missoula, Montana. These papers contain most of the speeches Mansfield made, beginning in 1939 with his first congressional race. The Montana Historical Society's Mike Mansfield vertical files contain copies of many newspaper and magazine articles written about Mansfield during his career. Speeches by Mansfield's colleagues on the occasion of his retirement from the Senate appear in the *Congressional Record* and are reprinted by the U.S. Government Printing Office in *Tributes to the Honorable Mike Mansfield of Montana* (Washington, D.C., 1976).

Specific election results for Mansfield are documented in Ellis Waldron and Paul B. Wilson, *Atlas of Montana Elections* (Missoula, 1978).

IX

Lee Metcalf,
the Modern Populist

There is no clearer lesson in history than that men and nations underwrite their own destruction as they violate the inexorable laws of nature—and unwisely use and waste basic resources.

"The Senate will be in order," demanded Senator Metcalf as he hammered the presiding officer's desk with the ivory gavel that Indian premier Nehru had given the country for moments such as this. The upper house had finally decided to take up the controversial civil rights bill and senators, abuzz on the floor, ignored the presiding officer. Metcalf, Democrat from Montana and acting president pro tempore of the Senate, glared at his colleagues who were nonchalantly chatting in the front row. He pounded the gavel again and his voice boomed through the chamber: "The Senate is now in order!" The Senate fell silent and the startled members quietly and quickly took their seats. They knew Metcalf meant business—and not business as usual.[1]

They had witnessed his fierceness many times. From the day he stepped into the House of Representatives in 1953, Lee Metcalf was an indomitable force. This was the man who had built a power base for young, liberal house members. This was the man who, after a few short years in Congress, had earned the title Mr. Education. This was the man who awakened America to its obligation of stewardship toward the earth and confronted the most powerful businesses in America with an

Senator Lee Metcalf. Metcalf served a term on the Montana Supreme Court before being elected to Congress in 1952. Drawing on his expertise as a utilities regulation lawyer, Senator Metcalf exposed excessive profits and public misrepresentations by investor-owned utilities, which he called "IOUs."
Courtesy of Montana Historical Society, Helena.

iron fist. Even as he commanded the Senate to order that day in 1964, this also was a man who was just getting started.

He rose from the land and the people of Montana and became their voice in the corridors of national power. His political world was a forum for advocacy—a battlefield on which the causes of real people were defended and advanced. By standing boldly for populist causes, he transformed citizen concern and grassroots effort into public policy. He inherited the legacy of the great western Progressives and carried their torch into the 1970s. Like his ancestors in that movement, Metcalf distrusted the captains of big business and fought their excesses openly.

His friends and foes called him tough, irascible, tenacious, loyal, shy, combative, compassionate, and smart. He raised the ire of many, but was the object of wide respect. The greatness of his career was underrated and underpublicized, partly because he shunned the spotlight of national media, partly because his passions concerned issues thought to be mundane by the press, and partly because his battles were fought in the shadows cast by his eminent colleague, Senate Majority Leader Mike Mansfield. Metcalf was called "the invisible senator," but the power of his presence in Congress as a champion for the "little guy" was undeniable.

Metcalf was burly, like a lumberjack, with rugged features and a bull voice. His intellect was equally formidable, and his quick temper could be unleashed explosively. He was a lawyer with a passion for the Constitution and an abiding faith in the American system of justice. His congressional career was built on this foundation. Metcalf did not join the Congress to wrap himself in the trappings of prestige and celebrity. He was a legislator with an agenda and a constituency. He served them aggressively and fearlessly, preserving and protecting America's natural heritage, exposing the inequities of the private utility industry, pushing open the gates for federal aid to education, and unveiling the secret consolidations of corporate America. Lee Metcalf did not stake out a haven near the middle of the road. He fought the power. "Take a position and stand up for it," he said, and that is what he did.

Lee Metcalf was born January 28, 1911, in Montana's Bitterroot Valley, later making him the Treasure State's first native-born

United States senator. Lee's father, Harold Metcalf, was the cashier of the First State Bank of Stevensville, but Lee grew up on the family's 300-acre farm outside of town. The Metcalf family was deeply rooted in Ravalli County. Harold's father was a contractor and the owner of a small lumber company, and his family had helped to build the Big Ditch that provided irrigation to the valley's vast orchards.

Lee's mother, Rhoda Smith, was a well-educated woman who attended the University of Montana until she was married. Perhaps because of her influence, Lee developed a voracious reading appetite and an early interest in public affairs. Rhoda's father, who lived in the Bitterroot, was from the Midwest and subscribed to the *St. Louis Globe Democrat*. Lee digested the paper's thorough analysis of public issues and listened to political talk from the Midwest on the crystal radio set that he built himself. As he did his schoolwork, Lee could follow the outspoken, populist campaigns of Sen. Robert LaFollette, Sen. George Norris, and others, including Montana's own firebrand radical, Burton K. Wheeler.

The Metcalfs' farm life was more a function of tradition than necessity. Harold's banking job was the family's primary source of income, but he believed in the virtues of the agrarian lifestyle, and the Metcalfs actively worked their small acreage. Lee plowed the fields and milked the cows. His mother ran the separator and Lee earned pin money delivering milk and cream to the townsfolk.

In high school, Lee was a strong student and dedicated athlete. He graduated from Stevensville High School in 1928 and enrolled at Montana State University in Missoula, where he played as a first-string tackle for the freshman football team. After a year at Missoula, Lee moved to California and spent a year working for the Los Angeles City School Gardens. Los Angeles was a flourishing, blooming area and Lee's experience at the gardens helped him develop a lifetime interest in horticulture. In 1930 Metcalf enrolled at Stanford University where he undertook his work for a bachelor's degree in economics and history. He played football at Stanford, as well, under the great Glenn "Pop" Warner, and won distinction on the Stanford track team until his career was cut short by knee injuries.

In 1933 Metcalf returned to Missoula and the law school of Montana State University. He was a senior with a successful scholastic record when he met Donna Hoover of Wallace, Idaho, a journalism student who was a columnist for the school paper and editor of the university's yearbook. "I was really very timid," says Mrs. Metcalf of herself in those days, but she was no shrinking violet in the field of journalism.[2] Remarkably, she was awarded the outstanding student journalist award by Sigma Delta Chi, the *men's* journalism society.

Donna got her bachelor's degree in 1935 and went to work as a secretary to the School of Journalism. She and Lee continued to date, but Lee was absorbed in his studies and fraternal activities with his classmates. "We were both pretty independent," Mrs. Metcalf recalls.[3] His studies paid off and Lee received his law degree at the top of his class in 1936.

He was just twenty-five years old, but Lee's sights were already set on political leadership. He returned to Stevensville, rented an apartment in an old house owned by his grandfather, and established a small law office on the second floor of a Main Street building across from the bank. A legislative seat in Ravalli County was open and Metcalf declared his candidacy. Although his parents were both Republican, Lee had developed an allegiance to the Democratic Party. A few years earlier, in 1932, he persuaded his parents to vote for Franklin Roosevelt, who promised to be the agent of change and stood for the same populist principles that Lee had read and heard about as boy. When he became a candidate himself, Lee drove around Ravalli County in a Chevy coupe plastered with big signs announcing "Metcalf for Legislature." His campaign was successful, and Lee took his seat in the Twenty-fifth Legislative Assembly at Helena in 1937.

Young Metcalf had considered himself a conservative—his friends from law school went on to become leaders in Montana's corporate community. During this first legislative term though, Metcalf's progressive colors surfaced. He later recalled:

> ... Every time I met the issues on a logical, reasonable and rational basis, ... I found myself voting with the working man, and all at once I was in trouble with the business community. ... Believe it or not, I introduced a bill to establish a thirty cent minimum wage in Montana and it failed.[4]

In the session of 1937, the Anaconda Copper Company still held sway at the capitol in Helena. Mining remained the state's biggest industry, and one of Metcalf's first acts was introduction of a bill that was antagonistic to the Company. It was a common practice in those days for the Company to leave miners sitting around for an hour or more at the bottom of a mine at the end of their shift while the ore was brought up first. The miners served the time, but the Company did not pay them for it. Metcalf's bill sought to force the Company to pay the miner from the time he went down the shaft until the time he came back. It was a courageous step for the twenty-five-year-old legislator, because it marked him as a troublemaker in the eyes of the state's power structure, but Metcalf believed in the working man and the working man began to believe in Lee Metcalf.

After completing his legislative service, Lee returned to Stevensville and his fledgling private law practice. Then, in August, Montana attorney general Harrison Freeborn asked Lee to serve as assistant attorney general. Metcalf accepted the appointment and, with this stable job, took Donna Hoover's hand in marriage.

At twenty-seven, Lee was the youngest assistant attorney general in Montana's history. He had earned a reputation in the legislature as a people's advocate and he retained that image defending the state Public Utilities Commission and other state regulatory agencies in lawsuits brought by the Anaconda Company, the Northern Pacific and Great Northern Railroads, and the Montana Power Company. These experiences were formative for Metcalf. In later years he frequently recounted his frustration with the disparity of legal power at the administrative hearings he attended. He faced corporate counsel and company executives many years his senior. As a senator, he recalled:

> So I would carry my briefcase into the rate hearing as one
> of my many extra-curricular duties, and there would be a
> whole retinue of attorneys for the private power industry.
> Some of them had been my instructors at law school, and
> I had only been out of school a couple of years. I resented
> the idea that the people's representative was so thoroughly overwhelmed.[5]

In 1940 Freeborn ran for the Senate and lost. In the final weeks of his term as attorney general, he tapped Metcalf to serve as chief assistant attorney general, but Metcalf also would leave as the office changed hands in 1941. Metcalf wrapped up his duties and returned to the Bitterroot a little older, a little wiser, and possessed of a commitment to redressing the imbalance between citizens and giant special interests.

By December 7, 1941, Lee had not practiced law for more than a few months in Hamilton, Montana, when the news of Pearl Harbor came to him and Donna over the radio, as it did to millions of other Americans. A day later the nation was at war. His country called, and thirty-one-year-old Lee Metcalf enlisted as a soldier in the United States Army.

After a going-away party and parade, Lee and other Montana recruits were sent to Fort Lewis, Washington, for basic training. After boot camp, Metcalf was shipped to southern California for desert warfare training and to Texas where he became a commissioned officer with the 607th Tank Destroyer Battalion. From Texas, the army sent Metcalf to Battle Creek, Michigan, for military-government classes, and to Boston University for instruction in the German language. In 1943 he was deployed to England where he continued his training.

Forty-eight hours after D day, when only a thousand yards of beach had been secured, Metcalf landed in Normandy. He took part in five campaigns through France, Belgium and Germany, including the Battle of the Bulge, serving with the 1st Army and 9th Infantry Division. After Allied troops captured the city of Aachen, Germany, Metcalf was sent to reorganize the police and court systems and to enforce military regulations on the civilian population. At the close of the war, Lee helped supervise the quartering, feeding, and repatriation of displaced people.

After two years of overseas service, Metcalf was honorably discharged in 1946 and returned to Montana where he was reunited with his wife and home. Returning veterans had already organized active new chapters of the Veterans of Foreign Wars and American Legion. The men who returned from Europe were heroes and those inclined toward government service came home with enviable political capital. Metcalf was one of them. Upon his return to Hamilton, Lee learned that

Justice Leif Erickson had given up his seat on the Montana Supreme Court to challenge Burton K. Wheeler for the United States Senate. Metcalf had barely unpacked his bags when he decided to file for Erickson's court seat.

At age thirty-five, Lee Metcalf was unusually young for a Supreme Court candidate. His opponents labeled him a "legal stripling" and dismissed his chances. "Nobody thought he could win," Donna Metcalf recalls, but the naysayers underestimated Metcalf's political acumen and popular support.[6] Donna's father lent the young couple a car on which they pasted campaign signs. With the donated wheels and a second-hand suit Lee bought from a friend of the Hoovers in Wallace, Metcalf began his journey around Montana to win support.

Metcalf was able to call upon a network of friends made during his term in the legislature. With the assistance of William Anthony "Tony" Boyle, who was then district representative for the United Mine Workers in Montana, Metcalf strengthened his ties with labor. "Tony Boyle and I went around to nearly every mine workers community," Metcalf later said. "He really helped me. Tony, so far as I was concerned in those days was a terrific individual. A militant, aggressive liberal, and I was certainly delighted to have his support."[7] Years later, in a speech on the floor of the United States Senate, Metcalf sympathetically described Boyle as "a man who bridles at injustice and arouses the indifferent to action."[8]

Metcalf served a full six-year term on the Montana Supreme Court, a chapter of his life that inspired an eternal love for the law and the adversary process that pervaded his actions as a legislator throughout his later career. He also developed a reputation as a jurist for his keen legal intellect. But one term on the court was enough and, in 1952, state Democratic Party leaders urged Metcalf to run for the congressional seat being vacated by Mike Mansfield.

Metcalf accepted the bid and captured the Democratic nomination for the Western District congressional seat. The First Congressional District, encompassing the mountainous, western third of the state was then still known as the "safest Democratic district in the West," because of the dominant roll played by the politically active and Democratically inclined labor camps of Butte and Anaconda. Justice Metcalf prevailed easily in the fall election and became Congressman Metcalf.

Metcalf's congressional career began in 1953. When he arrived in Washington, he learned the custom that younger members of the House were to be seen but not heard. They were to march deferentially in step with the party leadership, leaving little room for independent policy judgment. Since the inception of the Republic, the expectation of blind adherence by newcomers was never challenged. Metcalf, and a band of fellow liberals in the freshman class of 1953, however, chafed under the system's strict requirements. They believed that the newer members could and should be heard and that an effective liberal coalition was necessary to counterbalance the unified power of the southern Democrats and conservative Republicans.

Out of a coalition developed by Metcalf, Eugene McCarthy, and others, for conservation battles in the Eighty-third Congress, a growing group of young, liberal members began holding informal issue conferences and agreeing to vote together on matters of common concern. They called themselves the Democratic Study Group, or DSG, and they weighed in as a substantial new voting bloc in the House. As a principal leader of the group, Metcalf explained that new members of Congress were systematically thwarted in their efforts to provide effective representation to their constituents. The coalition was necessary both to ensure meaningful participation by new members and to reflect the contemporary forces of the country that had sent the new members to Congress. The leadership was not happy with this team of vocal rookies, but the voting power of the new alliance could not be denied.

On one occasion, a bill calling for higher interest rates was reported out of the Ways and Means Committee. DSG members firmly opposed the bill and hoped to stop it on the House floor. When it was announced that the bill would be considered on the floor without debate or amendments, Metcalf appeared in the offices of House Speaker Sam Rayburn and House Majority Leader John McCormack, demanding a meeting between DSG members and the House leadership. Rayburn and McCormack agreed and the meeting was set for that afternoon.

McCormack, apparently expecting only a handful of members, told Metcalf to bring his friends into McCormack's office. When three o'clock came, according to Metcalf, "a howling mob" of ninety-some congressmen descended upon McCormack's office. Aghast at the turnout, McCormack announced to the group, "I was a liberal before you were born!"[9] McCormack said that he agreed that debate on the bill should be extended and amendments allowed but that Ways and Means Chairman Wilbur Mills had insisted on the rule, closing the floor to debate and amendments. Metcalf's DSG was undaunted. The entire "mob" marched into Mills's office and demanded recognition on the bill. A defensive Mills was evasive and made no promises, but the message was clear enough— the bill never even came to a vote.

After several years, the DSG and the House leadership reconciled. The group was recognized formally as an official House organization in 1959 and Metcalf, then serving his fourth congressional term was elected as the group's first official chairman.

Metcalf's legislative achievements in the House were significant. As a freshman in the Eighty-third Congress, he helped defeat a grazing bill sponsored by Montana's conservative Eastern District Congressman Wesley D'Ewart, which would have raised grazing permits on federal lands to the level of ownership, for practical purposes. Metcalf charged that the bill would have made "monopolization of public ranges certain."[10]

In the second session of that Congress, Metcalf was floor leader of the members who stopped the Elsworth Timber Exchange Bill. Advocated by powerful lumber interests, the bill would have "swapped forested public lands for cutover private lands."[11] Metcalf argued that the proposal amounted to "trading trees for stumps."[12] Metcalf and his coalition stopped the bill, winning a major victory for conservationism. One writer later commented that "it was a remarkable victory for a freshman Congressman."[13]

Metcalf also played a key roll in efforts to block the proposed Echo Park Dam that threatened Dinosaur National Monument. In 1956 he cosponsored with Hubert Humphrey the nation's first wilderness bill, which was eventually embodied in the Wilderness Act of 1964. The same year he also instigated a comprehensive study of the effects of pesticides on fish and wildlife. The study caused funding to be provided for Rachel Carson's research, which led to the publication of *Silent*

Lee Metcalf at Canyon Ferry Lake, outside Helena. Metcalf was a father of American wilderness laws. He led the effort to enact the first wilderness designation legislation and forced changes in timber harvest practices.
Courtesy of Montana Historical Society, Helena.

Spring, a milestone exposé that helped to spawn the ecology movement of the 1960s and 1970s.

Metcalf's vigorous efforts to protect the earth and its resources in the 1950s predated the modern era of environmental consciousness, marking the young congressman as a brave forerunner in the area. In 1954 Metcalf was cited for distinguished service to conservation by the five major conservation organizations—the National Wildlife Federation, the National Parks Association, the Izaak Walton League of America, the Wilderness Society, and the Wildlife Management Institute.

Also in the House, Metcalf began his long series of legislative battles against the private power industry. When the air force attempted to purchase power for a massive communication system exclusively from private power companies, Metcalf spearheaded the effort to guarantee that purchases would be made from rural electric and telephone cooperatives as well. Again, Metcalf and his forces succeeded and law was enacted to require that cooperative and private power companies be treated equally by the air force in this communications program.

During his last term in the House, 1958–60, Metcalf intro-

duced a comprehensive bill providing for federal aid to education—legislation that would earn him the cloakroom title of
Mr. Education. The bill was originally introduced in the Senate
by Montana's senator James E. Murray. Metcalf sponsored the
House counterpart. The Murray-Metcalf Bill stirred fiery
protest, not only from conservatives but also from teachers
and leaders in education who vigorously opposed any federal
involvement in local education. Metcalf was unimpressed by
the opposition and pressed forward.

The bill was approved by the House Education and Labor
Committee, but was stalled by the Rules Committee and failed
to reach the House floor. Even the DSG, a securely ensconced
body by then, was unable to pry loose the grip of the Rules
Committee on the bill until after the election of the Democratic administration in 1960. Had the bill been passed by the
House in 1959, the effort would have been futile. The bill
failed by one vote in the Senate, as Vice President Richard
Nixon cast the tie-breaking vote against the measure.

As the career of James Murray demonstrated on many occasions, it often happens that failed legislation in Congress
plants seeds that, nurtured over time, eventually grow to
fruition. Such was the case with the Murray-Metcalf Bill. It
died in the Eighty-fifth Congress, but was resurrected in pieces
throughout the Kennedy administration and was finally embodied in the omnibus Elementary and Secondary Education
Bill of 1965. Metcalf, then acting president pro tempore of the
Senate, joined House Speaker John McCormack and President
Lyndon Johnson as signatories of the act.

Following final passage and signing of the new law, Sen.
Wayne Morse of Oregon acknowledged Metcalf's vital roll
from the Senate floor:

> I see on the back row a Senator who is not a member of
> the committee, the Senator from Montana (Mr. Metcalf),
> but when he was in the House of Representatives, he
> came to have a label attached to him, "Mr. Education."
> The Senator from Montana has consulted with me and
> other members of the subcommittee time and time again
> on bill after bill as we have taken this legislation through
> the committee.[14]

. . .

In 1960 Metcalf resolved to leave the House. Montana's great senator James Murray was old and had lost his vitality, but was considering running for a final term. Metcalf looked at the governor's race in Montana as well as Murray's Senate seat, but faced a difficult political decision given Murray's reluctance to leave office. *The People's Voice*, a staunchly liberal Helena newspaper, wrote:

> Metcalf is considered the strongest Democrat in Montana—he is a strong and respected Democrat in Washington, too, which is the source of his strength here at home, of course, and there aren't many politicians that would run against him in a campaign with much hope of winning—Republican or Democratic—whatever office he decided to take on.[15]

Metcalf received a letter from Judge Joe Strinisha of Hamilton, urging him to run for the Senate seat. "I would like to offer you this piece of humble advice," he wrote. "If you feel as you say in your letter, that Mr. Murray's physical condition is such, that his former capabilities are no longer dependable, that this could mean the loss of this important seat . . . then by all means file for the senator's seat."[16] A few days later, Metcalf announced his candidacy for the United States Senate. In his letter responding to Judge Strinisha, he wrote:

> My poll, my conversations with my friends, my mail, all confirmed the probability that Senator Murray would lose in the primary and, if nominated, would be decisively defeated in the general election. This was the decisive factor in arriving at my decision to file.[17]

House Speaker Sam Rayburn was sorry to see Metcalf go. He was widely believed to have picked Metcalf as the young House member most likely to rise to the speakership. Senator Murray, on the other hand, was rankled by Metcalf's decision to announce before Murray had released his retirement plans. Nevertheless, Murray ultimately bowed out and Metcalf prevailed in the 1960 election, narrowly defeating conservative Republican Orvin Fjare.

Fresh out of the blocks as a United States senator, Metcalf was appointed to the Migratory Bird Conservation Commission, where he served from 1961 through 1975. The commission received and judged proposals for additions to the National Waterfowl Refuge System. Metcalf attended every commission meeting during his tenure and participated in decisions to purchase a total of 525,000 acres of land and to create forty-three new refuges. One of the areas set aside by the commission was the national wildlife refuge just north of Stevensville in the Bitterroot Valley, which after Lee Metcalf's death would be renamed the Lee Metcalf National Wildlife Refuge.

Metcalf brought to the Senate his broad conservationist philosophy. In 1961 he wrote:

> There is no clearer lesson in history than that men and nations underwrite their own destruction as they violate the inexorable laws of nature—and unwisely use and waste basic resources. . . . America's ghost towns, once thriving communities, are tombstones to dead resources. They are monuments to exploitation in lumbering, grazing, commercial fishing and farming . . . men and interests who had a reason for doing so have fought conservation with bitterness and in many cases with success. The war is raging still, and it is yet very far from being won.[18]

In 1962 Metcalf introduced the Save Our Streams (SOS) Bill to protect fish, wildlife, and recreation resources threatened by the interstate highway system, which had been under construction since 1956. Montana residents had come to Metcalf fearing destruction of the Gallatin River Canyon as a result of highway construction. The SOS Bill would have required the secretary of the interior to ensure that recreation resources had been considered in highway planning.

The SOS Bill never became law, but Metcalf and his colleagues succeeded in persuading the Kennedy administration to issue an executive order requiring coordination of highway building and conservation activities. Metcalf's initiative was also reflected later in the National Environmental Policy Act of 1970, which did become law and required consideration of recreation resources in connection with every activity of the federal government.

Metcalf's record of conservation legislation was extensive in his first term. He cosponsored the Clean Air Act of 1963 and amendments strengthening the act in 1965 and 1966. He cosponsored the Water Quality Act of 1965 and the Clean Water Restoration Act of 1966, as well as the Solid Waste Disposal Act of 1965. The Wilderness Act of 1964 was the first comprehensive wilderness-preservation law and was the product of Metcalf's early efforts and prophetic voice in the 1950s, driving the need for wilderness protection to the forefront of national policy priorities.

In 1963 Metcalf was unanimously chosen by the members of the Senate to serve as acting president pro tempore, the presiding officer over the Senate. He served in that office longer than any senator and governed the deliberation on scores of the nation's most fiercely debated issues. Sen. Hubert Humphrey, captain of the forces behind passage of the Civil Rights Act of 1964, identified Metcalf as a key figure in the struggle.

Metcalf's power was illustrated early in that battle when the Civil Rights Act had passed the House and came over to the Senate. Majority Leader Mansfield met the bill "at the door" and moved that it proceed to immediate consideration on the floor, rather than to the Judiciary Committee where southern senators with seniority could bury the legislation. Metcalf ruled from the chair in Mansfield's favor. Georgia's senator Richard Russell, leader of the southern bloc, appealed the ruling, but Metcalf recognized Mansfield's motion to table the appeal and the motion carried.

Metcalf was regarded a "peerless order keeper who insists on schoolroom quiet during high moments."[19] His mastery of the Senate rules and commitment to the principle of civil rights was instrumental in the delicate and hazard-ridden path that led to the final passage of the 1964 act.

As the 1966 election approached, the enemies of Lee Metcalf and his aggressive stands as "the people's advocate" organized diligently to bring about his defeat. The instrument of the Republican Party was Montana governor Tim Babcock, a strong supporter of Barry Goldwater's presidential candidacy in 1964. While conservative, Babcock did not represent the right wing of the Republican Party. In April 1966, he and his supporters quelled attempts by arch-conservatives to seize control of the Republican Party.

Nevertheless, Babcock denounced Metcalf's ultraliberal record on national issues. Controversy over the Vietnam War had begun to emerge, and Babcock chastised Metcalf for his opposition to America's expanding roll in the conflict. Metcalf had been among fifteen senators that year who wrote to President Johnson asking that a temporary halt in bombing be extended indefinitely. Babcock also tagged Metcalf a "tax and spend" Democrat, the slogan of the Republican Party still heard today.

In September 1966, Metcalf and Babcock signed a "fair campaign code," pledging to wage "an honest, ethical and fair campaign."[20] A few days later, Metcalf formally launched his campaign in Stevensville. The fair campaign pledge was short-lived. Two weeks after the candidates signed the compact and shook hands smiling, Babcock publicly announced that he was returning the document to Metcalf, charging that Metcalf had misrepresented his positions in public speeches.

Accompanied by his longtime friend and faithful driver, Jack Condon, Metcalf traveled the state, attacking Babcock's veto of an air pollution bill, his moratorium on state water development, and his opposition to federal assistance to state government. Babcock had also opened himself to questions about his credibility. Eighteen months before he entered the Senate race, he said publicly, "I don't think it's right to win one office and hold it while running for another. . . . Even Bobby Kennedy had the integrity to resign when he sought another office."[21]

In October Metcalf received a glowing endorsement from *The New York Times*, which praised the senator as an outstanding public servant in the tradition of Thomas J. Walsh and Burton K. Wheeler. The *Times* hailed Metcalf's role as a leading protagonist of the 1965 act that committed federal financial aid to elementary and secondary schools, as a principal proponent of the Wilderness Act and the Land and Water Conservation fund in 1964, as the leading sponsor of the bill to create a national park to protect the California redwoods, and as the author of the SOS Bill, which led to executive actions to "curb the depredations which the interstate highway program initially made on the nation's streams because of careless planning of highway routes." The *Times* concluded:

> Senator Metcalf's many accomplishments during these
> past six years in behalf of both Montana and the nation
> would argue strongly for his re-election in any event. But

his re-election is even more desirable since his Republican opponent, Gov. Tim Babcock, though personally amiable, is a Goldwater Republican with a severely negative philosophy. He offers nothing to match Senator Metcalf's constructive record.[22]

Babcock told Montanans that Metcalf had lost touch with Montana and become an instrument of the eastern establishment. But Metcalf's conduct belied the accusation. When the senator filed for reelection, he wore the old felt hat he had worn twenty years before as he began his successful race for the state supreme court. The *Billings Gazette*'s front page headline: "Lee's Old Felt Hat in Ring for Main Event."[23]

Metcalf traveled the state in a modest campaign car, spending a relatively small sum on the race. When the expenditures were finally disclosed, Metcalf's $68,000 in spending compared to Babcock's reported $210,000. Metcalf was strongly supported by organized labor and small contributions from individuals, while Babcock drew his support from large individual contributors, the National Republican Committee, the American Medical Association, and the Business-Industrial Political Action Committee. When the votes were counted, Metcalf was retained by a vote of 137,214 to 120,503.

The narrow margin of victory over Babcock did not deter Metcalf from his fights for the people. In his second term, the senator waded even deeper into controversy. In 1969 Metcalf and his executive secretary, Vic Reinemer, published the book *Overcharge*, a scathing indictment of the activities of investor-owned utilities (IOUs). Reinemer was a native Montanan who had become an associate editor of the *Charleston* (North Carolina) *News*, and later served on the staff of Montana's senator James Murray.

Metcalf had begun to investigate the private-utility industry in his first term. In 1964 he and Reinemer prepared and published a public information pamphlet, "Twenty Questions about Your Loaded Light Bill." The pamphlet reported that IOUs reached huge profits in a noncompetitive, no-risk industry. IOUs comprised the largest industry in the United States, with about 12 percent of all capital invested in business in the nation. While 15,000 ordinary businesses failed each year, Metcalf reported that there had not been a failure in the giant electric light and power industry in more than a generation. "In their advertisements, some IOUs try to appear to be identical to other business," Metcalf said, "but the IOUs have a monopoly on an essential product, for which demand is unparalleled, along with the practical assurance of all expenses— including taxes—plus profit."[24]

Metcalf noted that 75 percent of power supplied in the United States was provided by private companies, while less than 25 percent was provided by nonprofit public systems. The pamphlet also explained that ninety-five IOUs had overcharged their consumers more than $2.2 billion in recent years. It also criticized the IOUs for contributing vast sums collected from the rate payer to right-wing political organizations.

Metcalf's allegations hit close to home. The Montana Power Company enjoyed the highest rate of return of any private utility company in the nation. In another publication, Metcalf cited a comprehensive survey of IOUs by the brokerage firm Merrill Lynch, which reported, over a sixty-year period, no other industry could match the remarkable growth of the electric utilities. Citing one example of abuse, Metcalf noted that utilities obtained approval for rate increases from the state regulatory commissions when new taxes were levied on them, but when tax reductions were granted, the rates remained the same, ballooning IOU profits. Metcalf argued that excessive rates of return resulted from the ineffectiveness of state regulatory bodies in their efforts to scrutinize the earnings and accounts of private utilities. This comment put Metcalf at odds not only with the IOUs, but with public service commissioners at home.

Another target of Metcalf's investigation was the large stock options enjoyed by utility executives. IOU executives were permitted to reserve options to purchase power company stock at an undetermined date in the future, for the stock value that existed when the option was exercised. "When the time comes for the executive to exercise his option, he does not buy the stock at its current price, but at the price as of the day his option was granted," Metcalf explained. "Thus he makes an automatic profit—and without risking a hair, since he has no obligation to buy the stock. If its value rises, he buys; if it doesn't, he doesn't."[25] Metcalf charged that the president of the Montana Power Company was able to supplement his

$75,000 annual salary this way, with a one-day transaction that netted him $370,000.

Metcalf's campaign against the IOUs gained national notoriety with the 1967 publication of *Overcharge*. The book compiled exhaustive research to substantiate Metcalf's arguments that electric bills were too high and that utilities were misusing rate-payers' money for political activities. A writer for *Forbes* magazine wrote: "A liberal Democrat, Senator Lee Metcalf of Montana naturally is an anathema to right-wingers in his state, who have fought to retire him to private life for over a dozen years. This he accepts as inevitable."[26]

The *Montana Rural Electric News* reviewed the book, saying that Montana's junior senator "has spit on his front sights and let loose" on the private power industry.[27] *Public Power* magazine's review called Metcalf "one of the most outstanding, courageous, and able members of the Senate. His record in support of natural resources, conservation, and public power *development is unsurpassed.*"[28] *Rural Electrification* determined:

> The results of this examination are frightening, for they show a pattern of moral decay and ethical deprivation far overshadowing Teapot Dome. It is a recital of economic subversion, intellectual dishonesty and connivance among people in high places. It demonstrates the futility of utility regulation as it exists in most states today.[29]

The New York Times Book Review called *Overcharge* "an extremely well written, tightly researched, intensely motivated condemnation of the private power industry," and concluded that Metcalf and Reinemer made "as strong a case as I have ever read for the proposition that in areas served by private power the public is being practically stolen blind."[30]

Hearings instigated by Senator Metcalf followed the publication of *Overcharge*. Out of the process came the Utility Consumers Counsel Act, first introduced in 1968, to establish an independent federal agency to represent utility consumers before state and local commissions. While the bill did not pass, its significant provisions were partly incorporated in the Consumer Protection Agency Act, which permitted that agency to intervene in proceedings before state commissions. The campaign also led to legislation providing federal grants to educate consumers about the regulatory process.

Metcalf's investigation of private utilities led him into broader inquiry about the power of giant corporations generally. Metcalf announced, "It is time to determine who owns America and who controls it, and then to reshape our institutions so that they will be responsive to the need of our times."[31] In 1971 Metcalf rose on the Senate floor and spoke these words:

> Mr. President, Aftco, Byeco, Cadco, Bebco, Ertco, Fivco, Floco, Forco, Jepco, Ninco, Octco, Oneco, Quinco, Sevco, Sixco, Tenco, Treco, Twoco. Mr. President, the above names may sound like a space age counting system. In reality, each is part of a corporate code. Each of these names is a nominee—a front name—used by the Prudential Insurance Company of America to hide some of its interests. . . . It is a practice which makes it impossible for us to know who owns America, or who is putting up the money to elect these politicians who make our lives miserable; it even makes it impossible for us to know who we work for.[32]

In 1970 Metcalf began hearings into the influence exercised by big-business interests over legislatively created boards and committees in the executive branch. He introduced and oversaw passage of legislation subjecting these government "advisory committees," such as the Civil Aeronautics Board, to congressional scrutiny. He also proposed the establishment of the Special Committee to Investigate Economic and Financial Concentration to establish and publish facts about ownership and control of American industry.

Metcalf's Corporate Ownership Reporting Act of 1972 (CORA) required corporations with gross revenues of more than $10 million per year to report quarterly to the Library of Congress the names and addresses of each person or institution voting 1 percent or more of the shares of the corporation. "The enforcement of law and order in the executive suites," Metcalf told his colleagues, "requires disclosure of the basic facts on ownership and control."[33] Metcalf knew the act would carry as much force in Montana as it would on Wall Street. He told a Billings newspaper: "CORA is a chinook. CORA will eat through the snow that comes out of Butte every time the Montana Power Co. runs a full page advertisement telling how the company is owned by widows and orphans."[34]

Metcalf demonstrated his courage and legal acumen again in 1970 during consideration of the organized-crime control act. The bill was heralded as an important step in law enforcement, but Metcalf believed that it improperly encroached upon individual civil liberties. Metcalf stood alone against the measure, as it passed by a seventy-two to one vote. He told a reporter that he was aware of the political risks of voting against the bill, but felt it was "the wrong way to curb crime to take away the basic rights of individuals."

He told his colleagues, "I stand here as a Senator ready to vote for more judges, more policemen on the street, more grants in aid to sheriffs and municipalities to help them train their police services, but I feel this will take away individual Constitutional rights that will not contribute to the law enforcement that we seek."[35] Metcalf's bold stand was vindicated by the Supreme Court, which subsequently struck down the act as unconstitutional.

The breadth of Metcalf's courageous public stands in his second term was as great as the controversy that surrounded them. In 1970 he supported Sen. Bob Packwood's bill authorizing physicians to perform abortions upon request. He explained:

> Young women from the United States are flying to Great Britain and the Scandinavian countries and many of them are being exploited by unscrupulous doctors and runners who meet every plane. It would appear that . . . these women who do not want children should have an opportunity to make their choice in their own community. After sitting through hours of hearings and reading many articles, I am inclined to vote for the Packwood Bill if given the opportunity.[36]

When President Nixon proposed stationing antiballistic missiles in Montana, the sentiment of his constituents, particularly those in the Great Falls area, supported the project. Metcalf opposed it and declared: "Why should I vote to make the people of my state the first and primary target? We don't need the bases anymore, I think we should get the hell out of Germany, get the hell out of Japan. I am not afraid of Russia. I am not afraid of dominos. If somebody overruns the Philippines, I don't think we'll have to have machine gun emplacements against the enemy in San Francisco."[37]

Lee Metcalf makes his point clear in a speech to Democrats in Billings.
Courtesy of Donna Metcalf.

In connection with that comment, a reporter asked Metcalf if he would say the same things to President Nixon. Metcalf replied:

> You're Goddamned right I would. If I were going to the White House every Tuesday, I'd tell Nixon every Tuesday that we've got to get the hell out of Vietnam. I would say it everyday to the President, if I could go to the White House everyday.[38]

In 1968 the United States Supreme Court was making considerable news with President Johnson's unsuccessful nomination of Associate Justice Abe Fortas to be chief justice. Metcalf's name began to surface as a prospective choice for the court. Sen. Mike Mansfield, among Metcalf's boosters, said

"He is one of the best legal minds in the Senate, if not the best. . . . he'd be a fine member of the Supreme Court."[39]

A news analysis in the *Billings Gazette* reported that Metcalf was a "top legal scholar," whose "first love is the law." It opined, "Metcalf's passion for law and justice is indisputable. He is also a man of recognized intellect and energy. While it may seem premature to consider him in speculation as a U.S. Supreme Court Justice, Metcalf by no means should be overlooked as a possibility for the future."[40] Sen. Hubert Humphrey was said to have wanted Metcalf for chief justice of the high court but such talk was indeed premature. With the election of the Nixon administration in 1968, another Democratic appointment was not to be made in Metcalf's lifetime.

In 1970 Metcalf challenged the Nixon administration to back up its words about pollution control. Testifying before the Senate Interior Committee's Appropriation Subcommittee, Metcalf blasted the administration's proposal to cut the Interior Department and forest service budgets. "I am dismayed that natural resource protection is again being slighted in the national budget," he said.

Metcalf acknowledged that the administration had recently "joined the chorus" for environmental quality, but noted that it then proceeded to propose funding reductions at odds with environmental protection. "One might expect that from this massive outpouring of words would issue a rash of innovative programs and action," Metcalf declared. "What we see, however, is neither programs nor action, nor even increase in budget priorities for the environmental agencies. These are only words, words, and more words."[41]

Metcalf's conservation efforts in his second term generated new heights of opposition. The timber industry was sagging in Montana and unemployment in the field was high. Timber workers, who had long been strong supporters of the senator throughout his career, became concerned that Metcalf's conservation efforts were partly responsible for their prevailing woes. In 1971 Metcalf commissioned a committee headed by Dr. Arnold Bolle, dean of the Forestry School of the University of Montana in Missoula, to conduct a study of the forest service's timber practices.

The Bolle Report, published in 1970, concluded that poor forest management created doubts that present harvest yield could be sustained. The report recommended additional research and policies consistent with recreation, watershed, wildlife, grazing, and sustained yield timber production. The report engendered a public outcry in the timber industry and Metcalf was blamed. Nevertheless, the report provided fundamental information to the policy debate about forest protection and profoundly affected legislative activity in the area throughout the 1970s.

As a result of the Bolle Report, Metcalf opened hearings in the Senate Interior Committee on clear-cutting practices in the national forests. While the hearings were held at Metcalf's behest, he was not chairman of the committee and, as the hearings drew to a close, timber industry advocates had dominated the proceedings while many citizen witnesses had not been given a chance to testify. Metcalf raised his voice and brought down his fist. The episode was vividly described by journalist Dale Burke:

> Hope had given way to disillusionment that late April afternoon in 1971 when the half dozen Senators and their aides filed out of the Senate Interior Committee hearing room in Washington. . . . It appeared that the crusade to improve forest management practices would be stymied at the very hearings called to bring the problem to national focus.
>
> Then, from behind the closed oak doors, a voice boomed loud enough to be heard in the hearing room: "No, dammit, we can't quit now. I can't go back in there and tell my people to go home. They haven't even had a chance to present their case.
>
> There was more arguing and again that booming voice, later likened to the bellowing of an enraged bull elk, demanding that the people be given a chance to "make their case." Lee Metcalf, United States Senator from Montana and a member of the committee's sub-committee on public lands, was on the prod. He won his point. The hearings continued through two more days until every witness had been heard.[42]

Cecil Garland, president of the Montana Wilderness Association, was at the hearings. He later explained that "it was typical of Lee to fight to give the little guy a voice in government decisions, and we'd never have had our say at the clear cutting hearings if it hadn't been for him. He gave us reason to believe that we could take our case to Congress and win."[43]

By 1971 Metcalf was uncertain about a third Senate term, "I want to go home," he said. "I really want to go home. For thirty years, except for the war, I have been running for public office in difficult, complex and involved political activities. And I think thirty years is long enough for a guy. I could live in Montana and not have to smell this stinking air."[44] Metcalf was tiring of the notoriety, as well, despite his image as the Invisible Senator.

In May 1971, he was the object of unwelcome national publicity when he stiff-armed a Washington, D.C., policeman during antiwar demonstrations near the Capitol. Metcalf was crossing a police line, trying to get from one part of the Hill to another, in an area where demonstrators were being arrested. The unfortunate cop unknowingly tried to restrain Metcalf and felt the consequences. Metcalf's ambivalence about a third term gave way. While he said he did not look forward to another six years of "smelling that stinky Potomac and fighting the traffic," Metcalf announced in late 1971 that he would run for a third and final term.[45]

Shortly after Metcalf's announcement, former Governor Babcock confessed his desire for a rematch with Metcalf. In 1968 Babcock had been defeated in his bid for reelection as governor by Attorney General Forrest Anderson. The Republicans, however, abandoned Babcock and nominated conservative rancher and state senator Hank Hibbard. Hibbard was heir to the 70,000-acre Sieben ranch operation, a working rancher, and a graduate of the Harvard Business School. As the Republican nominee, he charted a moderate course and attacked Metcalf for his support of presidential candidate George McGovern. Hibbard told the voters: "Like all crops, timber must be harvested once it matures," while declaring his opposition to "environmentally destructive methods of tree cutting."[46]

Hibbard called for welfare reform to "eliminate career welfare free-loaders," but advocated providing better care "for those who really need aid."[47] He called for a moratorium on coal strip mining, a position that Metcalf had held for years. Hibbard opposed national health insurance, but supported the Rural Development Act. He charged that Metcalf was "selling out the state of Montana to big city interests," and alleged that Metcalf voted with Senator McGovern 82 percent of the time.

Metcalf did not and could not ride two horses into the 1972 election. The lines were clearly drawn in Montana, and Montanans knew where they stood with Lee. In 1971 *The Missoulian* had written, "Metcalf has made many of the right enemies. He has fought special interests that SOMEBODY ought to be at least questioning but nobody ever has."[48] The Royal Logging Company found nothing admirable about Metcalf's conservation record and organized a group of women from logging families called WOOD—Women Opposed to Official Depression. At rallies convened by company representatives throughout western Montana, every fifth woman would be asked to step forward, representing the families who would soon be put out of work by Metcalf's radical preservationist initiatives in Congress.

Metcalf's stand on utility regulation invited equally virulent opposition. The power companies donated generously to Hibbard's campaign. One magazine reported: "For the utilities, Hibbard is a model candidate; he is eager to promote rapid power development regardless of the environmental consequences."[49]

As the election neared, Hibbard ran television spots showing Metcalf's face changing, like Jekyll and Hyde, into the unpopular visage of George McGovern. At a campaign rally, Metcalf quipped, "Maybe I should develop a TV spot showing Hibbard changing into a Neanderthal."[50] Although in jest, the remark may have been somewhat unfair, because Hibbard, though conservative, showed progressive problem-solving approaches to a number of issues. But Lee Metcalf did not pull punches.

In early November, Metcalf won the endorsement of *The Missoulian*, which said: "Metcalf is blessed with great human warmth and cursed by a fiery temper. He has a good mind, works hard and has more courage than most politicians. Metcalf comes across in this campaign as the more stable candidate. He is who he is, and takes pride in his record. Take him or leave him, he has no apologies."[51] Another paper wrote: "Metcalf was becoming a consumer's champion when Ralph Nader was in plastic pants and a conservationist when most Americans thought the Sierra Club was a fancy bar."[52]

In the end, Hibbard proved a tougher opponent than

Babcock. Metcalf squeezed into his third and final term 163,609 to 151,316, capturing less than 52 percent of the vote. Hibbard commented, "It was a hard fought race and I am proud of my showing." Then he wished Metcalf "the best of success for the next six years."[53]

Metcalf's final term was dominated by wilderness and timber issues. The Wilderness Act of 1964 created the National Wilderness Preservation System (NWPS) and instituted a process through which proposed lands could become part of the system: 9.1 million acres initially were designated as wilderness and 5.5 million acres of existing primitive areas were set aside for study by the forest service. The Wilderness Act was not considered a great victory for conservationists, but represented a foundation for further wilderness research and preservation. Broader research began in 1967 when the forest service undertook a national roadless area review and evaluation, which came to be known as RARE.

In June 1972, regional forest service directors highlighted 1,448 areas encompassing about 56 million acres, which merited further consideration for inclusion in the NWPS. The chief of the forest service reviewed the recommendations and, after a few months, recommended only 274 areas comprising some 17 million acres for further wilderness study. For Montana, the regional forester had proposed 5.2 million acres for further study and the chief of the forest service reduced the selected land to 1.5 million acres.

Metcalf was furious. He believed the Nixon administration had abrogated the responsibility delegated to the executive by the Wilderness Act of 1964, by failing to properly survey public opinion and by recommending unconscionably limited parcels for further wilderness study. In response, Metcalf introduced S393, the Montana Wilderness Study Bill.

Metcalf recognized the panoply of competing interests implicated in the wilderness debate. The Montana Wilderness Study Bill was designed to force discussion and compromise among forest service representatives, mining and timber companies, wilderness advocate groups, and regular Montana citizens. The bill was introduced in October 1974, and proposed to segregate nine areas for wilderness study. The response from lumber companies and timber workers was predictably antagonistic, but Metcalf did not recoil. The timber industry, he said, "is all hopped up about any sort of program which will keep them from exploiting every bit of national forest everywhere in America. . . . The industry has no concept of doing anything except cut, cut, cut, slash, slash, clear cut and go away."[54]

One industry forester complained that Metcalf did not understand the intent of his own bill. In his blunt manner, Metcalf replied:

> You are a professional forester skilled in marking trees for harvest, and probably work for a timber operator. If you are like other foresters working in private industry, you regard trees as first and foremost a cash crop. You enjoy their pre-harvest beauty, recognize their watershed and wildlife habitat value, but still regard them as destined for removal and replacement. If I shared this viewpoint, I would never have introduced S.393. But I do not share it, and it is presumptuous of you to suggest that I have "misconceptions about the intent" of my own bill. I know very well what I intend.[55]

Metcalf explained that S393 was "designed not so much to stop anything as to force Montanans and the Forest Service to step back and take a sober look at where we are going. . . . Many communities in our state may wake up fifteen or twenty years from now to find the timber gone, the mills closed, small trout streams barren and silt-laden, tourists repelled by visually disturbing clear cuts, and erosion and flooding heightened by damage to the watershed."[56] Metcalf further explained, "The commercial onslaught of our national forests pursued by two successive administrations makes it obvious that *only* those areas designated as wilderness are truly protected."[57]

Metcalf told his friends and foes in the wilderness-policy community that wilderness protection was not merely a matter of esthetics. Rather, he argued that it was fundamental to watershed protection, wildlife habitat, grazing, attraction of tourism, and recreation. According to one writer who was close to Metcalf, much of his motivation came from intimate knowledge. "He had seen that after World War II, too many mills were built in national forest communities. The result was mill capacity far exceeding the forest's sustained-yield potential, followed by ultimate economic collapse and community upheaval when the cut exceeded the forest's ability to re-generate itself."[58]

The Montana Wilderness Study Bill evolved and changed in the months and years following its introduction. Based on the testimony of witnesses elicited in extensive public hearings, the acreages designated for wilderness study were shifted and rearranged. Significantly, the bill did not designate a single acre of land as wilderness, but only identified the disputed parcels so that a longer-term debate could be organized and focused. Finally, on November 1, 1977, S393 became the Montana Wilderness Act, and the modern era of wilderness debate began.

Simultaneous and parallel to his consideration of wilderness issues, Metcalf remained locked in the struggle with the forest service over clear-cutting practices. Using information gleaned from the Bolle Report and the 1971 Interior Committee hearings, Metcalf developed legislation to redefine the legal concept "sustained yield" and to establish corresponding criteria for the selection of tree-cutting sites. When the 1972 election season arrived, Metcalf did not retreat—he marched straight through the stormy controversy swirling around the clear-cutting issue. When he emerged victorious, Metcalf pressed on and Congress followed. In 1976 they passed the National Forest Management Act, which accomplished the changes to the clear-cutting practices that Metcalf sought.

Lee Metcalf was never able to return to his beloved Bitterroot. He died of heart failure on January 12, 1978. In a fitting tribute to his legislative accomplishments and devotion to conservation, his congressional colleagues passed the two remaining Montana wilderness bills on Metcalf's agenda. The enactments established the Absaroka-Beartooth Wilderness on the Montana-Wyoming border and the Great Bear Wilderness, which bridged Glacier National Park and the Bob Marshall Wilderness area along the Continental Divide. Counting these posthumous additions, Lee Metcalf figured prominently in the designation of every acre of wilderness presently existing in Montana.

Metcalf's friends, both in and out of Congress, rose in tribute to him. Sen. Frank Church of Idaho remarked that Metcalf was motivated by "a fundamental belief that government exists to champion the cause of public interest over private gain." Church explained:

If he relished his battles on behalf of the consumer, or in favor of sound conservation, he was scrupulously fair, and he never lost the respect of those with whom he disagreed. . . . Throughout his public career, Lee Metcalf spoke for the ordinary people of his state and nation—the miners and loggers, consumers and housewives, young veterans, the disabled, the elderly—with the abiding conviction that they were the constituency most in need of representation.[59]

One Montana newspaper praised Metcalf's "agitated passion" and wrote:

Through his fiery and independent approach to problems, he thrilled some, agitated others, and provided an informative atmosphere for the rest who watched the cheerleaders and the hatchet-wielders battle. Love him or leave him, you didn't suffer from the aura of fuzzy uncertainty which sometimes surrounds politicians . . . he acted like he felt. Lee Metcalf didn't pretend.[60]

A Virginia newspaper editor wrote:

If one could have combined the virtues of our greatest leaders, Jefferson, Jackson, Lincoln, Norris, LaFollette, Carver, Booker T. Washington, and Truman . . . the result would have been Lee Metcalf. He was a rare breed of man. He was from the people and spoke for the people. . . . God has a special place in Heaven for this great man. And as long as America lives, Senator Metcalf has a special place in our history.[61]

Robert Kiesling, then director of Montana's Environmental Information Center, wrote:

The impact of losing Lee Metcalf is incalculable. For many of us, his death is more than a loss—it is a change of condition, of the framework of our confidence and hope. It is a loneliness of the spirit. . . . Lee Metcalf was the hoop of integrity in Montana's political life, the center of public trust. . . . To those who battle for wild lands preservation, for human justice, for rational control of irrational power structures, he was the core, the always-there intelligence, the strong, immediate, irascible, loved and loving father figure, unique and irreplaceable . . . [He] cared for honesty more than image, for action more than words, for dignity more than publicity—because, above all, he put courage before contrivance. Our best memorial to Lee Metcalf is to take upon ourselves and pass on to others the mandate of unsparing service to the earth and people that is his legacy.[62]

Eight years later, at the dedication of the Lee Metcalf Natural Resources and Conservation Building in Helena, former Metcalf campaign manager and distinguished State District Judge Gordon Bennett waxed nostalgic about Metcalf's rare qualities and "clarion blasts of reasoned outrage":

With the stilling of that wondrous voice, we need to be reminded that there was another time—another man, whose instincts and intellect told him what was in the public interest, whose ability, perseverance and courage enabled him to serve that interest brilliantly, and whose everlasting spirit and drive would never let him rest until he had done all he could to vindicate that interest.[63]

The tributes to Lee Metcalf were inspired reflections on the career of an uncommon man. Those in public life who stand for nothing of consequence will never be so eulogized. Lee Metcalf's course was a dangerous one, but the danger never dissuaded him. He stood for something, and that made all the difference.

Suggested Readings on Lee Metcalf

The two most comprehensive biographies about Metcalf are Richard D. Warden, *Metcalf of Montana, How a Senator Makes Government Work* (Sarasota, Florida, 1965) and Peter J. Petkas, *Lee Metcalf, Democratic Senator from Montana* (Washington, D.C., 1972). The former is one of a number in the "Congressional Leadership Series." The latter is part of the Ralph Nader Congress Project, which provided biographies and vote analysis of sitting senators. The most complete magazine article biography is Robert Scherrill's "Consider Lee Metcalf, The Invisible Senator," *The Nation* (May 10, 1971).

Metcalf's work on the wilderness issue is thoroughly studied by John Patrick Davis in his Carroll College honors thesis, "Lee Metcalf and the Montana Wilderness Study Act of 1977: A Case Study on the Wilderness Issue and Its Varying View Points" (Helena, 1982). Metcalf's contribution to wilderness and conservation in general is discussed by Dale A. Burke in various articles, including "Lee Metcalf's Conservation Legacy," *Montana Magazine* (March-April 1979) and "The Legacy of Lee Metcalf," an undated article contained in the Montana Historical Society's Lee Metcalf vertical files.

The source for examining evidence marshaled by Metcalf against the private power industry is Lee Metcalf and Vic Reinemer, *Overcharge* (New York, 1967).

Metcalf's voluminous papers are maintained at the Montana Historical Society Archives in Helena, Montana. The Historical Society's Lee Metcalf vertical files contain copies of many newspaper and magazine articles published during Metcalf's career.

Remarks made by Metcalf's colleagues following his death are compiled and published by the U.S. Government Printing Office in *Lee Metcalf, Late Senator from Montana* (Washington, D.C., 1978). Elections results for each of Metcalf's campaigns are found in Ellis Waldron and Paul B. Wilson, *Atlas of Montana Elections* (Missoula, 1978).

Conclusion

Ralph Waldo Emerson said: "There is properly no history; only biography." As history seeks to discover lessons that enhance society's capacity to meet the challenges of today and tomorrow, these chapters have looked into the biographies of nine remarkable political leaders to find examples of courage, integrity, and independence that inspire and guide.

Montana's most prominent political figures led colorful lives and approached public affairs with a bold style. These men and women brought the power of moral conviction to controversial debates. Their careers were marked by candor and determination in stormy times. The subjects of this book not only acted boldly but stood for the notion that government exists to pursue the ends of justice for all people and to actively promote the public good. As noted in the introduction, these leaders left a populist and progressive legacy. The question that begs attention now is whether these human qualities and populist-progressive approaches to public policy have retained relevance.

Montana and the world around it have been radically transformed by the strides of technology, economic mutations, and upheavals in geopolitical relations. Much has changed since the days of Walsh and Wheeler—even since the days of Metcalf and Mansfield. The world is closer. An international community is connected by satellite television, the Internet, and affordable, rapid air transport. A global economy has seen the export of American manufacturing jobs to third-world countries. The Soviet Union, the demonized center of European Communism, has collapsed, and with it, red scare politics. Now the biggest, most brutal Communist dictatorship in human history—China—has become a "most favored trading partner." The political influence of labor unions has declined as work places have become generally safer and wages relatively higher than in the earlier part of the century. Some of the largest social-welfare programs have been discredited by critics who argue that they breed dependence while subverting self-reliance and self-respect.

The demographics of Montana and its neighbors change

daily, as coastal city dwellers migrate in-land in search of a more intimate connection with nature. The consequent clash of cultures has engendered a host of issues in a region now called "the New West." Conflicts between the environmental movement and timber and mining workers throughout the New West have fractured the liberal alliance and made progressive policy choices more difficult.

The political bent of farm communities in the American West has also changed. Thousands of family farms have disappeared; rural land has been consolidated; and large-scale agriculture and agribusiness have undermined the roots of agrarian populism.

The class consciousness and conflict that motivated many of the battles recounted in this book have all but disappeared. Typical Montanans, like typical Americans, commonly hold a more complicated set of beliefs. There is wide sympathy for the old, the disabled, and the poor who truly cannot help themselves, but this is tempered by a precept that everyone who can work must pull his own weight. There is a common belief that every child should have access to decent education, good nutrition, and appropriate housing, but there is also an expectation that those benefits will culminate in a responsible, productive adult.

Blatant racial and gender prejudice offends most Montanans, but most do not favor special preferences for anyone. Montanans abhor waste in government and the taxes that support it, but they demand that government actively provide vital services in an efficient way. The very rich are still resented, but government redistribution of wealth wins little support. Suspicions about huge corporations linger, but big business is less vilified today than in years past. Many citizens have dumped personal savings into a more accessible stock market, tying their own fortunes to these same companies.

Inside Montana, the fundamental political dichotomy has shifted from management versus labor to economic development versus natural-resource conservation and environmental protection. The omnipotent Company is nearly forgotten. The average Montanan does not fear an evil corporate monolith. Throughout much of the Treasure State's history, urban Montanans gathered in the union halls to organize resistance to corporate abuses. The political leaders they elected, despite the power of the Company, often reflected this sentiment. To-day, much of the progressive community strongly supports strict environmental regulation while natural-resource labor-ers, the core of Montana's progressive vote historically, view such regulation as a threat to their livelihood. Cars sport bumper stickers proclaiming "Keep It Wild" or "This Family Supported by Timber Dollars" and the final designation of wilderness study lands has become the most troublesome is-sue for Montana's delegation in Congress.

The close battle in 1996 over Constitutional Initiative 122, proposing tougher clean water standards for mines, became the most expensive initiative campaign ever waged in Mon-tana. Although the opposition was financed by out-of-state min-ing companies, the families of blue collar mine workers waged an aggressive and emotional campaign against the measure as well and helped to defeat it. What used to be a vivid battle be-tween David and Goliath is now sometimes overshadowed by oblique skirmishes among Davids.

Montanans have in recent years voted more conservatively than at any time in the state's history. Like the rest of the na-tion, Montanans became enamored in the early 1980s with tax reductions and other policies touted by the New Right that emerged behind its spokesman, Ronald Reagan. By 1997 Re-publicans in Montana held one United States Senate seat, the state's lone seat in the United States House of Representatives, the governorship, and comfortable majorities in both houses of the state legislature. By and large, these have not been Rankin or Dixon Republicans, but conservative disciples of the New Right.

The rightward swing in recent Montana elections deviates from the pattern of progressive politics that runs through Mon-tana's history. Whether this phenomenon represents a truly energized electorate that has reconfigured the state deliber-ately or whether it is an impulsive response to certain effec-tive conservative campaign themes is not clear. It seems likely that the Republican tide will recede, but the political center in Montana among rank-and-file voters probably will settle some-where to the right of where the center has been in years past.

Despite broad socio-economic and political realignment, the lessons drawn from Montana's political past remain rele-vant because the fundamental tension persists between public interest reform and the establishment. In this century, America has made enormous strides toward eradicating social evils that motivated the early progressives. Legislation, union demands, social activism and litigation have given society safer work places, better pay and benefits, universal public education, high-quality medical care, safer foods and drugs, civil rights and meaningful suffrage for women and minorities, better nutrition for children, financial security for the elderly, and a wide array of environmental protections. A staggering amount of progressive work has been accomplished in less than one hundred years, but many challenges remain.

A widening gap between rich and poor underscores the importance of ensuring that every child has an opportunity to participate in the American dream. The export of unskilled jobs to developing countries signals the need to educate and train present and future American workers to fill increasingly sophisticated job descriptions. The remodeling of welfare necessitates public attention to child care and health insurance so that poor people can afford to go to work. The precious wonders of the earth are under greater pressure than ever as a growing world population increases its demand for natural resources. The heirs to Montana's progressive legacy will be needed at the front of these battles.

Progressive tasks loom ahead internationally as well. Most of the world's population languishes in countries that know none or few of America's twentieth-century progressive achievements. Low wages, dangerous working conditions, child labor, prohibition of union activity, and unabated industrial pollution abound in developing countries that now manufacture products for American consumers. In the coming millennium, as the world grows ever smaller, courageous progressives will be at the fore of the movements to extend basic human rights and social justice to all people. In Montana, a progressive vision will be indispensable to an ultimate solution to the dilemma of the New West, blending good jobs with a secure and pristine environment. These objectives are realistic but will not materialize easily.

Progressive politics will always demand courage. Those who seek to abolish the inequities of entrenched institutions will always suffer calumny. The opposition may come from industry or from government, from a special-interest group or from the politician's own party. It may come from constituents when the elected official's considered study of a controversial issue or commitment to the national interest causes him or her to act contrary to the fickle, but impassioned, preference of the voters back home. It will most certainly come from political opponents who, with increasing regularity, turn any controversial or unpopular position of an incumbent into scathing, sensational television advertisements.

Those who walk through fire for the public good place themselves in jeopardy. They may be driven from office or become heroes—or both. Dixon's assertive independence won him national fame but ultimately brought his defeat. The same can be said of Wheeler. Rankin's courage destroyed her political career twice, leaving just two brief flashes of valor for the record books, yet her statue is enshrined in the nation's Capitol as one of two Montanans so honored. Knowles never won elected office, but her daring adventures opened doors for Rankin and others.

Toole's strong leadership, progressive vision, and fearless words never disturbed his electoral popularity. Murray and Mansfield, less strident than some but no less courageous, were never defeated by their enemies. Metcalf practiced aggressive confrontational politics until his dying day, even though he was reelected repeatedly by the kind of narrow margins that make incumbents cringe. Often the politician cannot predict whether a bold profile on a contentious issue will bring glory or disdain. In the uncertainty lies the risk that made these champions rare.

If all history is biography, then it is more often the biography of controversial advocates than cautious moderates. It is the biography of explorers and entrepreneurs, inventors and adventurers, innovators and idealists. Acts of political courage and independence, when born of sincere public interest, distinguish politicians and give texture to the national character. They also breed confidence among voters and pique voters interest, thereby strengthening the democratic system.

American voters are more skeptical and cynical than ever before. They are fed up with false advertising, vicious slander, trivial shouting matches, and most of all, big money. Although the nation's fathers and grandfathers died to preserve the sacred right of self-government, and although others around the planet continue to die in quests for democratic freedom, America suffers the lowest voter participation levels in the Western world.

This irony is not easy to explain. It prompts a chicken-and-egg inquiry. Has a bland, insincere money-addicted political process turned people off to the point that they have given up on the system? Or are voters themselves to blame for ignoring the substantive political issues so that candidates are forced to win votes by pandering to the lowest common denominator?

Whichever came first, the solution lies in both quarters. Candidates and public leaders must apply creative political thinking to the problems of a new post-Soviet, global-economic community and in Montana to the challenges of the New West. They must speak candidly with voters and always attempt to elevate the quality of political dialogue. Voters must respond by studying problems and proposals, attending candidate forums, and involving themselves in issue-based organizations. In short, society must expand the roster of people who respect the miraculous privilege of living in a democratic society and understand that its success depends upon their direct participation.

Even when this goal is achieved, and perhaps especially then, political battle lines will be drawn. There rarely will be universal agreement. Citizens will clash over vital issues, just as the founding fathers intended, and people will fight the centers of power to achieve justice. When differences can be bridged, they should be. Yet when principle cannot be compromised—when reform no longer can be delayed—we will look into the ring for a Rankin or a Wheeler or a Metcalf: a progressive champion with a human heart, a determined mind, and the soul of a maverick.

Notes

Chapter 1

1. Warren Toole and John B. Ritch, "Joseph Kemp Toole," undated paper, Montana Historical Society, Joseph K. Toole vertical file. "Nestor," meaning a leader in a given field, derives from the Greek hero of the same name, who was associated with long life and wisdom.
2. *Congressional Record*, 50th Congress, 2nd Session, 1889, 20, pt. 1:821.
3. Ibid.
4. Ibid.
5. Ibid., 822.
6. Ibid., 829.
7. George F. Cowan to Joseph K. Toole, February 8, 1889, SC1003, Montana Historical Society. Reprinted in Dave Walter, "The Right Kind of Nail," *Montana, The Magazine of Western History*, Autumn 1987, 47.
8. William Wallace, Jr. to Joseph K. Toole, January 22, 1889. Reprinted in Walter, "The Right Kind of Nail," 57.
9. *Great Falls Tribune*, February 15, 1889. Reprinted in Walter, "The Right Kind of Nail," 53–54.
10. Governor's message, Gov. Joseph K. Toole, December 17, 1889. Reprinted in *Then and Now*, 1976, 19, Montana Historical Society, Joseph K. Toole vertical file.
11. Ibid.
12. Patricia Toole Whitehorn, "Joseph K. Toole," *Then and Now*, 1976, 22, Montana Historical Society, Joseph K. Toole vertical file.
13. *The Helena Daily Herald*, May 7, 1890.
14. *Address of J. K. Toole*, July 4, 1899, 5–6, Montana Historical Society, Joseph K. Toole vertical file.
15. *Message of Governor Joseph K. Toole to the Eighth Legislative Assembly of the State of Montana*, January 5, 1903 (Helena: State Publishing Co.), 54, Montana Historical Society.
16. Whitehorn, "Joseph K. Toole," 21.

Chapter 2

1. *New York Times*, July 17, 1892, quoted in Richard B. Roeder, "Crossing the Gender Line," *Montana: The Magazine of Western History*, 32 (Summer 1982) 67.

2. Ella K. Haskell, "My First Fee," *The Anaconda Standard*, February 3, 1907.

3. Ibid.

4. Ibid.

5. *The Bates Student*, 1992, 134.

6. Joaquin Miller, *An Illustrated History of the State of Montana* (Chicago: Lewis Publishing Co., 1894), 86.

7. *Progressive Men of the State of Montana* (Chicago: A. W. Bowen & Co., 1902), 474.

8. Dorris Buckward, "The Winning of Women Suffrage in Montana" (Master's thesis, Montana State University, June 1974), 35.

9. *Progressive Men*, 474.

10. *The Butte Miner*, January 28, 1911.

Chapter 3

1. K. Ross Toole, "Joseph M. Dixon," undated paper, Montana Historical Society, Joseph M. Dixon vertical file.

2. J. M. Dixon, "The Tyranny of Public Opinion," *The Earlhamite*, XIV, (July 1887), 227–30, cited in Jules A. Karlin, *Joseph M. Dixon of Montana*, pt. 1 (Missoula: University of Montana, 1974), 12.

3. Karlin, pt. 1, 8.

4. Ibid., 16.

5. *Bozeman Avant Courier*, October 3, 1902, cited in Karlin, pt. 1, 36.

6. Karlin, pt. 1, 40.

7. Ibid., 54.

8. Ibid., 100.

9. Ibid.

10. Ibid., 102.

11. Merrill G. Burlingame and K. Ross Toole, *A History of Montana*, vol. 1 (New York: Lewis Historical Publishing Co., 1957), 250.

12. Ibid., 251.

13. Ibid.

14. Ibid.

15. Ibid., 252.

16. Ibid., 253.

17. *The* (Miles City) *Independent*, January 4, 1911.

18. Ibid.

19. Helena *Daily Independent*, April 18, 1911.

20. *The* (Red Lodge) *Republican Picket*, August 3, 1911.

21. Karlin, pt. 1, 145.

22. Ibid., 146.

23. Ibid., 147.

24. *The Missoulian*, March 25, 1912, Special Supplement, Montana Historical Society, Joseph M. Dixon vertical file.

25. *The* (Hamilton) *Western News*, September 10, 1912.

26. Ibid.

27. *Western News*, April 12, 1912.

28. Karlin, pt. 1, 183, 190.

29. Burlingame and Toole, *History of Montana*, vol. I, 264–65.

30. *The Chinook Opinion*, March 12, 1920.

31. *The Daily Missoulian*, February 4, 1920.

32. *Ibid.*

33. Joseph Kinsey Howard, *Montana: High, Wide and Handsome* (New Haven: Yale University Press, 1943), 207–8.

34. Burlingame and Toole, *History of Montana*, vol. II, 363.

35. Full-page newspaper circular, "Reign of Special Privileges Is Ending in Montana: Governor Dixon Calls on People to Assert Rights," 1924, Montana Historical Society, Joseph M. Dixon vertical files.

37. Ibid.

38. Ibid.

39. K. Ross Toole, unpublished paper, Montana Historical Society, Joseph M. Dixon vertical file.

Chapter 4

1. Newspaper-style circular, "Editorial Page of Labor," 1930, Montana Historical Society, Thomas Walsh vertical file.

2. T. J. Walsh letter to Elinor McClements, November 6, 1887. Reprinted in J. Leonard Bates, *Tom Walsh in Dakota Territory* (Urbana/London: University of Illinois Press, 1966), 146–47.

3. T. J. Walsh letter to Mary McClements, August ____, 1890. Reprinted in Bates, *Dakota Territory*, 250–51.

4. T. J. Walsh letter to Elinor Walsh, September 17, 1890. Reprinted in Bates, *Dakota Territory*, 252. The governor was Joseph K. Toole.

5. "Editorial Page of Labor," 1930, Montana Historical Society, Thomas Walsh vertical file.

6. Josephine O'Keane, *Thomas J. Walsh, a Senator from Montana* (Francestown, New Hampshire: Marshall Jones Company, 1955), 21–22.

7. Ibid.

8. Ibid.

9. J. Leonard Bates, "T. J. Walsh: Foundations of a Senatorial Career," *The Montana Magazine of History*, October 1951, 23–24.

10. James E. Murray interview, quoted in Bates, "Senatorial Career," 28.

11. O'Keane, *Senator from Montana*, 27–28.

12. Ibid., 27.

13. Ibid., 29.

14. Ibid., 31.

15. Ibid., 34–35.

16. Ibid., 35.

17. Burton K. Wheeler, *Yankee from the West* (Garden City, New York: Doubleday & Co., 1962), 84.

18. Michael P. Malone and Richard B. Roeder, eds., *The Montana Past* (Missoula: University of Montana Press, 1969), 265.

19. Thomas Walsh, keynote address, Democratic State Convention, September 24, 1912, Billings, Montana, quoted in O'Keane, *Senator from Montana*, 45.

20. Merrill G. Burlingame and K. Ross Toole, *A History of Montana,* vol. 1 (New York: Lewis Historical Publishing Co., 1957), 257.

21. O'Keane, *Senator from Montana*, 53.

22. Ibid., 57.

23. Ibid., 59–60.

24. Ibid., 77.

25. *Congressional Record*, 66th Congress, 3rd Session, 1920, 60, pt. 1:150.

26. *Helena Daily Independent,* Helena, Montana, October 29, 1918, 3.

27. Ibid.

28. Burlingame and Toole, *History of Montana*, 258.

29. J. Leonard Bates, "Senator Walsh of Montana, 1918–1924, a Liberal Under Pressure" (Ph.D. diss., University of North Carolina, 1952), 93.

30. O'Keane, *Senator from Montana*, 105.

31. Robert M. Werner and John Starr, *Teapot Dome* (New York: Viking Press, 1959), 110.

32. Ibid., 113.

33. *The Congressional Record*, 68th Congress 1st Session, 1924, 65, pt. 3: 2065.

34. *Record News*, Wichita Falls, Texas, February 3, 1924.

35. *The New York World*, June 7, 1924.

36. *Cincinnati Times Star,* February 4, 1924.

37. Ibid.

38. *The Springfield Republican*, June 7, 1924.

39. *The New York World*, June 7, 1924.

40. Ann Hard, "A Democratic Dry Hope," February 19, 1928, Montana Historical Society, Thomas Walsh vertical file.

41. *The New York Evening World*, July 11, 1924.

42. O'Keane, *Senator from Montana*, 204.

43. Ibid., 213.

44. Ibid., 248–49.

45. *The New York Sun*, March 1, 1933.

46. *Congressional Record*, 73rd Congress, 2nd Session, 1927, 78, pt. 7:7561.

47. Ibid.

Chapter 5

1. Jeannette Rankin, "Why I Voted Against War," Montana Historical Society, Jeannette Rankin vertical file.

2. Jean M. Emery, "Jeannette Rankin: Ahead of Her Time," *Montanan* (University of Montana alumnae magazine), Winter 1993, 30.

3. "Quotes by and about Jeannette Rankin," compiled by the Montana Arts Council, 1985, Montana Historical Society, Jeannette Rankin vertical file, citing Jeannette Rankin's speech to the Montana House of Representatives, 1911.

4. Kevin S. Giles, *Flight of the Dove: The Story of Jeannette Rankin* (Beaverton, Oregon: The Touchstone Press, 1980), 55.

5. Ibid., 71.

6. Ibid., 73.

7. "Interesting Westerners," *Sunset*, November 1916, 33.

8. *The Daily Missoulian*, November 7, 1916.

9. Ibid.

10. *The Equity News,* August 23, 1917, Montana Historical Society, Jeannette Rankin vertical file.

11. Hannah Josephson, *First Lady in Congress: Jeannette Rankin* (New York: Bobbs-Merrill Co., Inc., 1974), 69.

12. Giles, *Flight of the Dove*, 82.

13. *The New York Times Magazine*, November 19, 1916, 15.

14. *The Daily Missoulian*, November 14, 1916.

15. Ibid.

16. Josephson, *First Lady in Congress*, 71.

17. Rankin, "Why I Voted Against War," 2.

18. Ibid., 2–3.

19. Emery, "Ahead of Her Time," 31.

20. Dave Walter, "Rebel with a Cause: Jeannette Rankin, 1941," *Montana Magazine*, December 1991, 66.

21. Emery, "Jeannette Rankin, Ahead of Her Time," 31.

22. Jeannette Rankin, speech on women's suffrage before the House of Representatives, January 10, 1918. Reprinted by government printing office, Montana Historical Society, Jeannette Rankin vertical file.

23. *Washington Star,* August 12, 1918, cited in *The Missoulian*, August 13, 1918.

24. Jeannette Rankin, "Twenty Years After," *The Christian Harald*, 1937, Montana Historical Society, Jeannette Rankin vertical file.

25. Remarks by Lt. Gov. Ted Schwinden at the dedication of the Jeannette Rankin statue in the Montana state capitol, June 11, 1980, Montana Historical Society, Jeannette Rankin vertical file.

26. Dave Walter, "Montana Congresswoman Stood Alone Against War," *Great Falls Tribune*, December 8, 1991.

27. Giles, *Flight of the Dove*, 181; Wilson, "Peace Is a Woman's Job," 47. Jeannette suspected, and some historians still postulate, that Pearl Harbor may not have been a complete surprise and that Roosevelt or others in the military allowed the attack to happen in order to mobilize strong support for immediate American entry into the war.

28. Walter, "Montana Congresswoman."

29. Wilson, "Peace Is a Woman's Job," 47.

30. Giles, *Flight of the Dove*, 183.

31. Walter, "Rebel with a Cause," 69.

32. Walter, "Montana Congresswoman."

33. Ibid.

34. Walter, "Rebel with a Cause," 71.

35. Walter, "Montana Congresswoman."

36. Ibid.

37. Walter, "Rebel with a Cause," 71.

38. Jeannette Rankin, "Some Questions about Pearl Harbor," speech before the House of Representatives, December 8, 1942. Reprinted by the U.S. Government Printing Office, Montana Historical Society, Jeannette Rankin vertical file.

39. Wilson, "Peace Is a Woman's Job," 49.

40. *Great Falls Tribune*, January 14, 1968.

41. Giles, *Flight of the Dove*, 210.

42. *San Francisco Chronicle*, May 9, 1972, Montana Historical Society, Jeannette Rankin vertical file.

Chapter 6

1. Richard L. Neuberger, "Senator Wheeler's Plight," *Current History*, August 1937, 29.

2. Ibid.

3. Burton K. Wheeler and Paul F. Healy, *Yankee from the West* (Garden City, New York: Doubleday & Co., Inc., 1962), 17.

4. Richard T. Ruetten, "Burton K. Wheeler and the Montana Connection," *Montana, The Magazine of Western History*, July 1977, 2.

5. Wheeler and Healy, *Yankee from the West*, 46.

6. Ibid., 56.

7. Ibid.

8. Ibid., 94.

9. Ibid., 142.

10. Ibid., 140.

11. Ibid., 140–41.

12. M. P. Malone, R. B. Roeder, and W. L. Lang, *Montana, a History of Two Centuries* (Seattle/London: University of Washington Press, revised edition, 1991), 276–77.

13. Wheeler and Healy, *Yankee from the West*, 163.

14. Malone, Roeder, and Lang, *Montana, a History of Two Centuries*, 279.

15. Ibid., 175.

16. Ibid.

17. Ibid., 179.

18. "Wheeler Rides the Storm," *Collier's*, July 8, 1944, 72.

19. Wheeler and Healy, *Yankee from the West*, 179.

20. Ibid., 183.

21. Ibid., 184.

22. Ibid., 186.

23. Ibid., 188.

24. Ibid., 191.

25. Ibid., 192.

26. Ibid., 196.

27. Ibid., ix.

28. "Wheeler Rides the Storm," 72

29. LaFollette-Wheeler campaign songs, 1924, Montana Historical Society, Burton K. Wheeler vertical file.

30. Ibid.

31. Wheeler and Healy, *Yankee from the West*, 266.

32. Ruetten, "Wheeler and the Montana Connection," 10.

33. "Wheeler Rides the Storm," 73.

34. Ruetten, "Wheeler and the Montana Connection," 11.

35. Ibid., 12.

36. Ibid.

37. Democratic State Central Committee circular, September 1934, Montana Historical Society, Burton K. Wheeler vertical file.

38. George Creel, "Man for Montana," *Collier's*, August 10, 1935, 12.

39. Ibid.

40. Ruetten, "Wheeler and the Montana Connection," 12.

41. *Encyclopedia of American History* (New York: Harper & Row, 1965), 356.

42. Wheeler and Healy, *Yankee from the West*, 325.

43. *Lewistown Democrat News*, September 12, 1938.

44. *Daily Missoulian*, November 2, 1938.

45. Richard T. Ruetten, "Showdown in Montana, 1938: Burton Wheeler's Role in the Defeat of Jerry O'Connell," *Pacific Northwest Quarterly*, January 1963, 19, 28.

46. *Congressional Record*, 76th Congress, 2nd Session, October 24, 1939. Reprinted and contained in the Montana Historical Society, Burton K. Wheeler vertical file.

47. "Wheeler Rides the Storm," 73

48. *Congressional Record*, October 24, 1939, Wheeler vertical file.

49. Democratic State Central Committee circular, September 1934, Montana Historical Society, Burton K. Wheeler vertical file.

50. Johnstown, Pennsylvania, *Democrat*, January 20, 1940. Reprinted in "The Wheeler-for-President Circular," Montana Historical Society, Burton K. Wheeler vertical file.

51. *Paducah, Kentucky, Sun-Democrat*, January 15, 1940. Reprinted in "Wheeler-for-President Circular."

52. M. D. Jamieson, "The Window Seat," syndicated column. Reprinted in "Wheeler-for-President Circular."

53. *Great Falls Tribune*, February 21, 1943.

54. Ibid.

55. *The Independent Record*, July 17, 1955.

56. Ibid.

57. *Forsyth Independent*, December 6, 1962.

58. *The Sunday Portland Oregonian*, February 27, 1972.

59. *Park County News*, 1971, Montana Historical Society, Burton K. Wheeler vertical file.

Chapter 7

1. Harry Billings, *The Helena People's Voice*, March 28, 1961.

2. *Congressional Record*, 86th Congress, 2nd Session, 1960, 106, pt. 7:8867.

3. *Great Falls Tribune*, September 8, 1936.

4. Donald E. Spritzer, *Senator James E. Murray and the Limits of Liberalism* (New York/London: Goland Publishing, Inc., 1985), 34.

5. Ibid., 38.

6. Ibid., 44, citing personal letters of Murray.

7. Ibid., 72.

8. *Congressional Record*, 78th Congress, 2nd Session, 1944, 90, pt. 5:6769–70. Hoovervilles were shantytowns of temporary dwellings during the Depression years.

9. *Congressional Record*, 79th Congress, 2nd Session, 1946, 92, pt. 6:6887.

10. James E. Murray, "World's Youngest Army," *Soviet Russia Today*, April 1943, 12; James E. Murray et al., "Allies in War and Peace," *Soviet Russia Today*, November 1943, 11; James E. Murray, "Tribute to Lenin," *Soviet Russia Today*, January 1945, 16; Spritzer, *Limits of Liberalism*, 62.

11. Spritzer, *Limits of Liberalism*, 106.

12. *Congressional Record*, 79th Congress, 1st Session, 1945, 91, pt. 11:A2041–43.

13. Ibid.

14. Spritzer, *Limits of Liberalism*, 109.

15. U.S. Senate, Committee on Education and Labor, hearings on S1606, a bill to provide a national health program, 79th Congress, 2nd Session, April 2, 1946, 46–52; Spritzer, *Limits of Liberalism*, 130.

16. Ernest Kirshten, "MVA: Stalled but Not Stopped," *The Nation*, August 17, 1946, 183–84; Spritzer, *Limits of Liberalism*, 151–53.

17. James E. Murray, *Missouri Valley Authority: Unified Integrated Program for Development of the Missouri Valley* (Washington, D.C.: U.S. Government Printing Office, 1947) reprinted from the *Congressional Record*, April 23, 1947, Montana Historical Society, James E. Murray vertical file.

18. Ibid.

19. J. K. Howard, "Jim Murray's Chances," *The Nation*, October 9, 1948, 397–98.

20. Ibid.

21. Ibid.

22. Ibid.

23. Spritzer, *Limits of Liberalism*, 168–75.

24. Ibid., 199–203.

25. Address, James E. Murray, National Lawyers' Guild, Washington, D.C., February 7, 1947; Spritzer, *Limits of Liberalism*, 177.

26. *Great Falls Tribune*, November 15, 1946; Spritzer, *Limits of Liberalism*, 178.

27. *Senator Murray and the Red Web over Congress*, compiled and published by the Montana for D'Ewart Committee, 1954, Montana Historical Society, James E. Murray vertical file.

28. Murray, Address to the Wildlife Motion Picture Show, Elk and Buffalo Barbeque, Butte, Montana, March 27, 1954; Spritzer, *Limits of Liberalism*, 239.

29. *Congressional Record* 86th Congress 2nd Session, 1960, 106, pt. 12:15564.

30. *Congressional Record*, 82nd Congress, 1st Session, 1951, 97, pt. 10:13495.

Chapter 8

1. *Dillon Examiner,* January 18, 1961.
2. *Great Falls Tribune,* September 29, 1963.
3. Charles Hood, "China Mike Mansfield, the Making of a Congressional Authority on the Far East" (Ph.D. diss., Washington State University, 1980), 136. Interview with Walter Scott.
4. *Hungry Horse News,* December 28, 1962.
5. Ibid.
6. Ibid.
7. Hood, "China Mike," 158, citing Mike Mansfield's academic file, University of Montana.
8. Ibid., 160.
9. *Hungry Horse News,* December 28, 1962.
10. Ibid.
11. Mike Mansfield, "American Diplomatic Relations with Korea, 1866–1910," (master's thesis, University of Montana, 1934), 21, 29.
12. Hood, "China Mike," 192–93, citing Mansfield, Labor Day speech in Butte, September 1939, Mansfield Papers; Armistice Day speech in Missoula, November 11, 1939, Mansfield Papers, University of Montana, Missoula.
13. Hood, "China Mike," 192–93, citing Mansfield, Labor Day speech in Butte, September 1939, Mansfield Papers; Armistice Day speech in Missoula, November 11, 1939, Mansfield Papers, University of Montana, Missoula. Hood, citing *People's Voice,* December 6, 1939.
14. *Dillon Examiner,* January 18, 1961.
15. Jim Ludwick, "Mansfield, the Senator from Montana," *The Missoulian,* November 13, 1988.
16. Hood, "China Mike," 208, citing *The New York Times,* March 9, 1943.
17. "What are we going to do about the Pacific?" Radio address, delivered over NBC blue network, April 30, 1943, speech file, Mansfield Papers, box 36, item 12, University of Montana, Missoula.
18. Ibid.
19. Hood, "China Mike," 284, citing Mansfield, China mission report, 21–22.
20. Ibid.
21. Hood, "China Mike," 318, citing Mansfield, letter to President Harry S Truman, November 7, 1945, Harry S Truman Papers, Truman Library, Independence, Missouri.
22. Ludwick, "Senator from Montana."
23. Mansfield, public statement, October 31, 1949, Mansfield Papers, box 36, item 42, University of Montana, Missoula.
24. Ludwick, "Senator from Montana."

25. Ibid.

26. *Time*, March 20, 1964, 24.

27. *Congressional Record,* 83rd Congress, 2nd Session, 1954, 100, pt 8:10001.

28. Ibid., 10002.

29. Ibid.

30. P. F. Healy, "The Senate's Reluctant Boss," *The Sign*, September 1961, 14.

31. Ludwick, "Mansfield, the Senator from Montana," booklet reprinting Ludwick's *Missoulian* articles of the same title, 20.

32. Healy, "Reluctant Boss," 14.

33. *Dillon Examiner,* January 18, 1961.

34. *The Christian Science Monitor*, April 9, 1962.

35. Ibid.

36. *Great Falls Tribune*, October 21, 1962.

37. *Los Angeles Times,* March 21, 1962.

38. *Great Falls Tribune*, November 27, 1960, citing the *Spokesman Review*.

39. *The New York Times Magazine*, July 30, 1961, 9.

40. *Congressional Record*, 88th Congress, 1st Session, 1963, 109, pt. 12:16326, 16330.

41. *Congressional Record,* 88th Congress, 1st Session, 1963, 109, pt. 16:21061.

42. Eulogy by Sen. Mike Mansfield, Montana Historical Society, Mike Mansfield vertical file.

43. *Time,* March 20, 1964, 22.

44. Ibid.

45. Ibid.

46. *Congressional Record,* 88th Congress, 1st Session, 1963, 109, pt. 17:22858.

47. *Great Falls Tribune*, July 11, 1964, citing *Washington Evening Star*, July 6, 1964.

48. *Great Falls Tribune,* July 11, 1964.

49. Andrew J. Glass, "Power Shy Mansfield Soft Sells in Tough Job," *Washington Post*. Cited in *Great Falls Tribune*, September 30, 1966.

50. Ludwick, "Senator from Montana," 21.

51. Ibid.

52. Ibid., 22.

53. Ibid.

54. *Great Falls Tribune,* September 30, 1966.

55. *Congressional Record*, January 31, 1966.

56. Statement of Senator Mike Mansfield, *Alumni Magazine of the University of Montana*, April 18, 1966, Mansfield Papers, box 43, item 33, University of Montana, Missoula.

57. Ibid.

58. Mansfield remarks, Indiana University Convocation, Bloomington, Indiana, February 23, 1968. Reprinted in *Congressional Record*, March 1, 1968, S1993, Mansfield Papers, box 44, item 17, University of Montana, Missoula.

59. Ibid., S1994.

60. Ibid.

61. *Congressional Record*, June 17, 1968, S7273, Mansfield Papers, box 44, item 37, University of Montana, Missoula.

62. *Congressional Record*, September 5, 1968, S10320, Mansfield Papers, box 44, item 46, University of Montana, Missoula.

63. *Congressional Record*, March 2, 1970, S2729, Mansfield Papers, box 45, item 73, University of Montana, Missoula.

64. Louis Baldwin, *Hon. Politician: Mike Mansfield of Montana* (Missoula: Mountain Press Publishing Co., 1979), 217.

65. Mansfield campaign brochure, August 1970, Montana Historical Society, Mike Mansfield vertical file.

66. *Helena Independent Record*, October 11, 1971.

67. Ibid.

68. "Cambodia: The Handwriting on the Wall," Senate floor speech, October 13, 1971, Mansfield Papers, box 47, item 68, University of Montana, Missoula.

69. Ludwick booklet reprint, 23.

70. Statement of Senator Mike Mansfield before the Senate Democratic Conference, January 25, 1972, Mansfield Papers, box 48, item 3, University of Montana, Missoula.

71. *The* (Carlisle, Pennsylvania) *Evening Sentinel*, January 17, 1973.

72. *Congressional Record*, April 18, 1973, S7682, Mansfield Papers, box 48, item 26, University of Montana, Missoula.

73. *The Evening Sentinel*, January 17, 1973.

74. *Congressional Record*, May 8, 1973, S8424, Mansfield Papers, box 48, item 31, University of Montana, Missoula.

75. Mansfield speech to Senate Democratic Conference, October 30, 1973, Mansfield Papers, box 49, item 67, University of Montana, Missoula.

76. Ibid.

77. *Congressional Record*, April 8, 1974, Mansfield Papers, box 49, item 106, University of Montana, Missoula.

78. *Congressional Record*, March 4, 1976, Mansfield Papers, box 58, item 57, University of Montana, Missoula.

79. Baldwin, *Hon. Politician*, 352.

80. Ludwick, booklet reprint, 28.

81. Ludwick, booklet reprint, 30, citing *Forbes* magazine.

82. Ibid., 28.

83. Ibid., 29.

84. *Helena Independent Record,* April 5, 1988.

85. Ibid.

86. Ludwick, booklet reprint, 29.

87. *Helena Independent Record,* February 15, 1989.

88. Ludwick, booklet reprint, 23.

89. *Great Falls Tribune,* December 7, 1986.

Chapter 9

1. "Metcalf Pounds Them Down," *Washington Sunday Star,* March 29, 1964.

2. Donna Metcalf interview with the author.

3. Ibid.

4. Robert Sherrill, "Consider Lee Metcalf, The Invisible Senator," *The Nation,* May 10, 1971, 584.

5. Ibid., 586.

6. Donna Metcalf interview with the author.

7. Sherrill, "Invisible Senator," 586.

8. Ibid.

9. Peter Petkas, *Lee Metcalf: Democratic Senator from Montana,* Ralph Nader Congress Project: Citizen's Look at Congress (Washington, D.C.: Grossman Publishers), 1972, 6.

10. Ibid., 8.

11. Sherrill, "Invisible Senator," 586.

12. Petkas, *Democratic Senator,* 8.

13. Sherrill, "Invisible Senator," 586.

14. *Congressional Record,* 89th Congress, 1st Session, September 2, 1965, 21810. Cited in Petkas, *Democratic Senator,* 8.

15. *The People's Voice,* September 4, 1959, Montana Historical Society, Lee Metcalf vertical file.

16. Joseph Strinisha, Hamilton, Montana, to Lee Metcalf, March 14, 1960, Lee Metcalf Papers, *Manuscript Collection* 172, box 391, file 3, Montana Historical Society, Helena, Montana.

17. Metcalf to Strinisha, March 21, 1960, Metcalf Papers, box 391, file 3.

18. Lee Metcalf, "The Resources Challenge," *Reader's Digest,* 1961, Montana Historical Society, Lee Metcalf vertical file.

19. *The Sunday Star,* March 29, 1964.

20. *The Livingston Enterprise,* September 7, 1966.

21. *Great Falls Tribune,* July 14, 1966.

22. *The New York Times*, October 17, 1966.

23. *Billings Gazette,* June 14, 1966.

24. *A Report to Consumers from Senator Lee Metcalf, Twenty Questions about Your Loaded Light Bill*, 1964, Montana Historical Society, Lee Metcalf vertical file.

25. Lee Metcalf, "Executive 'Incentive' v. Public Interest," *The Nation*, September 28, 1964, 151.

26. *Forbes* magazine, reprinted in part in *Montana Rural Electric News*, March 1967, 10.

27. Ibid., 10.

28. *Public Power*, February 1967.

29. "Book Review," *Rural Electrification Magazine*, undated copy in Montana Historical Society, Metcalf vertical file.

30. *The New York Times Book Review*, February 12, 1967.

31. Remarks of Judge Gordon R. Bennett, dedication of the Lee Metcalf Natural Resources and Conservation Building, Helena, Montana, April 11, 1986, Montana Historical Society, Lee Metcalf vertical file.

32. *The Washington Post*, 1971, Metcalf Papers, *MC 171*, box 684, file 3, Montana Historical Society.

33. *Congressional Record*, 92nd Congress, 1st Session, April 15, 1972, E 4244–4246. Cited in Petkas, *Democratic Senator*, 16.

34. "Metcalf Girds to Battle MPC," *Billings Gazette*, September 27, 1972.

35. "Metcalf Stands Alone Against Crime Measure," *The* (Butte) *Montana Standard*, January 24, 1970.

36. "Metcalf Supports Abortion Bill," *Billings Gazette*, August 6, 1970.

37. Sherrill, "Invisible Senator," 587.

38. Ibid.

39. "Boosters Pushing Metcalf for Top Court," *Billings Gazette*, October 6, 1968.

40. Ibid.

41. "Metcalf Challenges Nixon on Pollution Legislation," Gazette Washington Bureau, Metcalf Papers, *MC 172*, box 684, file 1.

42. Dale Burke, "The Legacy of Lee Metcalf," Wilderness Perspective II, 36, Montana Historical Society, Lee Metcalf vertical file.

43. Ibid.

44. Sherrill, "Invisible Senator," 588.

45. "Last Minute Switch for Lee Metcalf," *Billings Gazette*, November 14, 1971.

46. *Montana Pictorial News*, Hank Hibbard campaign material, Montana Historical Society, Lee Metcalf vertical file.

47. Ibid.

48. "Portrait of a Courageous Man," *The Missoulian*, May 14, 1971.

49. *Environmental Quality Magazine*, October 1972.

50. "Metcalf Campaigns Hard to Protect Senate Seat," Missoula Associated Press story, Montana Historical Society, Lee Metcalf vertical file.

51. *The Missoulian*, November 1, 1972.

52. "Metcalf Campaigns Hard to Protect Senate Seat."

53. "Hibbard: 'Time to Vacation,'" newspaper article in Montana Historical Society, Lee Metcalf vertical file.

54. Dale Burke, "Lee Metcalf's Conservation Legacy," *Montana Magazine*, March-April 1979, 30.

55. Burke "The Legacy of Lee Metcalf," 37.

56. Ibid., 38.

57. Ibid.

58. Ibid., 39.

59. Memorial services for Lee Metcalf, Senate document no. 95–104, 95th Congress, 2nd Session, 73–74 (1978).

60. "Thanks, Lee," *Tobacco Valley News* (Eureka, Montana) January 19, 1978.

61. "The Great Senator," *The Virginia Observer*, January 20, 1978, memorial services for Lee Metcalf.

62. Memorial services for Lee Metcalf, 164.

63. Remarks of Judge Gordon R. Bennett, dedication of the Lee Metcalf Natural Resources and Conservation Building, Helena, Montana, April 11, 1986, 6, Montana Historical Society, Lee Metcalf vertical file.

Index

Other Montana Titles
available from the University of Idaho Press

Monkey Mountain Madness
by Jeanne Phillips

A woman's impulse stop in Missoula begins an adventure in the wilderness of Sapphire and John Long mountains of Montana.

172 pp., cloth, 1996, 0-89301-192-4

Cowboy Memories of Montana
by Mark Perrault

Perrault reminisces about the life he and his family spent on a cattle ranch in Montana.

135 pp., cloth, 1997, 0-89301-207-6

For more information call
1 (800) 847-7377